How To Know The
IMMATURE INSECTS

An illustrated key for identifying the orders and families of many of the immature insects with suggestions for collecting, rearing and studying them.

by

H. F. CHU, Ph.D.

Zoologist, Institute of Zoology,
National Academy of Peiping,
Peiping, China

1946-47 Visiting Professor
Iowa Wesleyan College

WM. C. BROWN COMPANY

Publishers

DUBUQUE, IOWA

THE PICTURED-KEY NATURE SERIES

"How to Know the Insects," Jaques, 1947

"Living Things—How to Know Them," Jaques, 1946

"How to Know the Trees," Jaques, 1946

"Plant Families—How to Know Them," Jaques, 1948

"How to Know the Economic Plants," Jaques, 1948, 1958

"How to Know the Spring Flowers," Cuthbert, 1943, 1949

"How to Know the Mosses and Liverworts," Conard, 1944, 1956

"How to Know the Land Birds," Jaques, 1947

"How to Know the Fall Flowers," Cuthbert, 1948

"How to Know the Immature Insects," Chu, 1949

"How to Know the Protozoa," Jahn, 1949

"How to Know the Mammals," Booth, 1949

"How to Know the Beetles," Jaques, 1951

"How to Know the Spiders," Kaston, 1952

"How to Know the Grasses," Pohl, 1953

"How to Know the Fresh-Water Algae," Prescott, 1954

"How to Know the Western Trees," Baerg, 1955

"How to Know the Seaweeds," Dawson, 1956

"How to Know the Freshwater Fishes," Eddy, 1957

"How to Know the Weeds," Jaques, 1959

"How to Know the Water Birds," Jaques-Ollivier, 1960

"How to Know the Butterflies," Ehrlich, 1961

"How to Know the Eastern Land Snails," Burch, 1962

Other Subjects in Preparation

INTRODUCTION

NSECTS constitute the largest group of the animal kingdom. There are over seven hundred thousand species which have been named and described and still a large number of new species is being added to our knowledge every year. Because of the great diversity of their behavior and habits, their study is filled with interest. From the economic point of view, some insects are considered beneficial and others injurious to human beings. The better we know our insect enemies and insect friends, the better are our chances of anticipating protections or of preparing and conducting our defenses against them.

Insects are highly different in their young and their adult stages. For example, the butterflies fly in air and feed on nectar of flowers while their caterpillars live on plants and chew these coarse tissues; mosquitoes suck blood while their larvae dwell in water; many moths do not feed at all but their larvae do great damage to our crops. There are thousands of differences in their ways of living and also of the body structures between insect parents and their children. We need to know the adult insects and it is also necessary to know the immature insects. From either the economic standpoint or the evolutionary aspect the more we know of the immature stages the better we understand the adult insects.

Unfortunately our knowledge of the immature insects is still far away from complete. Much work must still be done in this interesting and very important field. This book is compiled from the available literature and designed to make it as easy as possible to acquire a ready knowledge of the immature insects. It contains a number of illustrated keys for identification of these insects to orders and their principal families. For advanced study, important references are given. In attempting this book the author feels like an explorer entering an uncharted region. At best there will be ommissions and mistakes. I shall be grateful for any corrections or constructive suggestions to put into later printings of the book.

The excellent instruction of Dr. W. P. Hayes, Professor of Entomology, University of Illinois on the immature insects during the time when the author was a student in his classes has made the book possible. Dr. H. E. Jaques, Professor of Biology, Iowa Wesleyan College, has given encouragement and invaluable suggestions. My wife, Y. S. Liu has helped with drawings and in many other ways. The author wishes to thank them most sincerely for all their kind help.

Peiping, China
January 1, 1949

We have found Dr. Chu not only a thoroughly trained Entomologist and an excellent teacher but also a most faithful friend. He has given much time and thought to the preparation of this manual in a comparative new and difficult field. We feel certain that students of insects will find it highly helpful.

CONTENTS

寄蜉蝣於天地
渺滄海之一粟

WHAT ARE IMMATURE INSECTS

DEVELOPMENT OF INSECTS. — When an egg and a sperm unite to form one cell fertilization results and the embryo begins to develop within the eggshell. This is called *embryonic development* and all that takes place after hatching or birth is *postembryonic development*. The life cycle is completed when the insect is fully grown and capable of producing young.

METAMORPHOSIS. — The term metamorphosis is derived from the Greek words, *meta*, change, and *morphe*, form, designating a change of form. The plural is *metamorphoses*. It is defined as the series of changes through which an insect passes in its growth from the egg through the larva and pupa to the adult, or from the egg through the nymph to the adult.

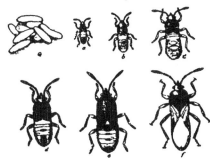

Fig 1. The life stages of chinch bug, **Blissus leucopterus** (Say): a-e, 1st to 5th instar nymphs; f, adult; g, eggs. (U S.D.A.)

a) *Gradual* or *simple metamorphosis*. — In many insect species the young are very much similar to the adult externally, except for the complete absence of wings. But after a period of growth the wing may appear, attached to the outside of the body as small wing pads. The more developed the young insect becomes, the more it resembles its parents. Such a development is called a *gradual* or *simple metamorphosis*. The young of such insects are called *nymphs*. They commonly have the same habits as their parents and the nymphs and adults frequently feed together. An example is the aphids where both adult and young are habitually found associated on the same plant. Grasshopper nymphs and adults both eat grasses and clovers and may be found hopping about together in the pastures. The insects of gradual or simple metamorphosis include the orders Plecoptera, Ephemeroptera, Odonata, Embioptera, Orthoptera, Isoptera, Dermaptera, Thysanoptera, Corrodentia, Mallophaga, Anoplura, Hemiptera and Homoptera. All these insects are collectively known as the *Heterometabola*.

b) *Complete* or *complex metamorphosis*. — In this type of metamorphosis, the young are very different from their adults. There are no external traces of wings. The young are known as *larvae* and the adult is preceded by a *pupal* stage. The insects having this type of metamorphosis are collectively called the *Holometabola* and include the orders Coleoptera, Neuroptera, Trichoptera, Lepidoptera, Mecoptera, Diptera, Siphonaptera, Strepsiptera and Hymenoptera.

1

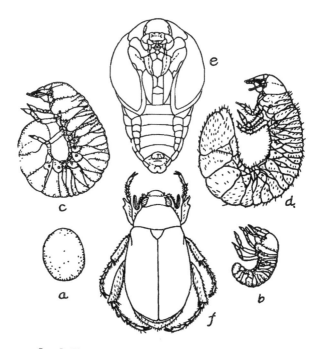

Fig 2. The life stages of **Anomala kansana** Hayes & Mc-
Colloch a, egg; b-d, 1st to 3rd instar larvae; e, pupa; f,
adult. (Redrawn from Hayes)

c) *No metamorphosis* or *Ametabola.* — The insect of this type of metamorphosis have no distinct external changes in development, except in size. When the young hatches from the egg it resembles its parents and scarcely shows any changes in appearance during the course of development. This is especially true of a small number of wingless insects belonging to the orders Protura, Thysanura and Collembola.

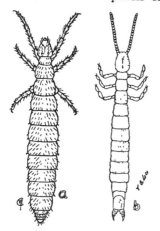

Fig 3. a, Protura; b, Thysanura.

These insects shed their outer coat (molt) from time to time to permit more comfortable growth, but all of these successive stages appear very much the same except in size. Some would call these immature stages "nymphs" but "young" seems to be a more accurate and preferred term.

Metamorphosis	Life		Stage	
Heterometabola or Gradual metamorphosis	Egg	Nymph		Adult
Holometabola or Complete metamorphosis	Egg	Larva	Pupa	Adult
Ametabola or No metamorphosis	Egg	Young		Adult

Fig 4. Metamorphosis and life stages.

IMMATURE INSECTS. — From the previous figure of the insect life stages, insects are seen to have *two* or *three* stages before they become adult or imago. The stages, egg, young (nymph or larva) and pupa are the immature stages of insects. We must consider all the life stages which precede the adult stage.

INSTARS. — Every insect during its growth sheds its skin one or more times. This process is known as a *moult* or *ecdysis*. The cast skin is termed the *exuviae* (this term does not exist in the singular). The intervals between moults are known as *stages* or *stadia* (singular, *stadium*), and the form assumed by an insect during a particular stadium is termed an *instar*. When an insect issues from the egg it is said to be in its *first instar*; at the end of this stadium the first moult occurs and the insect then assumes its *second instar*, and so on. The final instar is represented by the fully mature form and is known as the *adult* or *imago*.

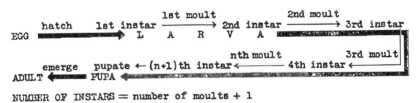

NUMBER OF INSTARS = number of moults + 1

Fig 5. Life stages and instars.

THE IMPORTANCE OF IMMATURE INSECTS

NUMBER OF SPECIES OF INSECTS. — According to Z. P. Metcalf (Ent. News 51: 219-222, 1940), approximately 1,500,000 species have been described during the period from 1758 to 1940. This would make the insects occupy almost eighty per cent of the species of the whole animal kingdom.

IMMATURE STAGES OCCUPY A LARGER PART OF THE LIFE CYCLE. — The egg stage usually lasts but a few days, sometimes even shorter, or the egg may hatch before it is laid, as is the case in

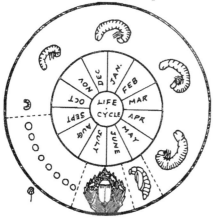

the aphids. Many insects hibernate in the egg stage in which event the egg period may last several months. The growing stage is usually much longer than other stages. The nymph of the periodical cicada, *Magicicada septendecim* (L.) Lives underground from 13 to 17 years as compared with the 30 or 40 days of its adult's life and 6 to 7 weeks of its egg stage. While some Mayflies live as adults for only a few hours, their nymphal stage is believed to occupy three years. Many insects spend their winter time in

Fig 6 Life cycle of the Japanese beetle, **Popillia japonica** Newman.

the pupal stage. In general, insects spend considerably more time in their immature stages than they do as adults.

LARVA AND NYMPH ARE HEAVIER FEEDERS. — When a survey of the feeding habits of insects is made, the nymphs are usually found to take the same kind of food as their adults. Larvae on the other hand, usually feed differently and consume much more than their adults. Take the order Lepidoptera as a good example; the caterpillars eat a large quantity of food while a good number of moths do not feed at all.

ANIMAL EVOLUTION AND ADAPTION. — The zoological position of some animals that are of degenerate form in the adult stages has been established only by study of their embryonic and larval stages. The larvae of barnacles show that these animals belong among the crustaceans, and the peculiar parasitic barnacle, *Sacculina* can be recognized as a crustancean only during its larval existence. Likewise, the tunicates were found to be Chordates only by a study of their larval characteristics. The adults of the Coniopterygidae look like aphids but are regarded as Neuroptera because of the structures of their larvae. The degenerate form of the adults gives no clue to their real position among animals. Among insects there are many highly interesting points to study in their evolution and adaptation. A knowledge of the immature stages makes for a much clearer understanding in both of these fields.

4

INSECT CONTROL. — The injurious insects give us a clear idea of the importance of immature insects. It is the larvae of the Codling moth, *Carpocapsa pomonella* Linne, for example which feed on our apples, not the adult moths. The maggots of the Mediterranean fruit-fly, *Ceratitis capitata* (Wiedeman), do serious damages to fruits, but the adult flies except for laying eggs are quite inoffensive. Note also the Gypsy moth, *Porthetria dispar* (L.), the Browntail moth, *Nygmia phaeorrhoea* (Donovan), and many Wire worms (Elateridae), White grubs (Scarabaeidae), Cut worms (Noctuidae); their larvae cost us millions of dollars every year. We need to know the morphological structures, life histories and habits of the immature insects in order to successfully conduct measures for their control.

WHAT IMMATURE INSECTS LOOK LIKE
EGGS

Insects develop from eggs which differ greatly in size and shape in different species. As a rule, insects tend to lay eggs proportionate to their own size. The smallest known eggs are those of the Collembola. The eggs of one of the small headed flies measure 0.15 by 0.18 millimeter. The eggs of the clover seed midge and of the Tingidae are also minute. The other extreme is found in the eggs of the giant silk moth, those of the polyphemus moth being 3 millimeters in diameter. The shapes of insect eggs are described in the following:

Fig. 7. Eggs of the codling moth, **Carpocapsa pomonella** L.

(a) Flat and scalelike (Fig. 7).—Take for example the eggs of the codling moth and the oriental fruit moth.

(b) Spherical (Fig. 8).—The eggs of many species, such as the swallow-tail butterfly, the green june beetle and many other Scarabaeidae are spherical.

Fig. 8 Eggs of a butterfly.

Fig. 9. Eggs of the fall armyworm, **Laphygma frugiperda** (Smith & Abbott).

(c) Conical (Fig. 9.)—The eggs of the imported cabbage worm, *Pieris rapae* (L.) and the violet tip, *Polygonia interrogationis* Fab., are conical in shape and deeply ridged.

5

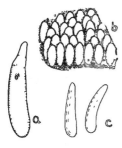

Fig 10 Eggs a, sugar-cane leafhopper, Perkin-siella saccharicida Kirk-aldy, b, Mexican bean beetle, Epilachna varives-tis Mulsant, c, housefly, Musca domestica L

(d) Elongate (Fig. 10).—Many eggs are elongate, as for example, the eggs of leafhoppers, tree-hoppers and tree crickets.

Eggs of this type are often inserted in narrow cavities such as hollow grass stems or in burrows made with the ovipositor or lend themselves readily to being laid in compact groups.

(e) With appendages (Fig. 11).—The eggs of a water scorpion have eight or more filaments radiating from the upper rim. Pentatomid eggs are usually beset with a circle of spines around the upper edge. Reduviid eggs have a definite cap at one end. The poultry louse has a striking egg,—white and covered with glass-like spines. The free end of this egg is furnished with a lid which bears at its apex a long lashlike appendage.

Fig 11. Eggs a, Podisus maculiventris Say, b, Mayfly, Tricorythodes al-lectus (Needham)

Fig. 12. a, Egg of the Western 12-spotted cucumber beetle, b, egg mass, c-d, sculpture of egg (From Webster)

(f) With sculpturing (Figs. 12 and 13).—The surfaces of insect eggs may be entirely smooth or with imbricated designs. Eggs that are laid in wood, leaves, or in the ground are frequently without sculpturing. The eggs of Curculionidae and Scarabaeidae are perfectly smooth. On the other hand, many eggs are reticulated or strikingly marked.

These reticulations are the imprints of the cells of the follicular epithelium. The eggs of the flower flies are chalky white and microscopically sculptured. The leaf-mining flies (Genus Pegomya) usually have eggs that are well marked by hexagonal or polygonal areas. The eggs of many butterflies and moths such as Pieridae, Noctuidae, etc. are deeply ridged and strongly sculptured.

Fig 13 Peridroma sau-cia Hubner. a, egg; b, egg mass.

NUMBER OF EGGS. — The sheep-tick and the true female of many aphids, for instance, produce but a few eggs (as few as 4). On the other hand, the egg mass of the dobsonfly may contain 3,000 eggs, and a parasitic fly, *Pterodontia flavipes* (Cyrtidae) has been reported as laying 3,977 eggs. The social insects lead the list. A termite queen may lay 1,000,000 eggs during her life. Queen ants and queen honey bees likewise are highly prolific.

WHERE THE EGGS ARE LAID — The whole story of where insects

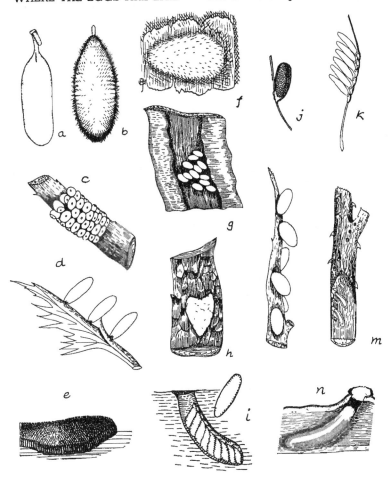

Fig. 14 Eggs a, Boll-weevil parasite, **Cerambycobius cyaniceps;** b, Boll-weevil parasite, **Eurytoma tylodermatis** Ashm , c, Range caterpillar, d, Asparagus beetle, **Crioceris asparagi** (L), e, egg mass of **Culex pungens** Wiedemann, f, egg mass of the gypsy moth, **Pothetria dispar** (L), g, Rosy apple aphid, h, apple leaf roller, i, grasshopper, j, sheep louse; k, **Hypoderma lineata** (De Villiers), l, katydid, m, Snow tree cricket, n, **Oecanthus niveus** (De Geer)

lay their eggs is a complicated one, but very interesting. Insect eggs are generally laid in situations where the young, upon hatching, may readily find food. Species that feed upon foliage usually lay their eggs upon leaves of the correct plant. The ability of adult to recognize the right species of food plant for its offspring often seems remarkable. Aquatic insects lay their eggs in or near the water. Parasites generally lay their eggs upon or within their host. Some flower flies lay their eggs in clusters of aphids or other soft-bodied insects. The Mallophaga and Anoplura lay their eggs upon the hair or feather of their hosts. There are also many special cases. Some insects lay their eggs upon foliage or in the ground and the young are compelled to seek their hosts. The twisted-winged insects (Stylopids) often lay their young upon plants where they must wait until certain solitary bees visit these plants. The young then grasp the legs of the bees and are carried to nests where they find their hosts. The eggs of walkingsticks lie dormant beneath leaves or other debris upon the ground. With the approach of Spring, the eggs hatch and the nymphs must find the leaves of their host plants. Insects such as leafhoppers and aphids, many of which feed upon herbaceous annual plants during the summer, seek woody plants on which to lay their eggs when winter approaches. Many leaf-mining insects of the orders Lepidoptera, Hymenoptera, Coleoptera and Diptera insert their eggs into wood, leaves, fruits and seeds, thus offering ready access to food for the young when they hatch. The Fruit Flies and many Snout Beetles insert their eggs directly into the fruit in which their larvae will develop. The tree crickets, treehoppers and leafhoppers lay their eggs within woody plants for protection of the eggs. Some Chalcids oviposit in seeds. Insect eggs are sometimes carried by the adult for better protection. The Hydrophilid beetles of the subfamily Sphaeridiinae carry the eggs attached to their hind legs. Certain Mayflies may carry two eggs adhering to the posterior end of the body until opportunity is found to drop them into the water. Roaches often carry an egg case (ootheca) at the tip of the abdomen. The females of the

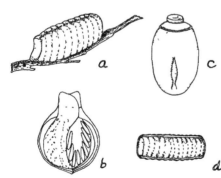

Fig. 15 Oothecae: a, Mantid; b, cross-section of mantid ootheca; c, phasmid; d, German cockroach.

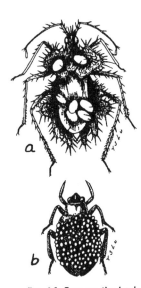

Fig 16 Eggs on the back of male insects a, **Phyllomorpha laciniata;** b, Western water bug, **Abedus** sp

giant water bugs, *Belastoma, Serphes* and *Abedus* deposit their eggs on the back of males where they remain until hatched. Some most interesting cases are those insects which impose upon other species. The water boatman, *Ramphocorixa acuminata,* attaches its eggs to the body of a crayfish. The human bot fly, *Dermatobia hominis,* uses the mosquito to transport its eggs to man. The botfly visits marshy places where mosquitoes are emerging. It seizes a mosquito and deposits 10 to 12 eggs on the abdomen and legs of the mosquito, after which it releases its hold. When the mosquito visits man, the warmth of his body causes the botfly eggs to hatch and the young maggots dig into the flesh of the victim. The females of the European beetle, *Clythra quadrimaculata,* deposit their eggs on the foliage of birch or other trees. These are covered with excrement and resemble small bracts of the plant. The ants pick these up apparently mistaking them for bits of vegetable refuse, and take them into their nests. When the eggs hatch the larvae live in the ant's nest as guests (called *inquilines*).

The ravenous larvae known as aphid lions hatch from eggs held erect on slender threads (fig. 17) and are thus supposedly prevented from eating the unhatched eggs.

Fig 17. Eggs of the aphid lion.

NYMPHS

The term nymph is obtained from the Greek word meaning bride or maiden. In mythology, a nymph was one of the inferior deities of Nature, represented by a beautiful maiden, who inhabited the mountains, forests and water. In entomology, a nymph is one of the immature instars of insects with a gradual metamorphosis. The immature stages of Orthoptera, Isoptera, Hemiptera, Homoptera, Thysanoptera, Anoplura, Dermaptera, Mallophaga and Corrodentia are known as nymphs. Nymphs have certain characters in common. The wings develop on the exterior of the body (some in the later instars). Compound eyes are usually present, and the species are mostly terrestrial.

9

They have no resting stage (pupae) before the adult is reached. The body form and structures as well as the feeding habits are generally similar to those of the adult.

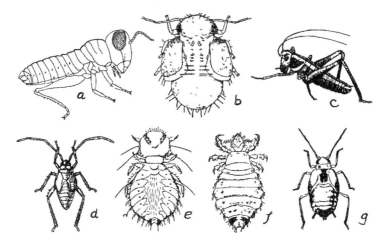

Fig 18 Nymphs a, grasshopper, b, pear psylla, **Psylla pyricola** Forster, (Redrawn from Conn Agr Expt Sta) c, Western cricket, **Anabrus simplex** Haldeman, d, plant bug, e, Mallophaga, f, Anoplura, g, aphid

In the Thysanoptera, there is no indication of wing pads until the second or third instar. In Corrodentia, the nymphs lack wing pads even in species that develop wings. In Thysanoptera and the male

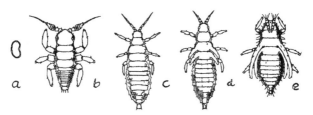

Fig 19 Bean thrips, **Hercothrips fasciatus** (Pergande). a, egg, b, newly hatched nymph, c, mature nymph; d, prepupa, e, pupa (USDA)

Aleyrodidae and Coccidae, there is what appears to be a pupa. In the male Coccidae, even a cocoon is formed. The nymphs of Notonectidae, Corixidae, Belostomidae, Nepidae and some other smaller families of Hemiptera are semi-aquatic. They descend beneath the waters and remain there for a considerable period of time, but they are air breathers.

10

NAIADS

In mythology, a naiad was one of the nymphs believed to live in, and give life and perpetuation to lakes, rivers, springs and fountains. In entomology, the term naiad is applied to the nymph with aquatic habits. There are altogether only three orders of insects which possess immature stages that are termed naiads. These are the Plecoptera, Ephemeroptera and Odonata. The naiads have some characters in common. All naiads are aquatic (except a few exotic species); they have closed spiracles, breathe by means of gills, and have mouth parts of the chewing type. Most

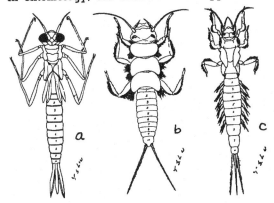

Fig 20   Naiads· damsel fly (Odonata); b, stonefly (Plecoptera), c, Mayfly (Ephemeroptera).

of them are predacious, but the naiads of Ephemeroptera are believed to be herbaceous.

Naiads are generally quite uniform in appearance. The legs are long, the body is flattened and campodeiform and they are very active in water. The naiads of Plecoptera and the Ephemeroptera have conspicuous caudal filaments, varying from two to three in number. In the damselflies (Zygoptera), the caudal appendages are modified into leaf-like form and known as *tracheal gills*. Tracheal gills are located on various parts of the body. In Plecoptera, they are usually located on the underside of the thorax, although some species have gills on the head or on the abdomen. In Ephemeroptera, the gills are located on the abdomen. In the dragonflies, the rectum is modified to form a tracheal gill chamber. In the damselflies, there are three plate-like gills at the posterior end of the abdomen.

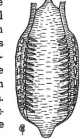

Fig. 21   Rectal tracheae of dragonfly.

LARVAE

The term larva is derived from the Latin word for mask, having reference to the ancient belief that the adult form was masked or obscured in the larva. In entomology, the larva applies to the immature stage between the egg and the pupal stages of the insects with complete metamorphosis. There are several characters in common. A larva has no trace of wings and compound eyes are never present. The

11

shape and the appendages ordinarily are very different from those of the adult; while the body is often soft, thin skinned, or weakly sclerotized.

TYPES OF LARVAE

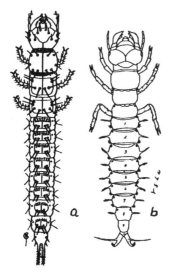

1. Campodeiform (Fig. 22).—The characteristics of a campodeiform larva are flattened body and long legs with cerci or caudal filaments usually present. The larvae of most of the Neuroptera, the Trichoptera, many of the Coleoptera, Dytiscidae, Carbidae, Staphylinidae, and the naiads of Plecoptera, Ephemeroptera and Odonata are campodeiform.

Fig. 22. Larvae: a, ground beetle, **Pterostichus** sp ; b, Dobsonfly, **Corydalus cornutus** (L.)

2. Carabiform (Fig. 23).—This is a modified form of the campodeiform in which the body is flattened but the legs are shorter. Generally there are no caudal filaments. The majority of the Chrysomelid beetles and many other Coleoptera (Lampyridae, Carabidae, Melyridae) exhibit this type.

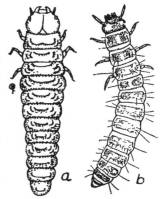

Fig. 23. a, Caraboid instar of meloid larva; b, saw-toothed grain beetle, **Oryzaephilus surinamensis** (L)

12

3. Eruciform (Fig. 24).—This type of larva is cylindrical, the thoracic legs and prolegs are present and the head is well formed. It is well illustrated in the Lepidoptera, Tenthredinidae and Mecoptera.

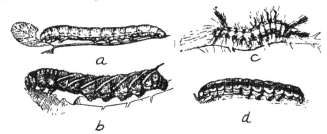

Fig 24 Larvae a, alfalfa caterpillar, **Eurymus eurytheme** (Boisduval), b, tomato hornworm, **Protoparce sexta** (Johnssen), c, tussock moth, **Hemerocampa vetusta** Boisduval, d, tomato fruitworm or corn earworm, **Heliothis obsoleta** Fabricius (U S D A)

4. Scarabaeiform (Fig. 25).—The scarabaeiform larva is cylindrical and curved in U-shape with a well developed head and usually with thoracic legs but without prolegs. There are a pair of spiracles on the prothorax and eight pairs of abdominal spiracles. This type of larva is typical of the Scarabaeidae. It is also represented by the Bruchidae, Ptinidae, Anobiidae, and other Coleoptera.

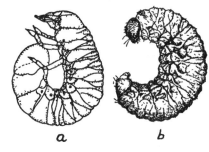

Fig. 25 Larvae· a, **Anomala kansana** Hayes & McColloch; b, clover leaf weevil, **Hypera punctata** (Fab.)

5. Elateriform (Fig. 26).—These larvae are cylindrical in shape with a thick tough body wall. The setae are much reduced, the legs are usually present but short. They resemble both the vermiform and carabiform larvae. This type is well represented by the Elateridae, Tenebrionidae, Alleculidae, Ptilodactylidae and Eurypogonidae.

Fig. 26. False wireworm, **Eleodes letcheri vandykei** Blaidell.

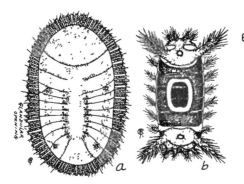

Fig 27 a, **Molamba lonata** Lec , (Redrawn from Boving and Craighead) b, Saddle-back slug caterpillar, **Sabine stimulea** Clemens.

6. Platyform (Fig. 27).—This type is short, broad and extremely flat. The legs are short, inconspicuous or absent. They are found in the genera *Microdon* and *Xanthogramma* of syrphid larvae, the larvae of some slug caterpillars and those of the water pennies, *Psepheus*, hister beetles, etc.

7. Vermiform (Fig. 28).—The larvae of this type are more or less wormlike. This designation is indefinite but is usually considered to include larvae that are cylindrical in shape, elongate and without locomotive appendages. Most of the larvae of Diptera are like that. This is also true of the larvae of woodboring beetles, some sawflies and the flea beetles of the genera *Systena* and *Epitrix*. The larvae of fleas and many parasitic Hymenoptera also belong to this type.

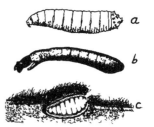

Fig 28 Larvae a, cabbage root maggot, **Hylemyio brassicae** (Bouche); b, buffalo-gnat, **Simulium pecuarum** Riley, c, common cattle grub, **Hypoderma lineatum** (De Villiers) under host skin. (U S D A.)

8. Hypermetamorphosis (Fig. 29). — This is a kind of complex metamorphosis in which there are several types of larvae, including: a minute active first instar, a more or less robust and sluggish second instar, and a similar but legless third instar. It is represented in the Neuroptera (Mantispidae), Coleoptera (Meloidae, Carabidae, Staphylinidae, Rhipiphoridae), Strepsiptera, parasitic Diptera (Acroceratidae, Bombyliidae, Nemestrinidae, Tachinidae), and Hymenoptera (Ichneumonidae, Pteromalidae, Perilampidae). The larvae of this type often have special names. The first instar of Meloidae, Strepsiptera and Mantispidae are called *triungulins*. They receive this name because the legs have three claws. The fifth instar of Meloidae

14

is called a *coarctate larva* or a *pseudopupa*. The first instar of *Platygaster*, a parasite of the Hessian Fly, resembles a crustacean

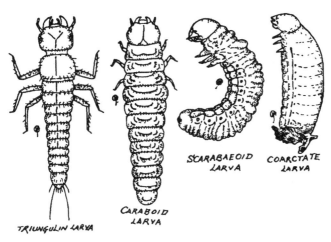

TRIUNGULIN LARVA

CARABOID LARVA

SCARABAEOID LARVA

COARCTATE LARVA

Fig 29 Life stages of **Epicauta vittata** Fabricius

and is called a *naupliiform larva*. The first instar of *Perilampus*, a secondary parasite of the fall webworm, is called a *planidium*, meaning a diminutive wanderer.

COMMON NAMES OF LARVAE

The importance of common names has been emphasized by many entomologists in recent years. We wish we could have common names for all the more important insects. Only a few orders now have common names. The larvae of Lepidoptera are known as *caterpillars*. The term *grubs* is applied to the larvae of Coleoptera. *Maggots* indicate the larvae of Diptera, *Cyclorrhapha* and *Caddisworms* the larvae of Trichoptera. A number of common names have been applied to the larvae of certain families: the Geometridae are called *inchworms* or *measuring worms;* the Limacodidae are known as *slug caterpillars;* the Psychidae are called *bagworms;* the Chrysopidae are named *aphid-lions;* the Myrmeleonidae are known as *ant-lions*. The Elateridae are called *wireworms* and the Sphingidae are known as *hornworms*.

Some common names are derived from the larval habits, such as

15

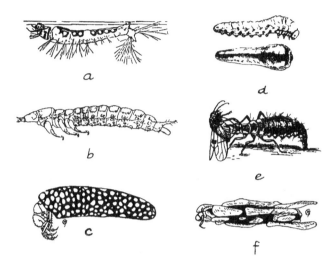

Fig 30 Larvae a, **Anopheles** sp , b, ground beetle, c, **Platyphylax** sp , d, sawfly larvae, e, aphid lion, f, **Stenophylax** sp (In part from U S D A)

leaf rollers, leaf miners, casebearers, webworms, tent caterpillars, leaf skeletonizers, cutworms, armyworms, borers, leaf tiers, loopers,

Fig 31 The formation of the bag in early stages of **Thyrido-pteryx ephemeraeformis** Hayworth. (U S D A)

leaf folders, gall makers, etc. Names of the hosts are usually used in indicating the insects of that particular host, for example, corn borer, tobacco hornworm, etc. The part of the host which the insects attack is also used in the common names of the larvae, such as the elder shoot borer, pink bollworm, tomato fruitworm, etc. Common names, unless standardized, are often confusing.

The common names of insects with economic importance have been standarized by the American Association of Economic Entomologists which include a number of names for the specific larvae.

PUPAE

The term pupa, derived from the Latin word meaning baby or child, was proposed by Linnaeus on account of its resemblance to a papoose or baby bound in garments. The term was first used in connection with the *chrysalis* of Lepidoptera. The pupa is defined as the resting stage or inactive period of all insects with complete metamor-

16

phosis, the intermediate stage between the larva and the adult. Another term *prepupa* refers to the last larval instar of some insects which retain the larval form and mobility but cease to feed. This condition exists in many orders of insects, notably the Diptera, Hymenoptera and Coleoptera.

TYPES OF PUPAE. — The pupae of insects can be classified with reference to the degrees of freedom of the appendages.

1. Obtect (Fig. 32). — If the appendages are closely appressed to the body, it is said to be an obtect pupa. This is a common type in the Lepidoptera, in many of the Coleoptera, and in more primitive Diptera.

Pupae of this type are covered with a tight-fitting, more or less transparent skin which holds all the parts except the end of the abdomen practically immovable. *Chrysalis* is a term often applied to the pupae of the Lepidoptera, especially of the butterflies, and by some would be restricted to those pupae bearing markings of silver or gold.

Fig. 32. pupae: a, leaf roller, **Cocoecia ros a c e a n a** (Harris); b, tobacco hornworm, **Protoparce quinquemaculata** Haworth.

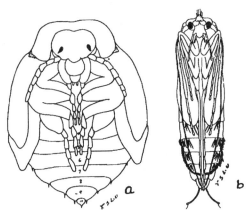

Fig 33 Pupae a, Colorado potato beetle, **Leptinotarsa decemlineata** (Say); b, **Hesperophylax** sp.

2. Exarate (Fig. 33). — When the appendages are not closely appressed to the body but are free, it is said to be an exarate pupa. The Neuroptera, Trichop t e r a, most of the Coleoptera and a few of the Lepidoptera (Tischeriidae) have exarate pupae.

3. Coarctate (Fig. 34). — The appendages are not visible at all and are obscured by the larval skin before the last moult, in the coarctate pupa. This type is found in the more specialized Diptera (Cyclorrhapha) and in certain Coccidae and Stylopidae.

The length of time in which an insect remains in its pupal state is highly variable. Much goes on within the pupal case before the adult is ready to emerge but the whole process moves so rapidly with some species that the insect remains as a pupa for only a few days. Many insects pass the winter or other unfavorable time in the pupa stage. When their growth is com-pleted many larvae travel for a day or two thus scat-tering the species and lessening the chances for total loss of a brood. These larvae usually select some pro-tected spot before settling down.

Fig 34 Cabbage root maggot, Hy-lemya brassicae (Bouche)

PROTECTION OF PUPAE. — Most pupae are concealed in one way or another from their enemies, and also from such adverse influences as excess of moisture, sudden mark-ed variations of temperature, shock and other mechanical disturbance. Pro-vision against such influences is usual-ly made by the larva in its last instar. Many lepidopterous and coleopterous larvae burrow beneath the ground and there construct *earthen cells* in which to pupate. The larger number of insects, however, construct *cocoons* which are special envelopes formed either of silk or of extraneous material bound togeth-er by means of threads of that sub-stance. Thus many wood-boring larvae utilize chips. Larvae which transform in the ground select particles of earth. Many Arctiid larvae use their body-hairs and Trichoptera use pebbels, veg-

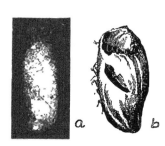

Fig 35. Cocoons a, braconid cocoon, b, empty braconid co-coon, c, cocoon of the clover-leaf weevil, d, cocoon of the aphid lion (U.S.D.A.)

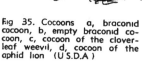

Fig. 36. Cases of the bagworm, **Thyridopteryx ephemeraeformis** Haworth.

etable fragments, etc., these larval cases functioning as cocoons. In these instances the substances are held together by means of a warp of silk and worked up to form cocoons. A large number of other insects, including some of the Neuroptera and Trichoptera, many Lepidoptera and Hymenoptera and the Siphonaptera, utilize silk alone in making their cocoons. Among the Tenthredinidae, cocoons of a parchment-like or shell-like consistency are frequent: in some cases the outer cocoon encloses an inner one of more delicate texture which may be called a *double* cocoon. The naked pupae of butterflies are suspended by silk on the cremaster at the caudal end of the abdomen. In the Diptera (Cyclorrhapha), instead of spinning a silken cocoon or constructing a case of extraneous material, the larva practices an interesting economy by retaining about itself one of its own cast, dry skins to form a case called a *puparium*. This next-to-the-last larval skin is not discarded at the time of pupation but is retained until the adult breaks out of the pupal skin.

Fig 37. A butterfly pupa.

WHERE TO COLLECT IMMATURE INSECTS

Insects are so highly diversified in their food and ways of living that one may find at least a few insects almost any where he looks. When we consider their habits the insects fall into groups which may be rather definitely located.

A. CHARACTERIZED HABITATS:

1. Aquatic Insects — Those insects that dwell in water or are more or less closely related with water are said to be aquatic About five per cent of all the insects are aquatic and still another three per cent are closely related with water. In a strict sense, the truly aquatic insects are those which employ gills to separate the oxygen from the water in which they live. Other insects·obtain their oxygen from the air but because they are closely related with water are said to be semiaquatic insects. If we take a count of the insect orders, almost half of them have aquatic or semiaquatic species. The Ephemeroptera, Odonata, Plecoptera and Trichoptera, with rare exceptions, are strictly aquatic.

The Neuroptera, Hemiptera, Diptera, Lepidoptera, Coleoptera and Hymenoptera are only partly aquatic. Some Collembola live on the surface of water.

2. Phytophagous Insects. — Most insects feed on plants. We can find them on or in the plants. Others in like manner feed in dead woods or decaying plant materials. All these are said to be phytophagous.

3. Parasitic Insects. — Those insects that secure their food by living within other animals are known as *endoparasites*. *Ectoparasites* live and feed on other animals from the outside as with lice. Many insects live within dead or decaying animal and plant materials and are said to be *saprophagous*.

4. Subterranean Insects. — These insects exist beneath the surface of the soil. Most of the orders contain some species with subterranean habits. Remarkable examples are ants, termites, social wasps and bees which live together of their own. Numerous insects lay their eggs in the soil, such as the grasshoppers, earwigs, beetles, flies, etc. Among the Coleoptera, the Cicindelidae, Carabidae, Scarabaeidae, Meloidae and Elateridae are outstanding examples. With the Diptera, the Tipulidae, Bibionidae, Dolichopodidae, Rhagionidae, Empididae, Asilidae, Bombyliidae and Anthomyiidae commonly hide the eggs within the ground. Lepidopterous larvae and pupae frequently hibernated in the soil. Comparatively few nymphs dwell in the soil except certain root-feeding Aphididae and Coccidae and the immature mole crickets. The cicada nymphs on the other hand spend a long time underground.

B. SOME CHARACTERISTIC MARKINGS:

1. Damaged Plants. — Defoliated plants, skeletonized or partial eaten leaves, holes bored in plant stems or in fruits, etc., are good indications for locating the insects which did this damage.

2. Associated Animals. — When a collector sees busily working ants, he can find aphid colonies near by. From the noise of bees or flies, we can often find their nests or their larval breeding places. On the host animals, we can usually find predators and parasites.

3. Sweet Secretions. — A number of insect families, such as the Chirmidae, Aphididae and Coccidae give off a molasses-like sweet secretion known as "Honey dew". This is easily observed and helps to locate the insects producing it.

4. Insect Feces. — Many caterpillars for instance eat such large quantities of coarse foods and discharge such large amounts of waste material from the digestive tract as to give a clue to their presence. Furthermore, from the characteristic shape of the feces, certain species can be identified.

5. Abnormality of Plants. — Not only the abnormal growth of plants but also the malnutrition of plants can lead us to find the insects re-

sponsible for these stunted conditions. The gall-insects and leaf miners are readily located within the galls and the mined leaves. Many other insects can be found on malnutritive plants even though the insect pests are feeding underground.

Fig 38 a, Wool sower gall, **Andricus seminator** Harr , b, Spring rose gall, **Rhodites bicolor** Harr , c, goldenrod ball gall, **Eurosta solidaginis** Fitch, d, Dryophanta galls, **Dryophanta lanata** Gill, e mine of **Phyllocnistis populiella** Cham

HOW TO COLLECT IMMATURE INSECTS

1. Sweeping. — There are usually numerous nymphs and larvae that live or hide in grass, weeds, shrubs and trees. Sweep the net back and forth on those plants in order to get those insects into the net. This method of collecting can usually give large returns. The contents of the net should be examined often and the specimens removed before they are damaged by this vigorous treatment.

2. Trapping. — Many insects are attracted to food, certain chemicals, or places of shelter. We can use cans or bottles sunk into the ground and baited with molasses, fruits or meat. Not only the nymphs or larvae can be trapped in this way, but the eggs may also be laid by the adults.

3. Digging. — Many subterranean insects can be collected by digging in the earth. You will be surprised at the large numbers of insects a square foot of soil may contain.

4. Hand Picking. — This is the simplest method to collect insects. As a matter of fact, we use it frequently. When we see the insects we can simply pick them up in our hands. However, some insects have nettled hairs or strong mouth parts which may hurt the hands, therefore, it is advisable to use a pair of tweezers or forceps on some species.

5. Netting in Water. — For the aquatic insects, a water net can be used for scraping the bottom or passing through vegetation in water. Occasionally the aerial net is used in water, but it is quite poor economy.

21

6. Sifting. — Rinse the aquatic plants or bottom mud in a sifter. Many insects can be collected on the screens of the sifter (See Fig. 41). Subterranean insects may be easily secured by running the ground litter or soil through a sifter.

7. Separating. — Field soils, debris and animal nests or discharges can be put in a separator with a light on the top for heating. Some separators employ a stream of water to remove the insects from the debris. A good number of unusual insects may be collected in the receptacle. Those insects are usually small and active, or they feign death when disturbed, and can not be collected readily by ordinary methods. If heat is being used as in the Berlese trap, great care should be taken that the material does not catch fire. Your specimens may not only be damaged in this way but you could also have no place to work the next morning.

COLLECTING APPARATUS

1. Sweeping Net. — The sweeping net needs to be strong enough to stand rough beating and sweeping. For the bag, 6-ounce drill, heavy

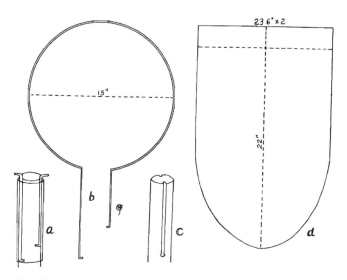

Fig 39 Sweeping net a, net handle with metal cylinder to hold the ring in place, b, ring, c, net handle with grooves, d, bag

muslin or light canvas is usually recommended. The handle with a length of three to four feet and a diameter about an inch is desirable.

22

Many prefer a shorter handle; a few strokes of a saw will take care of that.

2. Water Net. — The triangular dredge has some advantages over

other types because no matter which side rests on the bottom one of the blades will cut into t h e ground when the instrument is dragged.

Fig. 40. A triangular dredge.

This dredge has a net of fairly close mesh, sturdy fabric. It may be drawn behind a boat or the net may be rolled into a compact body and thrown out to some distance from the shore then drawn back by its long cord. In the absence of a dredge net, a garden rake can be used to good advantage. The debris at the bottom of the water course is dragged out on the bank and examined for the insects that are hiding within it. As the water runs out of the debris the insects try to get back to the body of water also.

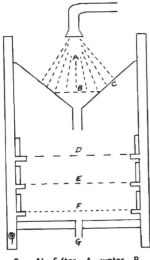

3. Sifter. — Any container with a wire-mesh bottom will serve this purpose. The size of the meshes in the screen depends upon the size of the insects, but for general purposes eight meshes to the inch will be found useful. Figure 41 shows a sifting box which is good for collecting soil insects.

Several sieves with different sized meshes will help separate the insect catch. The process should not be rushed, but the water turned on gently or many of the specimens will be damaged.

Fig 41 Sifter A, water, B, screen, C, funnel, D-F, screens, from coarse to fine, G, water exit.

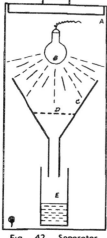

Fig 42 Separator
A, container, B, light,
C, funnel, D, screen,
E, preservative

4. Separator. — This is also known as the Berlese funnel. It consists of a funnel over which a sieve is placed. The funnel leads into a receptacle which contains liquid preservative. Over the top of the funnel a light bulb is placed by which the heat and light drive the insects down until they fall into the receptacle. A rack or special container is often employed to support the funnel. Where a constant source of hot water or steam is available the funnel may be surrounded by a water jacket or coils of hollow tubing which greatly reduces the fire hazard.

5. Aspirator. — This is also known as a suction bottle. It is conven-

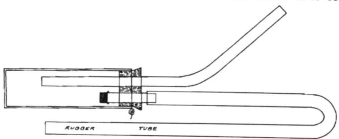

RUBBER   TUBE

Fig 43 Aspirator

ient to collect small insects either from the sweeping net or from under stones, bark, etc. Its construction is illustrated in the figure 43.

6. Other Apparatus. — Different sizes of bottles and vials are needed for storing insect specimens. Tweezers, forceps, pocket knife, small shovel or spade, note book, labels, etc., are all important in collecting insects. It is preferable to have a collecting bag to store those tools for fieldwork.

HOW TO PRESERVE SPECIMENS

For facilitating permanent study and handling, the insects must be killed and carefully preserved to make good specimens. It is important that the specimens be kept in as good condition as possible. The insect body should retain its correct shape and the colors should likewise be kept as true to life as possible. No one method is entirely satisfactory to cover all these aspects.

Immature insects are not ordinarily mounted on pins, but 70% to 80% alchohol or other special liquid preservatives are used. Occasionally the small-bodied specimens need to be mounted on slides for microscopic study. Before the insect is placed in the preservative it should be killed by putting it into boiling water for one to five minutes. The length of time in boiling water depends entirely upon the size of the specimen. It will be sufficient when the specimen become swollen up. This method of fixing is found even better than by injecting the preservative into the insect body.

For exhibition purposes, the larvae are often inflated and kept in dry condition. However, that is not desirable for scientific study, for during the process of inflation, many cuticular appendages could be damaged and the body color is sometimes changed. Inflating larvae is rather simple; place the larva on a clean blotter or a piece of paper and press the body contents out by gently rolling a round pencil from just back of the head to the end of the abdomen. Insert the drawn end of the glass tubing into the anal opening of the larva and secure it in place with the clips. Blow gently into the glass tubing so that the larva is distended to its normal size but not

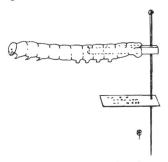

Fig 44 An inflated and mounted larva

distorted, and warm it gently in an oven until dry. A lamp can be used for heating and a chimney or a tin can can be used as an oven. For blowing air into the body, it is better to use a hand bellows. An expansion bulb is desirable to give an even flow of air. When the specimen is thoroughly dry, remove it from the glass tubing and mount it on a kitchen match by inserting the match stem into the anal opening and then mount the match stem on a pin (see Fig. 44). If the specimen is too loose on the match stem, glue may be added.

Specimens must always be accompanied by labels in which brief information of date, locality and collector are recorded. For the liquid preserved specimens, the label should be written with India ink or black pencil and the label put in the preservative with the specimen. For the pinned specimens, the label should be pinned below the speci man.

Peterson recommends the following preservatives:

1. X A. mixture:

Xylene ... .1 part.
95% ethyl alcohol ....1 part.
Good for caterpillars, coleopterous larvae and Tenthredinid larvae.

25

2. X.A.A.D. mixture:

Xylene ....4 parts.
Commercial refined isopropyl alcohol ....6 parts.
Glacial acetic acid ... .5 parts.
Dioxan .... 4 parts.
Good for lepidopterous larvae and coleopterous larvae.

3. K.A.A.D. mixture:

Kerosene .. ..1 part.
95% ethyl alcohol or
refined commercial isopryl alcohol ....7-9 parts.
Glacial acetic acid ....1 part.
Dioxan ....1 part.

Good for maggots, lepidopterous larvae, hymenopterous larvae and pupae, coleopterous larvae and neuropterous larvae. But it does not produce satisfactory specimens where larvae possess a thick exoskeleton, namely wireworms and similar species or among some aquatic insects especially immature stages of Zygoptera and Ephemeroptera.

Larvae collected in the field are dropped into the killing solution and kept submerged until they are completely distended. If narrow vials are used for large larvae they should be places in a horizontal position until the larvae straighten out and become firmly set. This may take from one to several hours depending upon the species. At the end of this period the larvae should be transferred to ethyl alcohol. Larvae possessing a firm exoskeleton may be preserved in 75% ethyl alcohol, while soft bodied forms killed in K.A.A.D. mixture should be preserved in 95% ethyl alcohol to prevent any collapse.

HOW TO REAR IMMATURE INSECTS

For studying the life history or identifying the adult stage, the immature insects are often reared in the laboratory. Rearing insects is quite a technical job. The natural conditions under which the immature insects were found should be simulated as closely as possible. The following is just a brief account of the more important aspects.

1. Cage. — Screen cages of different sizes are desirable for rearing immature insects. The food plant can be cultured in soil or in water and put in the cage. For rearing a large number of isolated individual insects it is usually difficult to provide a large number of cages and bottles or vials are used instead.

2. Food. — The kind of food material the insect feeds on must be determined at the start. Ordinarily the rearing container is not large enough for putting the entire food material inside, so fresh food should be supplied every day. For example, leaves or the other parts of plants should be provided for the phytophagous insects and they always should be kept fresh. Insects that infest seeds and those that

cause plant galls may be reared by enclosing the seeds or galls in a tight container. Parasitic wasps may be reared from their hosts by keeping the host until the adult parasites emerge. Boring insects can be left in the original food material and kept in a cage until they emerge.

3. Humidity. — Humidity plays an important part in rearing insects. If the condition inside of the container is too dry the food material becomes unsuitable for the insects. On the other hand, if the humidity is too high, moisture will be deposited on the sides of the container and frequently the death of the insect will result. To adjust the humidity of a vial or a bottle, changing of the materials of the stopper is sometimes found practicable. A cork stopper can keep the humidity much higher than a stopper of cotton. Insects that feed on decaying animal matter should have the cage provided with slightly moist soil or sand.

4. Pupation. — Insects that are being reared often die during the pupal stage. This requires a careful study of the pupation habits. Some insects make silk or soil cocoons and some just pupate in the soil without forming any covering. Soil must be added to the cage to meet the needs of the insect, otherwise a successful rearing will not be obtained. The cocoon should not be removed artificially from its enclosed pupa for it is necessary to protect the insect. The over-wintering pupae should be kept in good condition. Cold can kill the pupae and too high temperatures may cause the pupae to emerge too early.

5. Preserve the different stages. — For life history study, not only the different stages, and different instars need to be preserved, but also the cast larval skins, pupal cases and cocoons which are very important in scientific study. These should all be carefully labeled.

6. Recording. — Every change of the insect, both morphological and physiological, should be recorded at once. The student may devise his own form of records but should keep them uniform and with all the necessary details. Careless observations and records are worse than none at all; the latter can not be misinterpreted.

The following form is recommended for recording the life history:

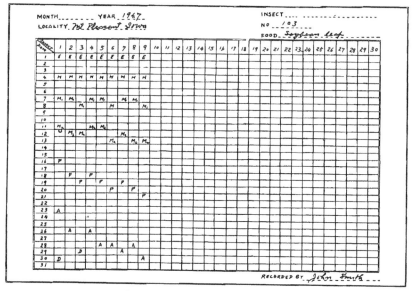

Fig. 45 Life history recording form

For recording the following abbreviations can be used:
E for egg; L for larva; N for nymph; A for adult; H for hatch; M for molt; P for pupa; D for died.

PICTURED-KEY TO ORDERS OF IMMATURE INSECTS*

1a. Mouth parts of chewing type, often retracted within head; 3 pairs of legs present; tarsi frequently single-segmented and usually with 2 claws; wing pads never present; sides of thoracic segments and sterna not divided into small sclerites; abdomen may possess cerci, forceps or furcula and collophore. Fig. 46. 2

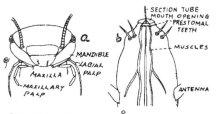

Fig. 46 a, Mouth parts of the firebrat, **Thermobia domestica** (Packard), b, Mouth parts of the long-nosed cattle louse, **Linognathus vituli** (L.)

---

* The orders and families of insects follow the same terminology in this book as that used in the revised edition of "How to Know the Insects" (1947). For a phylogenetic list of these orders and families see ,'How to Know the Insects" pages 171-193

1b. If mouth parts of chewing, rasping, or piercing and sucking types, they are not retracted within head; if retracted the mouth parts are usually hook-like (legless maggots) or of usual sucking type (Anoplura, etc.); legs ordinarily present, tarsi composed of 1 to 5 segments, when one-segmented, possessing only one claw; wing

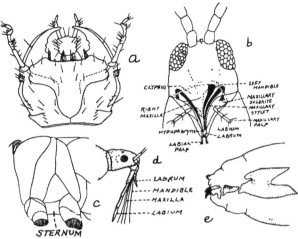

Fig 47 a, Head of **Harpalus vagans** LeConte with chewing mouth parts, b, Head of a thrips with piercing and rasping mouth parts, c, Lateral aspect of the thorax of a damselfly; d, Piercing and sucking mouth parts, e, Head of a maggot and mouth hooks

pads present in some orders, when present the sides of the thoracic segments and sterna are usually divided into smaller sclerites; all appendages absent among some larvae and puparia. Fig. 47. 4

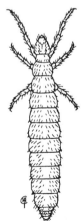

2a. Antennae absent. Fig. 48. . . . .
Order PROTURA page 54

The members of this order are very minute, slender, whitish, wingless insects with retracted mouth parts, no eyes but with a pair of pseudoculi, pointed head, nine-segmented abdomen in young and twelve-segmented abdomen in adult. Less than a hundred species have been described.

Fig 48 **Microentomon perposrilom.**

29

2b. Antennae present. 3

3a. Antennae consisting of 10 or more segments; cerci usually multi-articulate, long and filiform, or specialized into forceplike structures; abdomen usually 11-segmented, without a furcula or collophore; mesothorax never overlapping and concealing the prothorax. Fig. 49. ... .Order THYSANURA page 55

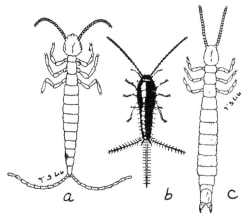

They are known as bristletails, silverfish and slickers. About 400 species have been described. They are found in the soil, in rotting wood, under stones, or in leaf-deposits of forest floors, and also live in the nests of ants and termites.

Fig. 49. a, **Campodea fragilis** Meinert, b, **Lepisma** sp., c, **Japyx minemus.**

3b. Antennae consisting of not more than 8 segments; cerci never present nor specialized into forcep-like structures; abdomen 6-segmented, if segments are visible; generally possesses a furcula and a collophore may be present; mesothorax may overlap and conceal the small prothorax. Fig. 50...... Order COLLEMBOLA page 58

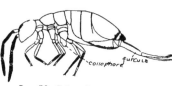

Fig 50 **Entomobrya comparata.**

Springtails are small insects rarely exceeding 5 mm. in length, and occur in almost all situations. They are found in the soil, in decaying vegetable matter, among herbage, under bark of trees, etc. A few species live in the nests of ants and termites, other occur on the surface of fresh water and several are littoral or marine. In habits they are saprophagous or phytophagous. About 1,500 species have been described.

30

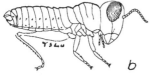

Fig 51 a, **Adelphocoris rapidus** (Say); b, **Melanoplus differentialis** (Thomas).

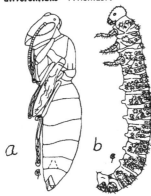

Fig 52 a, Pupa **Vespa maculata** Kirby, b, Larva **Pteronidea ribesii** (Scopoli).

4a. Tarsi usually consisting of 2, 3, or 4 segments, rarely of 5, and very rarely of a single segment. Legs very rarely wanting. Thorax with all 3 segments exposed and generally different in form; pleural and sternal sclerites usually distinct and never concealed; wing pads usually present; epicranial suture does not extend to the clypeus; external genitalia may be evident in later instars.

Fig. 51. .. .... NYMPHS.........5

4b. Tarsi usually consisting of a single segment, or legs wanting, or segmentation of tarsi difficult to determine; more rarely tarsi of 2, 3, or 4 segments; thorax with all three segments similar in form and wing pads wanting; or, wing pads present, laterally and ventrally, the thoracic segments not exposed; the pleural and sternal sclerites never distinct, either not differentiated from notum or concealed by legs and wing pads; epicranial suture usually extends to clypeus; external genitalia not evident..

Fig. 52. ..LARVAE and PUPAE..17

NYMPHS

5a. Mouth parts adapted for piercing and sucking, or for piercing and rasping.

Fig. 53. 14

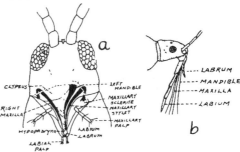

Fig 53 Mouth parts a, piercing and rasping, b, piercing and sucking

5b. Mouth parts adapted for chewing. Fig. 54. 6

MANDIBLE
LABRUM
MAXILLARY
PALPUS
LABIUM
LABIAL
PALPUS

a

b

Fig 54 Chewing mouth parts a, carabid larva, b, grasshopper

6a. Labium when extended, usually **4** or more times as long as broad, scoop-like in structure and when folded serves as a mask that covers the other mouth parts; plate-like gills may occur at caudal end of abdomen: aquatic life. Fig. 55. Order ODONATA page 67

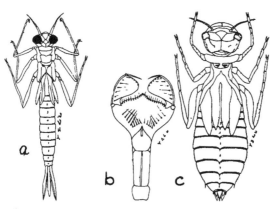

a

b   *c*

Fig 55 a, **Agrion** sp , b, labium of **Libellula luctuosa** Burmeister, c, **Libellula luctuosa** Burmeister.

The damselflies and dragonflies are the members of this order which includes about 5,000 described species. The naiads are extensively aquatic, living in various situations in fresh water. Many live hidden in sand or mud, etc. Without exception all the naiads are predacious, feeding upon various forms of aquatic life. The principal external changes involved during metamorphosis include an increase in the size of the compound eyes, and during the last few instars, ocelli become evident; the antennal segments increase in number, and the wing-rudiments undergo certain changes with the result that the developing hind wings overlap the anterior pair; the caudal gills change in the Zygoptera.

6b. Labium of normal type, not modified into a scoop nor hinged....7

7a. Tracheal gills (plate, feather, tassel or finger-like) usually occur on abdomen or thorax (none in some small Plecoptera); 2 or 3, long, many segmented tails present at caudal end of abdomen; aquatic life. Fig. 56. 8

7b. Abdomen or thorax without tracheal gills and without long segmented tail-like filaments at caudal end; short cerci may exist. 9

Fig. 56 A Mayfly naiad showing the tracheal gills.

The presence of gills as well as their type is more easily determined if the specimen is floated in water or preservative. They are often so fine and may lie so close to the insect as to not be readily apparent in dry specimens. The function of the gills, of course, is to extract oxygen from the water. The gills are extensions of the tracheal tubes.

8a. Tracheal gills (plate, feather, or tail-like) located on lateral margins of abdominal tergites only; 3 tails (in some family only 2), fringed with rather long setae, occur at caudal end; tarsi possess 1 claw. Fig. 57. ....Order EPHEMEROPTERA page 62

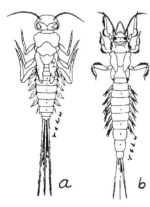

Fig. 57 a, **Heptagenia** sp , b, **Hexagenia bilineata** Say

About 1,500 species of Mayflies are described. Their naiads are aquatic and long lived, in some cases, this period is believed to occupy three years. Between the naiad and the imago, there is a subimago stage which differs from the mature imago in its duller appearance and its somewhat translucent wings which are usually margined by prominent fringes of hairs. They are essentially herbivorous, feeding upon fragments of the plant tissues. Certain forms, however, are believed to be carnivorous.

33

8b. Tracheal gills, usually finger-like bunches or single, often located
on the ventral aspect of the thoracic segments; in some cases they
occur on the jaw, on the proximal and the last segments of the
abdomen; (may be absent in Nemouridae and Capniidae); 2 distinct tails (cerci), usually without long fringes of setae, occur at
the caudal end of the abdomen; tarsi possesses 2 claws.
Fig. 58. . . . . Order PLECOPTERA page 59

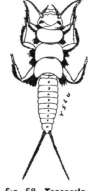

The stoneflies constitute a small order, about
1,500 species being described. The naiads are
aquatic, they live under debris in eddies or under stones in clear fresh water and feed largely
upon the larvae of Mayflies and midges, but
some are thought to feed upon vegetable debris. The time occupied in development appears
to range from about a year to four years.

Fig 58. **Topoperla
media** (Walker).

9a. Antennae not more than 5-segmented; body strongly depressed;
head larger and broader than prothorax; ectoparasitic life.
Fig. 59. . . . . Order MALLOPHAGA

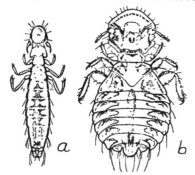

The biting lice or bird lice are
ectoparasites of birds and mammals. About 2,800 species have
been described. Their food consists of dry and nearly or quite
dead cuticular substances. Eggs
are glued separately to the feathers or hair. The nymphs closely
resemble their adults except in
size. The distribution of the biting
lice is quite limited to their definite hosts.

Fig 59 a, Variable hen louse, **Lipeurus
caponis** (L) (Ohio Agr Expt Sta), b,
Large chicken louse, **Goniocotes gigas**
(Taschenberg) (Ohio Expt Sta).

9b. Antennae more than 5-segmented. 10

10a. Prothorax usually subequal to mesothorax or larger; if prothorax
is much smaller than mesothorax then cerci are present, tarsi are
5-segmented and the legs are greatly elongated. 11

10b. Prothorax shorter than and smaller than mesothorax or metathorax; cerci wanting; tarsi 2 or 3-segmented; labial palp 1-seg-
mented; resemble aphids in shape. Fig. 60. Order CORRODENTIA

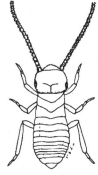

The psocids, booklice, or dustlice are the members of this order which includes about 1,000 described species. They feed upon the paste of book
bindings, fragments of animal and decaying vegetable matter, and cereal products. They are found
in houses, on tree trunks, under bark, in bird's
nests, etc. Eggs are laid in small groups on bark
or leaves and are protected by a meshwork of
silken threads. After hatching, the changes of development are slight. Six instars are recorded in
certain species.

Fig. 60 **Peripsocus
phacopterus.**

11a. Long axis of head and mouth parts usually vertical; in one family (Blattidae) the mouth parts project caudal and in another
family (Phasmidae) cephalo-ventrad; among the Phasmidae the
prothorax is much smaller than the mesathorax or metathorax
and the legs are greatly elongated; the mouth parts of all the
species are of a generalized chewing type; antennae with many
segments. Fig. 61.. ... .   Order ORTHOPTERA page 69

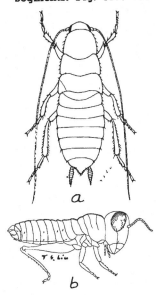

The number of recorded species is
about 22,000. They possess greatly developed powers of running and leaping. The eggs are mostly cylindrical
and some are deposited in oothecae.
In many Mantidae and Locustidae the
nymphs shed a membranous covering
shortly after hatching. The wing pads
are usually present in the second or
third instar. There are commonly 6 instars passed in the nymphal stage.

Fig 61 a, German cock-
roach, **Blattella germanica**
(L), b, **Melanoplus** differ-
entialis (Thomas)

35

11b. Long axis of head and mouth parts project cephalad or cephalo-ventral; the antennae usually located on the head capsule near the mandibles; compound eyes may be absent. 12

12a. Head longer than broad; legs of moderate length and tarsi 4-seg-mented (frequently inconspicuous); color usually dirty white; exo-skeleton frequently soft; ant-like in shape; live within sapwood or dead wood. Fig. 62. . . . . .Order ISOPTERA

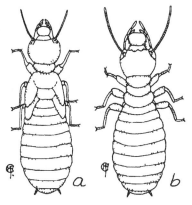

The members of this order are known as termites or white ants. There are about 1,900 described species. The social life of the ter-mites includes different types of castes: the reproductive castes which have functional wings, the short winged forms and the wing-less forms. The sterile castes are divisible into workers and sol-diers.

Fig. 62. Termites a, young queen, b, young worker.

12b. Head distinctly broader than long, tarsi 2 or 3-segmented. 13

13a. Proximal tarsal segments of prothoracic legs as long or longer than the tibia and strongly dilated (bearing openings to silk glands on ventral surface); proximal tarsal segments of other legs of normal size and shape. Fig. 63. . . . . .Order EMBIOPTERA

About 150 species have been described. These insects generally avoid daylight, living beneath stones or under bark, etc. Silken tunnels are al-ways constructed. When disturbed in these re-treats they are able to run backwards or forwards with equal agility. Eggs are elongate-cylindrical with a conspicuous operculum at one pole and are laid in small groups. The newly hatched young of both sexes do not differ in any important charac-ters from the female parent.

Fig 63. Embia major Imms.

13b. Proximal tarsal segments of prothoracic legs not dilated nor do they differ greatly from the same segments of the other legs; forcep-like structures occur at caudal end of abdomen. Fig. 64. . ... .Order **DERMAPTERA**

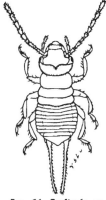

About 1,000 species of earwigs are known. They are probably omnivorous but seem to prefer animal food. When alarmed or molested, the extremity of the abdomen is often upraised and the forceps widely opened in a threating manner. The eggs are deposited in the soil in a group and the female rests over them. The nymphs resemble their parents except the forceps are simple and more or less styliform. They pass 4 to 6 molts before reaching the adult stage.

Fig 64. **Forficula** sp

14a. Mouth parts external, visible and in form of a trough-like tube or a cone; wing rudiments usually visible. Fig. 65. 15

14b. Mouth parts internal, short piercing stylets withdrawn into head parallel with meson, with no external labium; wing rudiments absent; tarsi scansorial type.
Fig. 66. ....Order **ANOPLURA**

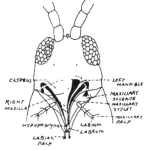

Fig 65 Head of thrips

The sucking lice are blood-sucking ectoparasites of mammals and around 500 species have been described. Of these, two species infest man and about a dozen occur on domestic animals. The louse lays up to 300 eggs, which are usually attached to a hair or fibre. The egg period is about a week. Three moults occur during the life and the young resemble the adult in external features.

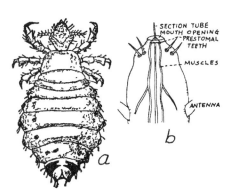

Fig. 66. Hog louse, **Haematopinus adventicius** Neum. (U.S.D A); b, its mouth parts.

37

15a. Mouth parts in form of a cone located between the ventro-caudal margin of the head and the prothorax showing maxillary palpi and inconspicuous labial palpi; mouth parts are asymmetrical in that only one functional mandible exists which may project a short distance from tip of mouth-cone; tarsi small, apparently 1-segmented, clawless and possess single, protrusible pads; body cylindrical, usually less than ⅛ inch long and pointed at caudal end. Fig. 67. .. ..Order THYSANOPTERA

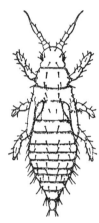

Fig. 67. Green house thrips, **Heliothrips haemorrhoidalis** (Bouche).

Approximately 3,100 species of thrips have been described. They are found among all kinds of growing vegetation, as well as in wood and fungi. They have the habit of curving the apex of the abdomen upwards. They are generally four instars before the adult stage is reached. Parthenogenesis is of frequent occurrence.

A favorite feeding ground for thrips is within the flowers of plants where they often do heavy damage. Both adults and nymphs may be readily shaken from flowers out upon a white cloth or paper and picked up by a small brush moistened in the preservative in which the specimens are being placed. A separate vial should be kept for each species of plant and the species of plant recorded on a paper slip with lead pencil and put in the vial.

15b. Mandibles and maxillae usually enclosed within a trough-like tubular labium which usually projects caudad between the thoracic legs; labium may be absent, if labium is cone-shaped, maxillary palpi and labial palpi are absent. Fig. 68. 16

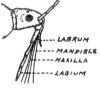

Fig 68 Piercing and sucking mouth parts.

16a. The mouth parts, consisting of a segmented labium enclosing needle-like mandibles and maxillae, arise from the cephalic portion of the ventral aspect of the head capsule; in some aquatic species the mouth parts appear to rise from the caudal portion of the head capsule; among these the legs usually show some kind of adaptation for aquatic locomotion and the prothoracic legs may be modified for grasping.

Fig. 69......... . .. .Order HEMIPTERA page 129

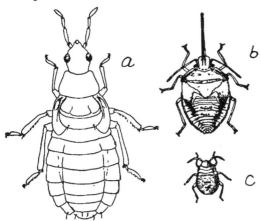

Together with the order Homoptera there are approximately 52,-000 species recorded. The Hemiptera are true bugs. The great majority of the species are phytophagous and feed upon the juices of living plants, causing great losses to agricultural c r o p s , b u t some are predacious and also attack birds and mammals, including man. Most of them are terrestrial and others aquatic or semi-aquatic.

Fig 69. a, **Triphleps tricticolor** (White) (Redrawn from U S D.A), b & c, Green stink bug, **Acrosternum hilare** (Say).

16b. The mouth parts, consisting of a labium (may be absent) and needle-like mandibles and maxillae, arise distinctly from the caudal portion of the head capsule or from the meson between the thoracic legs; no aquatic species.

Fig. 70.. ..   . .Order HOMOPTERA page 135

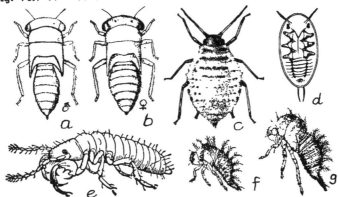

Fig 70 a & b, **Idiocerus provancheri** Van D : c, Aphia, d, **Aleyrodes** sp , e, **Magicicada septendecim** (L), f & g, Two different instars of **Stictocephala** sp (USDA)

There are about 52,000 species when counting the Homoptera and Hemiptera together. Practically all the members of Homoptera are phytophagous and mostly injurious to agriculture. Except for the cicadas, the Homoptera are mostly small insects. The aphids or plant lice, the scale-insects, the spittle bugs or froghoppers, the treehoppers, the leafhoppers, the whiteflies, the jumping plant lice and the planthoppers are all destructive insects.

17a. Never any trace of wings or wing pads; compound eyes never present; wormlike; a feeding and active stage. Fig. 71...LARVAE..18

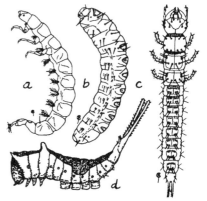

The members of this active feeding stage of the insects developing by complete metamorphosis vary widely in structure, size, habits, color, etc. They are usually heavy feeders and often represent the most destructive stage of the species. They may be short or long lived which has much to do with the length of the life cycle.

Fig 71 a, **Hydropsyche** sp , b, Plum curculio, **Conotrachelus nenuphar** (Herbst), c, **Pterostichus** sp , d, **Cerura vinula** L.

17b. Legs and wing pads encased in an extra membrane, not used for locomotion, usually incapable of being moved; compound eyes visible unless adults are eyeless; a nonfeeding and resting stage.
Fig. 72. PUPAE.45

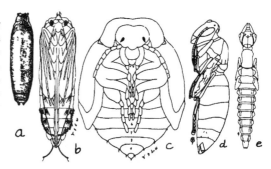

Fig 72 a, Puparium of frit fly, **Oscinella frit** (L); b, Pupa of **Hesperophylax** sp ; c, Pupa of **Leptinotarsa decimlineata** (Say); d, Pupa of **Vespa maculata** Kirby, e, Pupa of **Corydalus cornutus** (L.).

LARVAE

18a. Thoracic legs absent or represented by paired fleshy swellings on mesothorax and metathorax or on all thoracic segments. 19

18b. Segmented thoracic legs always present on 2 or all thoracic segments. .34

19a. Thoracic legs represented by unsegmented, fleshy, paired protuberances (called pedal lobes) on 2 or 3 thoracic legs. Fig. 73. 20

19b. Thoracic legs never present. 22

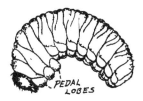

Fig 73. **Dendroctonus frontalis** Zimm.

20a. Adfrontal areas, spinneret, and one or more pairs of simple eyes usually present; prolegs with crochets on 3rd to last abdominal segments (except Nepticulidae without crochets on prolegs of 2-7th abdominal segments). Fig. 74. . Order LEPIDOPTERA page 149

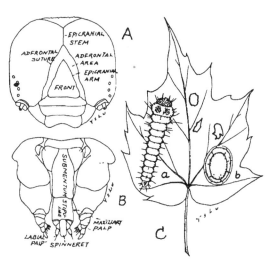

Fig 74 A, Cephalic aspect of the head of **Ceramica picta** (Harr), B, Caudal aspect of the labium of **Cirphis unipuncta** (Haw), C, The maple case-bearer, **Paraclemensia acerifoliella** (Fitch) a, larva, b, case

The order is a large one numbering about 110,000 species. Eggs are highly variable in size, shape, sculpturing, color and arrangement. Larvae are known as caterpillars, and have 3 pairs of segmented thoracic legs. The abdominal segments bear prolegs which are armed with crochets. The head bears adfrontal areas.

20b. Not so. 21

21a. Body straight and of more or less uniform diameter throughout; usually 2 spiracles on thorax (pro- and meso-).
Fig. 75. . . . . .Order HYMENOPTERA page 210

Fig 75 Clover seed-chalcid, **Bruchophagus funebris** Howard (U S D.A)

At the present time, at least 120,000 described species are known. The ants, bees and social wasps live in colonies. The larvae vary in form ranging from caterpillar-like sawfly larvae to the legless larvae of bees and ants. They live in nests constituting a colony or are solitary. Most are phytophagous but many are parasitic. Hypermetamorphosis occurs among many parasitic forms. Gall-makers and leaf-miners are also found among the members of this order.

21b. Body U-shaped with mid-abdominal segments of greater diameter than those near the caudal and cephalic ends; usually with 1 spiracle on mesothorax. Fig. 76. . . . Order COLEOPTERA page 72

Fig 76 Large Chestnut weevil, **Curculio proboscideus** Fab (U S D A)

This is the largest order of insects and comprises about 40 percent of all the known members of the class Insecta and no less than 264,000 described species. The habits of the larvae vary greatly, most are terrestrial and phytophagous; some are predacious, or carnivorous, or saprophagous; some are aquatic or semiaquatic. Many species are also inquilines in the nests and communities of other insects.

22a. With partial (caudal portion non-sclerotized or absent) or completed head capsule. 23

22b. Without a distinct sclerotized head capsule. 29

23a. With partial sclerotized head capsule. 24

23b. With complete sclerotized head capsule. 25

24a. Mouth parts of normal chewing type and antennae distinct. . . .30

24b. Mouth parts highly modified, frequently by hook-like mandibles or· apparently absent. Fig. 77. . . . . .Order DIPTERA page 189

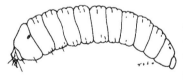

Fig 77 **Sparnopolius fulvus** Wied

It includes about 80,000 described species. The larval habits present a great diversity: phytophagous, fungivorous, saprophagous, predacious and parasitic. Most are terrestrial, some aquatic–or semiaquatic.

42

25a. Head capsule directed distinctly cephalad. 31
25b. Head capsule directed ventrad or somewhat cephalo-ventrad...26

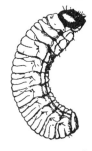

26a. Usually with one or more distinct cephala-caud-
al folds or depressions on the lateral and ventro-
lateral aspects of the abdominal segments; body
U-shaped.
Fig. 78. ....Order COLEOPTERA page 72

Fig 78 Black
Hills beetle,
**Dendroctonus
ponderosae**
Hopk

26b. Usually without such folds or depressions on lateral or latero-
ventral aspects; body not U-shaped. 27

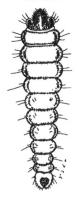

27a. Adfrontal areas, spinneret, 1 or more pairs of
simple eyes and prolegs with crochets usually
present. Fig. 79....Order LEPIDOPTERA page 149

Fig 79 **Tischeria
malifoliella**
Clem

27b. Not so. 28

28a. Larvae may be pointed at one or both ends and
U-shaped; live within plant tissues, or in mud or
paper-like cells; one pair of simple eyes may
occur. Fig. 80....Order HYMENOPTERA page 210

Fig 80 Clover
seed chalid, **Bru-
chophagus gib-
bus**-(Boheman).

28b. Larvae usually long and slender: (a) terrestrial species: spiracles on several abdominal segments, the caudal pair is much larger; (b) aquatic species may have gills or breathing tubes at caudal

end of abdomen. Fig. 81. Order DIPTERA page 189

Fig. 81. Myiatropa florea L.

Fig 82 Monomorium minimum (Bruckley) (U S D A.)

29a. Larvae usually U-shaped, more or less pointed at both ends and larger in mid-region; live within plant tissues or live in cells or nests; mouth parts may be reduced to a pair of opposable (or nearly so), sharp-pointed mandibles or to sclerotized plates fused with the cephalic segment or to more fleshy sensoria. Fig. 82...Order HYMENOPTERA page 210

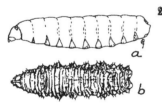

Fig 83 a, Rhagoletis cingulata (Loew), b, A syrphid larva

29b. Larvae spindle-like or peg-like with cephalic end pointed and mouth parts usually 1 or 2 hook-like structures embedded in the prothorax; or the mouth parts greatly reduced; aquatic species may show 1 or several ventral prolegs and a caudal breathing tube or gills.

Fig. 83..... .Order DIPTERA page 189

Fig 84 a, Flat-headed apple tree borer, Chrysobothris femorata (Oliv) (U S D A), b, Round-headed apple tree borer, Saperda candida Fab (U S D A)

30a. Labrum a single lobe; ambulatorial warts may occur on abdomen; many species live in wood.

Fig. 84. ..Order COLEOPTERA page 72

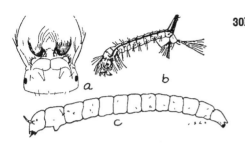

Fig 85 a, Head of **Culex**; b, **Culex** sp; c, **Camptocladius byssinus** Schrank.

30b. Labrum and sometimes clypeus subdivided laterad into 3 parts with groups of setae or spines on the lateral portions; h e a d deeply retracted within prothorax; aquatic or semi-aquatic. Fig. 85.

Order DIPTERA page 189

31a. Head capsule peg-like, etc., variable in shape and size, not of usual rounded or depressed type. Fig. 86.

Order DIPTERA page 189

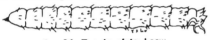

Fig 86 **Tupula eluta** Loew

31b. Head capsule round type or depressed type. 32

Fig 87 **Biblio albipennis** Say.

32a. Mouth parts opposable or parable. Fig. 87.

Order DIPTERA page 189

32b. Chewing mouth parts usually distinct. 33

33a. Abdomen with 11 segments; spiracles, if present, inconspicuous; several long setae on thorax and abdomen. Fig. 88. ....Order SIPHONAPTERA

There are approximately 1,100 described species. The larvae are small, cylindrical, nonparasitic and feed upon a miscellaneous diet of vegetable and animal debris and even the feces of their adults. They frequent the floors of human habitations and the nests of their hosts. When fully grown, the larvae spin small cocoons in which they transfer into the pupae.

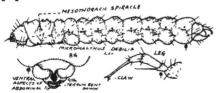

Fig 88 **Ceratophyllus fasciatus** Bosc

33b. Abdomen with 9 or 10 segments; spiracles usually present on mesothorax and most abdominal segments. Fig. 89.

Order COLEOPTERA page 72

Fig. 89. **Micromalthus debilis** Lec.

34a. Prolegs absent on 1st to 8th abdominal segments (rarely present on 8th). 35

34b. Prolegs present on 2 or more abdominal segments. ...,......39

35a. Head directed cephalad. 41

35b. Head directed ventrad or cephaloventrad. 36

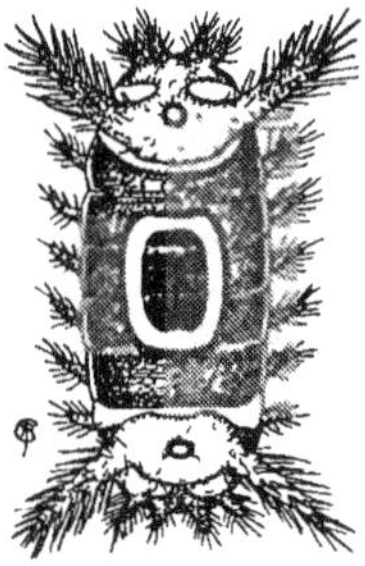

36a. Head capsule may be deeply imbedded in prothorax; may also possess adfrontal area; many species slug-like in form.

Fig. 90.........Order LEPIDOPTERA page 149

Fig 90 Saddle back-
ed slug caterpillar,
Sabine stimulea
(Clemens).

36b. Head capsule not deeply embedded in prothorax and without adfrontal areas. 37

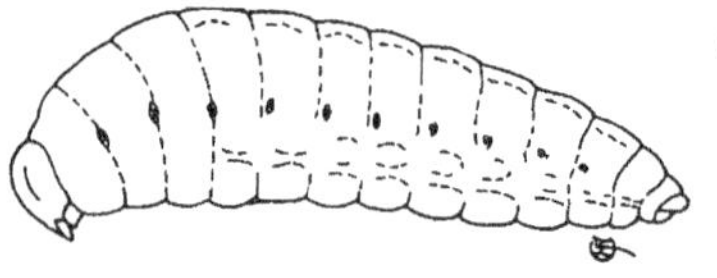

37a. One pair of simple eyes present or absent; 2 pairs of spiracles on thorax (pro- and meso-); body usually eruciform. Fig. 91.
Order HYMENOPTERA page 210

Fig. 91. **Vespa maculata** Kirby.

37b. Several pairs of simple eyes present. 38

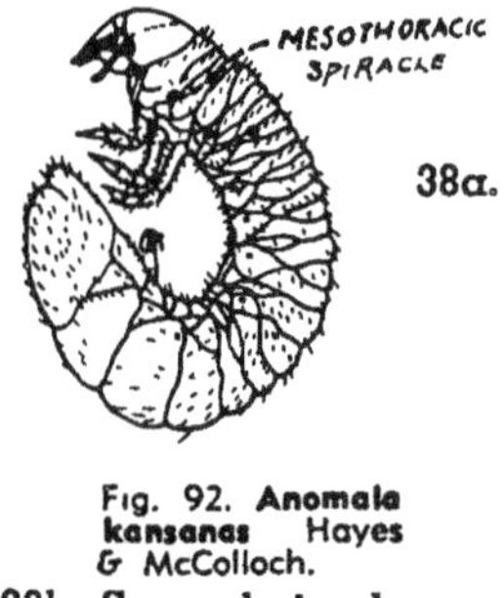

38a. Several pairs of simple eyes may be present; spiracles usually present on mesothorax only; body U-shaped.

Fig. 92.. ....Order COLEOPTERA page 72

Fig. 92. **Anomala
kansanas** Hayes
& McColloch.

38b. Several simple eyes and in a close cluster usually present; meso-thoracic and metathoracic legs distinctly larger and project more laterad than the prothoracic legs. ....Order MECOPTERA

This small order represents some 350 species. The larvae are most-ly carnivorous, few feed upon vegetable matter. The larvae bear a close resemblance to caterpillars.

Fig. 93 **Panorpa rufescens** Miyake.

39a. Head usually with more than 10 simple eyes on each side, closely grouped; prolegs on abdominal segments 1st to 8th or 3rd to 8th inclusive; anal end resembles a sucking disk.
Fig. 93. ......Order MECOPTERA

39b. Head with never more than 10 simple eyes on each side or entirely wanting. 40

40a. Prolegs usually present on abdominal segments 3rd to 6th and last, crochets present; adfrontal areas usually present; 1 to 8 pairs of simple eyes usually present.
Fig. 94......... ... . .most LEPIDOPTERA page 149

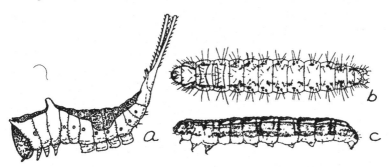

Fig 94 a, **Cerura vinula** (L , b, Corn earworm, **Heliothis armigera** (Hbn), c, **Euxoa auxiliaris** Grate

Fig 95 Imported currantworm, **Pteronidea ribesii** (Scopoli).

40b. Prolegs usually present on abdominal segments 2nd to 8th and last, sometimes 2nd to 6th, 2nd to 7th and last; no crochets present; no adfrontal areas; one pair of simple eyes usually present. Fig. 95.
Order HYMENOPTERA page 210

41a. Thoracic legs with single claw (stout spines about base of claw may create impression that there are 2 or more claws). 42

41b. Thoracic legs with 2 distinct claws. 44

47

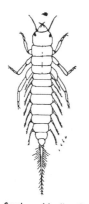

Fig 96 Smoky alderfly, **Sialis in-fumata** Newman

42a. Single claws on thoracic legs; sickle-shaped mandibles and maxillae. Fig. 96.
Family SISYRIDAE,
Order NEUROPTERA page 140

This family contains some 20 species of rather small insects known as spongilla flies since the larvae feed on Spongilla and other freshwater sponges, as well as on algae and bryozoa. The small, elongate eggs are laid in clusters on objects overhanging water from which the larvae drop into the water upon hatching. Pupation takes place under objects along shore or within the soil above the water line. The pupa is covered with a double walled silken cocoon.

Perhaps less than 5000 species of Neuroptera are known and many of these are rare. Some of the larvae are helpful friends of man. Only a few of the families have larvae that are aquatic but all the families are similar in having pupae that are enclosed in a rather spherical cocoon.

42b. Single claws with spur or spine about the base; chewing mouth parts. 43

Fig 97 **Pelto-dytes** sp

43a. Thoracic legs elbowed and may possess stout spines at base of claw; prolegs and cerci may occur at caudal end of abdomen; aquatic forms may possess abdominal gills.
Fig. 97.. .... .Order COLEOPTERA page 72

This odd appearing larva belongs to the crawling water beetles (family Haliplidae), and is similar to other members of the family. They are small and slender and not likely to be observed unless one is looking for them.

48

43b. Larvae live in cases or webs in water; thoracic legs possess spurs on or about the base of claw; no prolegs, but the caudal hooks; gills may be present on thorax and abdomen.

Fig. 98. . . . . .Order TRICHOPTERA page 146

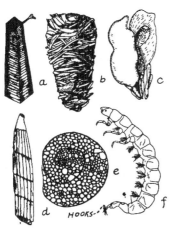

Fig 98 a, Case of **Brachcentrus** sp , b, Case of **Limnephilus indivisus** Walker, c, Case of **Astenophylas** sp , d, Case of **Triaenodes flaviscense** Banks; e, Case of **Helieopsyche** sp , Larva of **Hydropsyche** sp.

The order has approximately 4,200 described species. The larvae are known as caddisworms and are mostly aquatic, but a few are terrestrial. The eggs are deposited in the debris at the bottom of water or attached to aquatic plants and other objects in the water and are protected with gelatinous masses or strings. The larvae construct characteristic cases or silken retreats. Their food habits are varied, most of them are likely herbivorous but some are known to be carnivorous.

The immense numbers to which these interesting larvae develop make them very important as food for fish and doubtless a very large percentage of the larvae contribute to the growth of fish. Naturally they are used extensively as fish bait. They may be found in abundance in the debris of flowing streams or attached to rocks under water.

Pupation usually takes place within the water, often within the larval case but sometimes outside it and within a silken cocoon. Some species burrow in submerger logs or in crevices in the rocks to pupate. The adult may emerge under water or bring the pupal case to the surface of the water to effect its escape.

44a. Mandibles and maxillae usually of normal chewing type; on the abdomen among terrestrial species cerci usually occur on the 9th

Fig 99 **Harpalus vagans** LeConte

segment; among aquatic species the caudal segment(s) may be tube-like or gills may be present. Fig. 99.

Order COLEOPTERA page 72

44b. Mandibles and maxillae long and sickle-shaped, of mandibulo-suctorial type; aquatic species may possess abdominal prolegs with hooks at caudal end; gills may be present on most abdominal segments. Fig. 100..........Order NEUROPTERA page 140

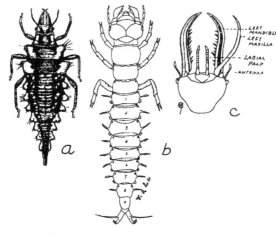

About 5,000 species of the order have been described. The larvae exhibit great diversity of structure and mode of life, but they are all carnivorous; in a considerable proportion of the species they are aquatic.

Fig 100 a, Golden-eye lacewing, **Chrysopa oculata**. Say (Redrawn from Smith); b, **Corydalus cornutus** (L); c, Mandibulo-suctorial mouth-parts

PUPAE and PUPARIA

45a. Appendages, including mouth parts, invisible on exterior, or, if visible, they are fused with each other and to the body wall to form a continuous covering; obtect type.
(see Figs. 107 and 109). 51

45b. Appendages distinctly visible and free, even though held in a fixed position; resembles a mummy; exarate type.
(See Figs. 101-106). 46

Fig 101 Pupa of dog flea, **Ctenocephalides canis** (Curtis).

46a. Body strongly compressed; length less than 3 mm.; wing pads absent; antennae minute; mandibles of piercing type; compound eyes absent. Fig. 101. .... Order SIPHONAPTERA

46b. Body rounded or flattened, not strongly compressed; antennae and wing pads usually prominent. 47

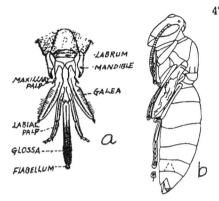

Fig 102 a, Chewing and lapping mouth parts; b, Pupa of **Vespa macutata** Kirby.

47a. Mouth parts for chewing and lapping; mandibles present; usually a median or bifurcate lobe or tongue (the hypopharynx) arises from the labium; distal segments or ends of the 12 or more segmented antennae usually adjacent to and frequently parallel with the meson; paired ovipositors frequently visible at caudal end; a distinct constriction usually present between the thorax and abdomen. Fig. 102.

most HYMENOPTERA page 210

47b. Mouth parts for chewing only; no distinct tongue or paired ovipositors present. 48

48a. Antennae long, always with 12 or more segments; wing rudiments not elytra-like. 49

48b. Antennae shorter than body, if elongated, with numerous stout segments and much longer than the body, usually 11 or less segments and distal segments usually far removed from meson; wing rudiments always elytra-like and located between the distal portion of mesothoracic and metathoracic legs on the ventral aspect; legs elbowed sharply at end of femur. Fig. 103...........................most COLEOPTERA page 72

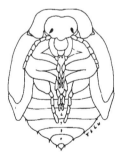

Fig. 103 Pupa of the Colorado potato beetle, **Leptinotarsa decimlineata** (Say)

The pupae are mostly of exarate type, but in some of the Staphylinidae they are obtect. Pupation takes place mostly in earthen cells in the soil, but also occurs within the food plant. Certain Curculionidae make cocoons with the product of the Malpighian tubes, while several of the Lamellicornia use the contents of the posterior caecum. Many Cerambycidae construct pupal cells largely impregnated with carbonate of lime. The pupae of the Coccinellidae are often protected by the persistent remains of the last larval skin.

51

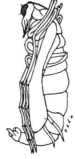

49a. Head abnormal in shape; head capsule and mouth parts elongated; antennae with 16 or more segments, arise from the head capsule near the compound eyes and not from the beak as in some weevils (Rhynchophora).

Fig. 104. . . .Order MECOPTERA

Fig 104 Pupa of **Bittacus pilicornas** Westw

49b. Head normal in shape; mouth parts not greatly elongated. ...50

50a. Mandibles short, stout, curved, nearly cylindrical; they usually project cephalad or nearly so and cross each other; thorax and abdomen frequently bearing filamentous gills; usually found in cases or webs constructed by the larvae (Micropterygoidea of the Lepidoptera may also fall into this group, but they are non-aquatic and not over 4 mm. in length).

Fig. 105. . . .. .Order TRICHOPTERA page 146

The appendages are quite free from the body, and the abdomen is armed with dorsal spines which enable the pupa to work its way out of its habitation. The pupae of some species are able to swim freely.

Fig 105 Pupa of **Hesperophy- lax** sp.

50b. Mandibles large and stout never overlapping or crossing each other. Fig. 106.. . . . . .most NEUROPTERA page 140

The pupae of this order are free, enclosed in a silken cocoon, curved with the head and tip of abdomen near each other, and with all the appendages visible. Pupation occurs in the soil or in moss, etc. The pupae are able to work their way out to the surface.

Fig 106 Pupa of **Corydalus cornutus** (L).

51a. All appendages invisible on exterior, the ectal surface smooth or made up of concentric rings, usually resembling a barrel with two ends somewhat similar (blunt); caudal and thoracic spiracles of last larval stage usually visible as remnants or scars; this hardened or leathery larval exuviae (called puparium) contains a pupa or a hibernating larva within; coarctate type. Fig. 107.

Fig 107 Puparium of **Zonosemata electa** (Say).

chiefly CYCLORRHAPHA. Order DIPTERA page 189

51b. The cases possessing the appendages of the developing adult visible on the lateral and ventral aspects of the thorax, yet more or less fused to each other and in most instances to the body covering; obtect type. . . . . ⌐ .52

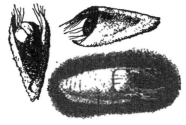

52a. Distinct respiratory projecting organs present on the dorsocephalic region; one pair of wings. Fig. 108.

chiefly NEMATOCERA. Order DIPTERA page 189

Fig 108. Pupa and cocoon of **Simulium venustum** Say. (U.S.D.A.)

53

52b. Distinct respiratory projecting organs absent on the dorsocephalic region; spiracles usually present on mesothorax and some of the abdominal segments; functional mandibles absent (except among Micropterygoidea); paired galeae of maxillae usually present along ventro-meson; antennae adjacent to mesal margins of wings; 2 pairs of wings, outer pair may conceal inner pair.
Fig. 109...........................most LEPIDOPTERA page 149

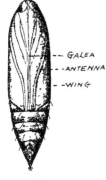

GALEA
ANTENNA
WING

The lepidopterous pupae are of 2 main types: (1) the Incompletae which have the appendages often partially free and more than 3 of the abdominal segments are mobile. Dehiscence is accompanied by the freeing of segments and appendages previously fixed. The pupae exhibit considerable power of motion, usually emerging from the cocoon to allow of the escape of the adult. (2) The Obtectae which are smooth and rounded and the only free segments in both sexes are the 4th, 5th and 6th. Dehiscence takes place by an irregular fracture. The pupa rarely emerges from the cocoon and a cremaster is generally present.

Fig 109 Pupa of the European corn borer, **Pyrausta nubilalis** (Hubner)

PICTURED-KEYS TO FAMILIES

———o———

ORDER PROTURA

1a. Meso- and metathoracic spiracles and trachea present.
Fig. 110. ....Family EOSENTOMIDAE

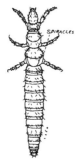

SPIRACLES

Practically nothing is known concerning the life histories of the proturans. They have been found in damp situations under leaves, bark and stones, in rotten wood, decaying vegetation, turf and humus soils.

Fig 110 **Eosentomen ribagai** Berlese

1b. Spiracles and trachea absent. 2

2a. Abdominal terga each with one or three transverse sutures.
Fig. 111. ....Family ACERENTOMIDAE

The proturans are minute whitish organisms. The largest species scarcely attain 2 mm. in length. They are widely distributed in Europe, Asia and America.

Fig 111 Aceren-
tomon doderoi
Silvestri.

2b. Abdominal terga without transverse sutures.
Fig. 112. ....Family PROTENTOMIDAE

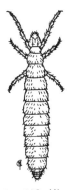

Proturans are peculiar in that they walk only on the middle and hind legs and hold the fore legs in front and above the head.

Fig 112. Micro-
entomon perpo-
sillom.

ORDER THYSANURA

1a. 3 caudal appendages; compound eyes present (Suborder Ectotrophi). (See Figs. 113 and 114). 2

1b. 2 caudal appendages; compound eyes absent (Suborder Endotrophi). (See Figs. 115 - 118). 3

2a. Compound eyes large, more or less contiguous; ocelli present; styli present on thoracic coxae, also on abdominal segments 2-9. Fig. 113. ....Family MACHILIDAE

Bristletails, silverfish, and slickers are the common names. The family contains about 150 described species. They inhabit grassy and woody areas. Some are tenants in caves and some inhabit the nests of termites. At least six instars have been reported. In the first two instars scales and styli are absent.

Fig 113 **Machi-**
lis maritima
Leach.

2b. Compound eyes small, widely separated; ocelli absent; styli absent on thoracic coxae, but present on abdominal segments 7-9 or 8-9. Fig. 114. ....Family LEPISMIDAE

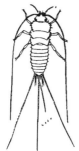

About 200 species are known. They are commonly called the bristletails, fish-moths or slickers. They are found in dry hot places, among leaves, under stones, debris, caves, buildings and the nests of ants and termites. They feed upon dry vegetation or plant products. They are also fond of paste, glue and rayon cloth. The silverfish, *Lepisma saccharina* L. and the fire brat, *Thermobia domestica* (Packard) are common in buildings.

Fig. 114 **Thermobia**
domestica (Packard)

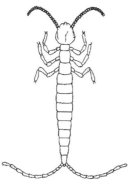

3a. Styli absent on 1st abdominal segment. Fig. 115. ...... .Family CAMPODEIDAE

About 75 species have been described. Most species are from the Palaearctic, Nearctic and Neotropical regions with very few known in the Oriental regions. They are blind and occur in damp places.

Fig. 115 **Campodea fragil-**
is Meinert

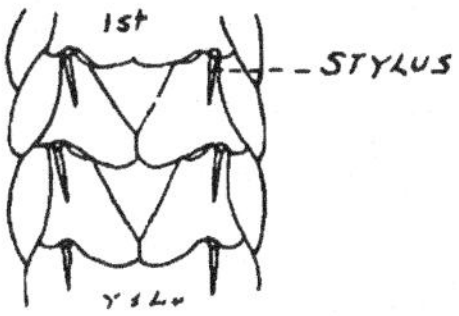

3b. Styli present on first abdominal
segment. 4

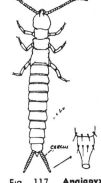

Fig. 116 Ventral aspect
of 1st to 4th abdominal
segments

4a. Cerci with glandular opening at apex.
Fig. 117. .... Family PROJAPYGIDAE

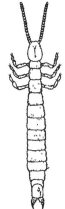

There are only 5 species known, distributed
in the Mediterranean regions of Southern Europe
and Northern Africa, and in Mexico and South
America. They are small blind insects with a
pair of short segmented cerci.

Fig 117 **Anajapyx
vesiculosis** Silvestri.

4b. Cerci without opening at apex.
Fig. 118. ....Family IAPYGIDAE

About 100 species are described. The young have
segmented cerci which are replaced in the last moult
by pincerlike cerci. It is reported that the eggs and
young are carried beneath the body of the female for
protection.

Fig. 118. **Iapyx
minemus.**

57

ORDER COLLEMBOLA

1a. Body more or less cylindrical and elongate; abdomen plainly segmented. ....(Suborder Arthropleona)....... 2

1b. Abdomen subglobular, segmentation obliterated or vestigial. ....(Suborder Symphypleona)............3

2a. Prothorax well developed, with a definite tergum; cuticle usually granulated. Fig. 119. ... .Family PODURIDAE

Fig. 119. **Achorutes armatus** Nicolet.

These are the springtails and snow-fleas including about 315 species. The young live a secluded life and are often white or colorless. The snowflea, *Achorutes nivicolus* Fitch is a widely distributed species which often occurs on the surface of snow.

2b. Prothorax greatly reduced, without a tergum; cuticle not granulated. Fig. 120. ....Family ENTOMOBRYIDAE

Fig 120 **Entomobrya laguna** Bacon

There are some 600 described species. The marsh springtail, *Isotoma palustris* (Muller), is a widely distributed species. It may be found in wet leaves, moss and soil and often appears on the surface of fresh water pools.

3a. Antennae stout, not longer than head; thorax very large. Fig. 121. ....Family NEELIDAE

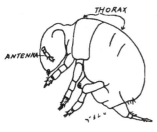

Fig 121 **Neelides folsomi.**

A small family composed of 4 species. They are globular and bristly with very short antennae inserted on the middle of front of the head, with eyes present or absent and with the furcula about twice the length of the antennae. They may be found under dead bark and in decaying vegetation.

3b. Antennae more slender longer than head; thorax not exceptionally
large. Fig. 122. ....Family SMINTHURIDAE

Fig 122 **Sminthurides lepus**
Mills.

The family is composed of about
200 species. These springtails are
very active and often occur in immense numbers in moist places on
the surface of the soil or water. The
head is vertical and the antennae
inserted on the back portion of the
head. Various species of living plants
constitute their food.

ORDER PLECOPTERA

(This key is compiled from Claassen and Frison.)

1a. Gills present on first 2 or 3 abdominal segments.
Fig. 123. ....Family PTERONARCIDAE

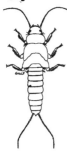

The naiads of this family are all herbivorous. They
live in the small upland spring brooks and are un-
able to move rapidly, getting around awkwardly.
Upon being taken out of the water, they curl up, remaining motionless for some time.

Fig 123 **Pteronar-
cella badia** Hagen.

1b. Gills absent on first 2 or 3 abdominal segments. 2
2a. Venter of thorax covered with large over-lapping shield-like plates.
Fig. 124. ....Subfamily PELTOPERLINAE, PERLIDAE

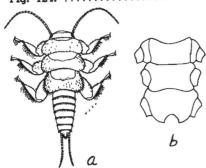

b

a

The single genus *Peltoperla*
is distributed over the Eastern,
Southern and Western United
States. The naiads are herbivorous and can be distin-
guished from other families by
the large shield-like pro-, meso-
and metanotum, short abdomen, wide legs, short cerci and
head bent under the body.

Fig 124 a, **Peltoperla arcuata** Ndm, b
Ventral aspect of thorax.

2b. Venter of thorax not covered with large over-lapping shield-like plates. 3

3a. Gills present on thorax. ...... · 4

3b. Gills absent on thorax. 5

4a. Gills on the venter of prothorax. Fig. 125. ..Family NEMOURIDAE

The naiads are herbivorous and live mostly in the small upland spring brooks. They are uniform through out in color.

Fig 125 **Ne-moura sinuata** Wu

4b Gills on all three thoracic segments. Fig. 126. ....Family PERLIDAE

The naiads are all carnivorous and brightly col-ored. They are mostly found in rather swift run-ning water.

This is the best represented family of stoneflies. It furnishes in its immature as well as its adult stages great quantities of food for fish, but at the same time competes with them for many of the smaller forms of insect life in the water.

Fig 126 **Togoperla media** (Walker)

5a. 1st and 2nd tarsal segments together less than half as long as 3rd; labrum 3 to 4 times as wide as long; lab-ium 2-lobed; body flattened and brightly colored. Fig. 127. ....Family PERLIDAE

The eggs of stoneflies are very small but are pro-duced in immense numbers,—as many as 6000 for one individual. They are laid directly into the water.

Fig 127 **Perla verticalis** Banks.

5b. 1st and 2nd tarsal segments together as long as 3rd or at least more than half as long; labrum not very much wider than long; labium 4-lobed; body more or less cylindrical, not brightly colored; herbivorous. Fig. 128. 6

Fig 128 Labium a, **Perla hastata** Banks, b, **Nemoura venosa** Banks.

6a. Hind wing pads diverging considerably outward from the body. Fig. 129. ....Family NEMOURIDAE

The members of this family are widely distributed. Their tails are characteristicly short. The adults are usually dark colored.

Fig. 129. **Leuctra decepta** Classen.

6b. Hind wing pads wider than fore wing pads and not divergent outward from the body. Fig. 130. ....Family CAPNIIDAE

The smallest known stoneflies belong to this comparatively small family.

The naiads are herbivorous and live in small water-courses. The color of the naiads is brown or blackish.

Fig 130 **Capnia vernalis** Newport.

ORDER EPHEMEROPTERA

1a. Thorax shield-like covering most abdominal segments; gills invisible. Fig. 131. ....Family PROSOPISTOMATIDAE

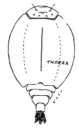

The naiads are flat and disk-like. The gills are concealed by a large shield-like thorax. Their three caudal filaments are short. They live in swift running water, and are vegetable feeders. It belongs to the old world.

Fig 131 Prosopistoma foliaceum Fourcroy

1b. Thorax not shield-like; gills visible. 2

2a. Mandibles extending anteriorly far beyond the head; gills plumose. 3

2b. Mandibles short; gills not plumose. 6

3a. The projecting part of mandible shorter than head; gills extending laterally. Fig. 132. ....Family POTAMANTHIDAE

The naiads live upon silt-covered stones and muddy bottoms. The mandibles are tusk-like but short. The gills are long and plumose. They feed on the vegetation of their area.

Fig. 132. Potamanthus sp.

3b. The projecting part of mandible almost as long as head; gills extending dorsally. 4

62

4a. Front of head with 2 tubercles; mandibles curved outwards at tips; antennae with long cilia. Fig. 133. . . . .Family EPHEMERIDAE

The naiads live in muddy bottoms or muddy water. The body is elongate and more or less cylindrical. The mandibles are long and tusk-like. The caudal filaments are long and almost equal in length.

Fig 133 Hexa-
genia bilineata
Say.

4b. Not so. 5

5a. Abdomen with 6 pairs of gills; median caudal filament shorter than the lateral ones. Fig. 134. .. Family PALINGENIIDAE

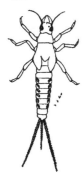

The mandibles are large and protruding. The median caudal filament is shorter than the lateral ones. They live in Europe and Asia.

Fig. 134. Palin-
genia sp.

5b. Abdomen with 7 pairs of gills; median caudal filament as long as, or longer than the lateral ones.
Fig. 135. ... .Family POLYMITARCIDAE

The naiads sometimes dig into mud. The mandibles are long and tusk-like. The caudal filaments are equal in length.

Fig. 135 Campsurus sp

63

6a. Eyes dorsal; body distinctly flattened. 7

6b. Eyes lateral; body more or less cylindrical. 8

7a. Caudal filaments shorter than abdomen; 1st pair of gills inserted on the ventral side of 1st abdominal segment.
Fig. 136. . . . . .Family OLIGONEURIELLIDAE

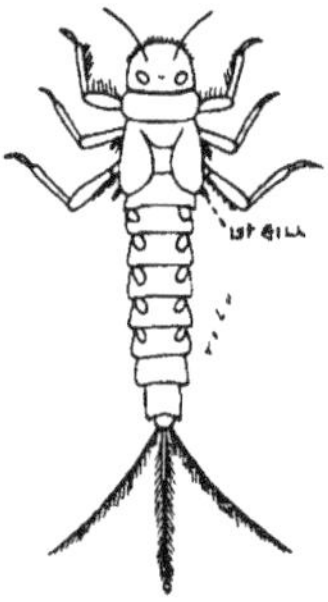

The body is more or less cylindrical with small and short gills. Long hairs may be present on the fore legs.

Fig 136 **Oligoneuria** sp

7b. Caudal filaments longer than abdomen; 1st pair of gills inserted on the lateral sides of 1st abdominal segment.
Fig. 137. . . . . .Family ECDYURIIDAE

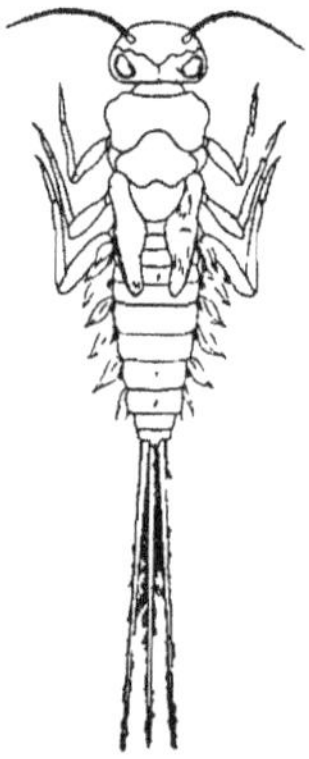

The naiads live in rapid waters, clinging to stones and other objects, where the waves break over lake shores and on the margins of gently flowing streams. The body and appendages are flattened, the head large and the gills leaf-like.

Fig 137 **Hepta-genia** sp

8a. Abdominal gills inserted dorsally. 9

8b. Abdominal gills inserted laterally. 10

9a. The 2nd pair of abdominal gills normal, not covering the remaining pairs. Fig. 138. .... .Family EPHEMERELLIDAE

The naiads are often strikingly colored. In some species the venter of abdomen forms a sucking disk. They often cling to the underside of stones in swift waters.

Fig 138 Ephe-merella sp.

9b. The 1st pair of abdominal gills very small; 2nd pair exceptionally large and covering the remaining pairs.
Fig. 139. ....Family CAENIDAE

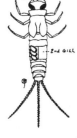

The naiads live in sand or mud bottoms. They are peculiar in having the second pair of gills covering the succeeding pairs. The members of this family are mostly of small size.

Fig 139 Tri-corythus sp

10a. Claws of middle and hind legs as long as the tibiae.
Fig. 140. ....Family AMETROPODIDAE

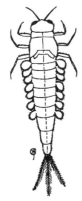

There is rather wide variation in the naiads of the Mayflies. A few are even thought to be predacious. They apparently molt many times during their development. They belong in the eastern hemisphere

Fig. 140. Amethropus sp.

10b. Claws of the middle and hind legs shorter than the tibiae. ....·11
11a. Lateral caudal filaments with very short hairs, or with longer
hairs fringed on both sides.
Fig. 141. ....Family LEPTOPHLEBIIDAE

The naiads are elongated with three
equal caudal filaments as long as the
body and with long slender leaf-like
or string-like gills.

Fig 141. **Blasturus cupidus** Say

11b. Lateral caudal filaments with long hairs on the inner side only..12
12a. Latero-caudal margin of the abdominal segments with tooth-like
projections. Fig. 142. ....Family SIPHLONURIDAE

The naiads live in rapidly running
water and sometimes occur in cataracts
and waterfalls. They have small head
and slender legs.

Fig. 142 **Siphlonurus alterna-
tus** Say.

12b. Latero-caudal margin of the abdominal segments without tooth-
like projection. Fig. 143. ....Family BAETIDAE

The naiads are found in waterfalls, cataracts, slow currents and open waters. They
may be also found among aquatic plants in
still pools. The family is large and widely
scattered.

Fig. 143. **Gallibaetis fluctuans** (Walsh)

ORDER ODONATA

1a. Abdomen stout, usually wider than head, with 3 short, triangular or spine-like appendages at tip (Suborder Anisoptera, dragonflies). Fig. 144. 3

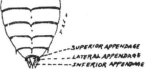

Fig 144 Dorsal aspect of abdominal segments of a dragonfly naiad

1b. Abdomen slender, usually narrower than head, with 3 long, leaf-like tracheal gills at tip (Suborder Zygoptera, damselflies). Fig. 135. 2

It will be noted that both the imature stages and the adults of the damselflies can be separated at sight from those of the dragonflies. One does not always find distinguishing characters so obvious.

Fig 145 Dorsal aspect of abdominal segments of a damselfly naiad.

2a. 1st antennal segment shorter than the remaining segments together: lateral gills 2-sided.

Fig. 146. ....Family COENAGRIONIDAE

The naiads of this large and prolific family are very abundant. A large percentage of these delicate creatures are eaten by fish and other aquatic associates, but large numbers escape to become adults.

Fig 146 a, **Isch-nura** sp , b, a lateral caudal gill.

2b. 1st antennal segment as long as the remaining segments together; lateral gills 3-sided. Fig. 147. . . . . .Family AGRIONIDAE

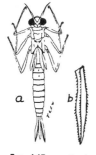

This family of broadwinged damselflies is much
smaller than the preceeding one. The naiads are
larger and sturdier.

Fig 147 a, **Agrion**
sp, b, a lateral
caudal gill

3a. Labium spoon-like. Fig. 148. . . . . .Family LIBELLULIDAE

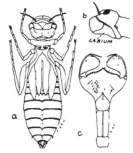

This is the large family of dragonflies in
point both of abundance and numbers of
species. The immature forms may be found
among the debris of almost any shallow
body of water.

Fig 148 a, **Libellula
luctuosa** Burmeister, b,
Lateral aspect of head,
c, labium

3b. Labium not spoon-like. Fig. 149. . . . . .Family AESCHNIDAE

The members of this family average larger
than those of the preceeding family, though
there are much fewer individuals and species.
Their naiads while not as abundant may be
collected rather readily.

Fig. 149. a, **Aeschna** sp.,
b, Lateral aspect of
head.

68

ORDER ORTHOPTERA

1a. Hind tarsi with 1 segment or obsolete.
Fig. 150. .... Subfamily Tridactylinae, GRYLLIDAE

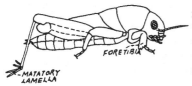

Fig 150 **Ellipes minuta** Scudder

They are pigmy crickets, scarcely more than 10 mm. long, with the fore tibiae fossorial and the hind femora enlarged for jumping. The terminal end of hind tibiae provided with movable elongated plates called matatory lamellae. They inhabit damp places and near water. They can also burrow into sand.

1b. Hind tarsi with more than 1 segment. 2

2a. Fore legs greatly modified, either adapted for grasping Fig. 151a or for digging Fig. 151b. 3

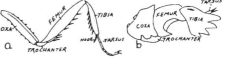

Fig 151 a, Fore leg of a mantid, b, Fore leg of a mole cricket

2b. Fore legs normal. 4

3a. Fore legs adapted for digging.
Fig. 152. ....Subfamily Gryllotalpinae, GRYLLIDAE

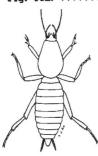

The subfamily consists of about 50 species. They are called mole crickets, because of their fossorial fore tibiae and their burrowing habits. They live in mud along waterways and are vegetable feeders.

Fig 152 Mole crick-et, **Scapteriscus dida-ctylus** Latr

3b. Fore legs adapted for grasping. Fig. 153. . . . .Family MANTIDAE

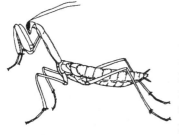

About 1,550 species are describ-ed. The name, praying mantids, is applied because their fore legs are held in front of the face as if pray-ing. They appear to be wholly car-nivorous and devour only living prey.

Fig 153 Chinese mantis, **Teno-dera aridifolia sinensis** Saussure

4a. Hind legs much larger than other pairs, adapted for jumping. (See Fig. 159). 5

4b. Hind legs of usual size, not adapted for jumping. (See Fig. 161). 9

5a. Antennae usually much short-er than the body; auditory or-gan when present, near the base of the abdomen. Fig. 154. 6

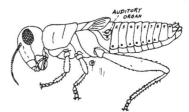

Fig 154 A grasshopper, showing the auditory organ on abdomen

5b. Antennae usually as long as or longer than the body; auditory or gan, when present, near the base of the fore tibiae. Fig. 155. 7

Fig 155 A fore leg with audi-tory organ on tibia

6a. Fore and middle tarsi 2-segmented, hind tarsi 3-segmented; prono-tum greatly extended, often beyond the tip of the abdomen. Fig. 156. ....Family TETTIGIDAE

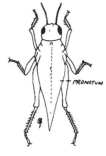

About 650 species have been described. They are herbivorous and found in wet places. They can swim and dive in water. Eggs are laid in the soil. These are the pygmy or grouse locusts.

Fig 156 **Acrydium granulatum** (Kirby)

6b All tarsi 3-segmented; pronotum normal size.

Fig. 157. . . . . .Family LOCUSTIDAE

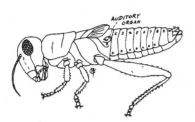

Fig 157 **Melanoplus femur-rubrum** (DeGeer), 3rd instar

The family contains about 8,000 known species. The common name grasshopper is generally applied to the nonmigratory species and locust is applied to the migratory forms. They are all destructive to crops. The migratory locust, *Locusta migratoria* L. is the most serious pest and is distributed widely in most of the Eastern Hemisphere. It breeds in dry grassy areas. Grasshopper eggs are often laid underground.

7a. Tarsi 4-segmented. 8

7b. Tarsi 3-segmented. Fig. 158. . . . . .Family GRYLLIDAE

Fig. 158 Snowy tree-cricket, **Oecanthus niveus** (DeGeer) (N Y A.gr Expt Sta)

About 1,150 species have been described. They are generally called crickets, and are both herbivorous and carnivorous. They hide themselves in holes in the ground or under stones and debris and some live on trees, shrubs and grass. Nymphs and adults are often found together.

8a. Auditory organ usually present on the fore tibiae.

Fig. 159. . . . . .Family TETTIGONIIDAE

Fig 159 Mormon cricket, **Anabrus simplex** Haldeman.

They are commonly called long-horned grasshoppers or katydids, about 7,000 known species. They can produce stridulatory sounds by the fore wings of the males. They are both herbivorous and carnivorous, living in grass or trees. The eggs are often inserted in the stems of plants.

8b. Auditory organ never present on the fore tibiae.

Fig. 160. . . . . .Subfamily Stenopelmatinae, TETTIGONIIDAE

Fig. 160 **Stenopelmatus longispina** Brunner.

The subfamily includes about 300 described species. They are mostly carnivorous, living in caves, in holes, under stones and other concealments. These camel crickets and related forms are given their own family by some systematists. The adults are wingless and strongly resemble the nymphs.

71

9a. Prothorax small, meso- and metathorax modified either long and in linear form or short and in leaf form; antennae shorter than the body; cerci not segmented. Fig. 161. .....Family PHASMIDAE

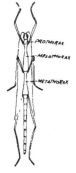

They are commonly known as walkingsticks and leaf insects because of their body structures closely resemble the twigs or leaves. Over 700 species are described. All of them are vegetable feeders. The nymphs and adults of many species appear much alike for most adults are wingless. The eggs are often dropped at random.

Fig 161 Walk-ingstick, **Dia-pheromera fe-morata** (Say)

9b. Prothorax large, projecting over the head; antennae as long as or longer than the body; cerci segmented.
Fig. 162. ....Family BLATTIDAE

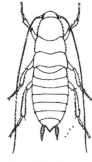

About 1,200 species of cockroaches are known and they occur under dead leaves, moss, refuse and on flowers and bushes. The most familiar do-mesticated species are the German cockroach, *Blat-tella germanica* (L.), the American cockroach, *Periplaneta americana* (L.), and the Australian cock-roach, *Periplaneta australasiae* (Fab.). They have been distributed throughout the entire world and are household pests. The females may often be seen carrying their egg cases which are presently left for hatching.

Fig 162 German cockroach, **Blat-tella germanica** (L)

ORDER COLEOPTERA

(The key is mainly compiled from Boving and Craighead, 1931, and Van Emden, 1942.)

1a. Legs consisting of 5 segments (coxa, trochanter, femur, tibia and tarsus) and 1 or 2 distinct claws (except in instars of *Micromalthus* which are legless or have 2-segmented legs). Fig. 163.....2

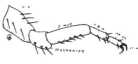

Fig 163 A leg

1b. Legs consisting of 4 segments (coxa, trochanter, femur and tibiotarsus) and 1 claw; or less than 4 segments; or even vestigial or absent. Fig. 164...13

Fig 164 A leg

2a. Mandible with molar structure. Fig. 165. 3

The food habits of an insect possessing chewing mouth parts can usually be judged fairly accurately by the size and character of the mandibles. These structures are "first line" organs when it comes to securing food. It is interesting to note that insect jaws meet on a vertical plane instead of a horizontal one as with the mammals.

Fig. 165. A right mandible.

2b. Mandible without molar structure. Fig. 166. 4

Fig. 166. A left mandible.

3a. 9th abdominal segment extended terminally into a single, conical, straight process; ventrally with a simple, transverse, narrow sternal plate; legs short, conical; claws of subequal size. Fig. 167. ....Family CUPESIDAE

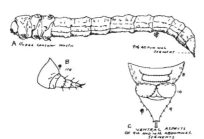

Fig 167 a, **Cupes concolor** Westn , b, a leg, c, ventral aspect of 9th and 10th abdominal segments

A very small family ranging into both hemispheres, including Australia. The larva of Cupes is a wood borer, as are most of the other members of the family. They are medium sized borers, and may be found under bark.

3b. 9th abdominal segment with terminal process bent downward and directed toward a similar but upward bent process from the sternal plate; leg (in instar in which fully developed) provided with a long, slender tarsus carrying 2 claws of equal length.
Fig. 168. ....;... ....Family MICROMALTHIDAE

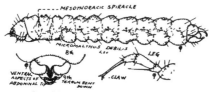

Fig 168. **Micromalthus delibis Lec.**

It consists of a single North American species, *Micromalthus debilis* Lec. The biology of this insect is most remarkable. It combines in its life cycle 7 or 8 forms of larvae. and exhibits both oviparous and ovoviviparous paedogenesis.

4a. Cardo very large; 2 pairs of gills on the tip of 9th abdominal segment. Fig. 169. ....Family GYRINIDAE

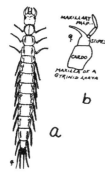

They are called whirligig beetles or surface swimmers. There are about 450 described species. The eggs are laid on objects in water. The larvae are aquatic and predacious. They pupate in flimsy cocoons attached to rocks, water plants, etc.

Fig. 169. a, **Dineutes** sp; b, Maxilla of a gyrinid larva.

4b. Cardo of normal moderate size or small; never have 2 pairs of gills on the tip of 9th abdominal segment. Fig. 170. 5

Fig 170 Maxilla of a carabid larva.

5a. Labial palpi latent; mentum and ligula fused into an unpaired anteriorly bilobed piece. Fig. 171. ....Family RHYSODIDAE

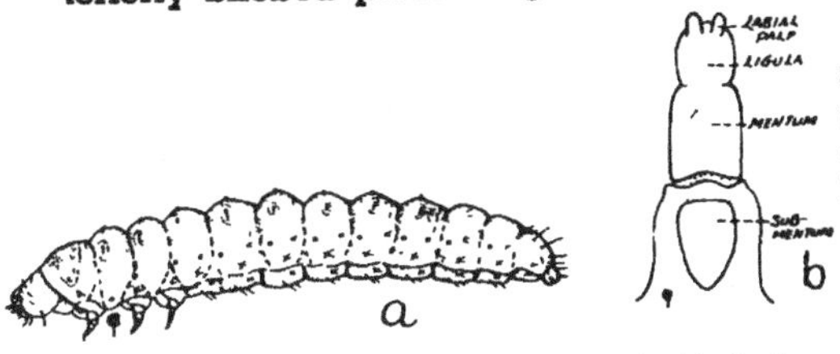

Rather more than 100 species have been described. Nothing appears to be known about their metamorphoses. The larvae are probably predacious. Look for them under decaying bark.

Fig 171. a, **Clinidium sculptile** Newn:; b, Ventral aspect of labium.

5b. Labial palpi distinct and segmented. Fig. 172. 6

6a. 9th abdominal segment present; 8th abdominal segment never terminal. (See Fig. 174). 7

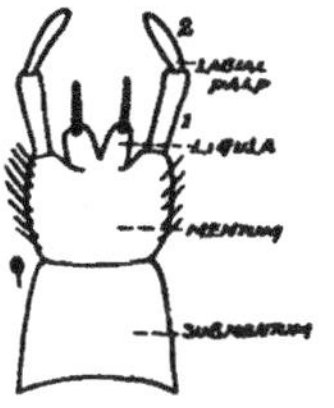

Fig. 172. Ventral aspect of labium.

6b. 9th abdominal segment rudimentary; 8th abdominal segment long, conical, appearing as the terminal segment of the body. (See Fig. 177). 10

7a. 10th abdominal segment developed as a pygopod for locomotory purpose. 8

7b. 10th abdominal segment not developed as a pygopod. Fig. 173. ....Family HALIPLIDAE

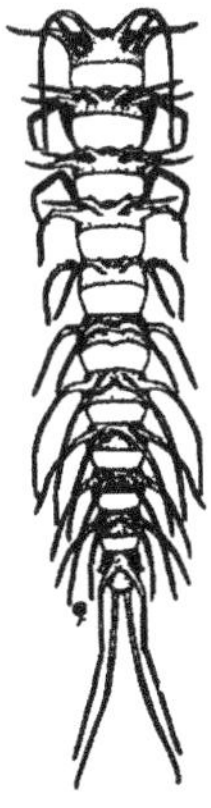

They comprise about 100 widely distributed species. Their larvae possess segmentally arranged groups of freshy process and are aquatic insects. Larvae and adults live together among aquatic plants and may be collected readily by raking these plants out on to the shore.

Fig. 173. **Pelto-dytes** sp.

8a. 2 or 3 pairs of hooks present on tergum of 5th abdominal segment. Fig. 174. ....Family CICINDELIDAE

Fig 174 **Megacephala carolina** (L.).

The family consists of about 2,000 species and their adults are called tiger beetles. The larvae live in vertical or slanting, cylindrical burrows often a foot or more deep in which they can move up and down by aid of the dorsal hooks of the fifth abdominal segment. They are predacious and found along the sandy banks of rivers and bodies of water, in wet meadows, and in damp partially shaded canyons.

8b. No hooks on 5th abdominal tergum. 9

9a. Terminal setae of tarsus much shorter than claws; retinaculum single or absent. Fig. 175. ....Family CARABIDAE

Fig 175 **Harpalus viridiaeneus** Beauvois

The family is very large, comprising around 21,000 described species. The larvae are carnivorous and living in the soil, grass, under debris or dead bark. Pupation takes place in a cell in the ground. They are elongate, usually flattened and grublike, and often very active.

9b. Terminal setae of tarsus much longer than claws; retinaculum bicuspidate. Fig. 176. ....Family OMOPHRONIDAE

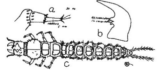

Fig 176 a, leg of **Omophron;** b, Mandible of **Omophron;** c, **Omophron** sp

The members of this small family live in the sand and debris along water courses. They are comparatively rare.

10a. Head nutant; mandible falcate and simple; 8th abdominal spiracle absent. Fig. 179. ....Family HYGROBIIDAE

This is a small family comprising all aquatic species. They are found in the Eastern Hemisphere.

Fig 177. **Hydrobia tarda** Herbst (Redrawn from Boving and Craighead).

10b. Head porrect; mandible not simple; 8th adbominal spiracle terminal. (See Fig. 178). 11

11a. Mandible with distinct retinaculum, inner margin neither sulcate nor tubular; legs fossorial.
Fig. 178. ....Subfamily Noterinae, DYTISCIDAE

The members of this small subfamily are rather minute in size. Their larvae must feed, of course, on tiny animal forms.

Fig 178 a, **Noterus** sp , b, mandible.

11b. Mandible without distinct retinaculum, inner margin either sulcate or tubular; legs ambulatory or natatory.
(See Fig. 179). 12

12a. Prothoracic presternum large and subquadrate; gula present, subquadrate or triangular; gular suture double or anteriorly bifurcate. Fig. 179. ....Family DYTISCIDAE

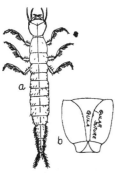

The family contains more than 2,000 species. Their adults are known as predacious diving beetles, water beetles and dytiscids. The larvae are predacious and feed upon many kinds of aquatic animals including mollusks, worms, tadpoles, salamanders and fishes. Because the hunting life, the larvae are sometimes called water tigers. Their pupae are terrestrial and pupation takes place above the water line.

Fig 179 a, **Dytiscus** sp , b, Ventral aspect of head

12b. Prothoracic presternum transverse, narrow and band-shaped; gula absent; gular suture median and simple.
Fig. 180. ....Family AMPHIZOIDAE

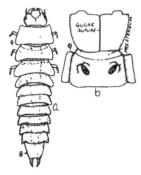

The family consists of the single genus, *Amphizoa,* with only 3 aquatic species. They inhabit rocks and logs in fresh water streams along the Pacific coast of N. America and 1 species in Tibet.

Fig 180 a, **Amphizoa** sp, b, Ventral aspect of head and prothorax.

13a. 8th abdominal segment glandular, discoidal and terminal.
Fig. 181. ....Family PAUSSIDAE

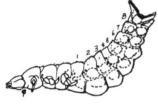

More than 300 species are known. They are adapted to a myrmecophilous life. The metamorphoses of this family have received very little attention. Its known members are all exotic.

Fig 181 **Paussus kannegieteri** Wasm.

13b. 8th abdominal segment not glandular and not discoidal. 14

14a. Cerci segmented, individually movable. 15

14b. Cerci solid or absent. 28

15a. (a) Galea usually inserted on the palpifer; if absent, then the abdomen with only 8 distinct segments; or (b) galea less often inserted on stipes (to the outside of lacinia), but then the mandible serrate, the cerci 2-segmented, and the 10th abdominal segment almost always with a pair of recurved ventral hooks.
Fig. 182. 114

Fig 182 Maxilla.

15b. Galea never inserted on the palpifer; often absent or fused with the lacinia; abdomen always with 9 to 10 distinct segments; if the mandible is serrate, the cerci absent or 1-segmented. Fig. 183. 16

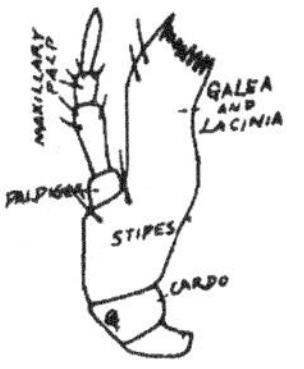

Fig 183 Maxilla.

16a. Mandible with a usually large, asperate or tuberculate molar part. Fig. 184. ... .17

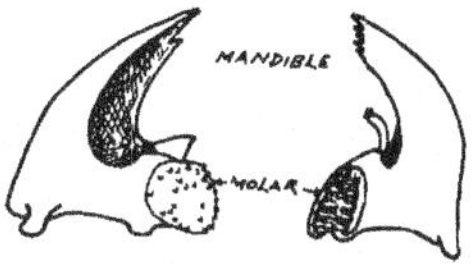

Fig 184 Two mandibles.

16b. Mandible without asperate or tuberculate molar part, usually without molar part. 21

17a. 10th abdominal segment provided with a pair of recurved hooks. Fig. 185. ....Subfamily Limnebiinae, HYDROPHILIDAE

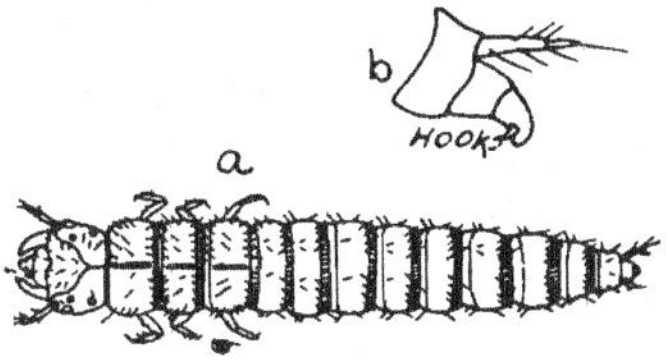

The members of this small subfamily are for the most part found on the Pacific coast, and are comparatively small in size.

Fig 185 a, **Ochthebius mipressus**; b, Tip of abdomen.

17b. 10th abdominal segment without terminal hooks but sometimes with a pair of long setae. ... .18

18a. Spiracles absent; balloon-like appendices on prothorax, 1st and 8th abdominal segments; antenna very short and 2-segmented. Fig. 186. ....Subfamily Hydroscaphinae, HYDROPHILIDAE

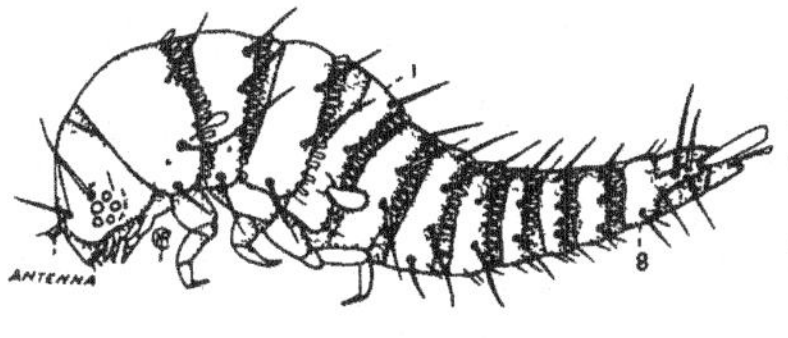

It is a small subfamily, comprising only 4 or 5 species adapted for an aquatic life. They occur in running water, including hot springs. The one American species is found in our Southwest.

Fig. 186 **Hydroscapha natans** Lec

18b. Spiracles present; no balloon-like appendices; antenna 3-segmented. 19

19a. Apex of mandible multiserrate; cerci short, 1-segmented.
    Fig. 187. ....Family PTILIIDAE

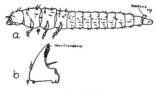

Fig. 187 a, **Nossidium ameri-
canum** Mots, b, Mandible

The larvae and adults of these 'feather-winged" beetles live in decaying
wood, fungi and in ant's nests. They
are very minute, some of the smallest
known beetles belong to this family.

19b. Apex of mandible bifid or trifid; cerci 2-segmented, last segment
    often multiannulated. (See Fig. 188). 20

20a. Mandible with vestigial retinaculum.
    Fig. 188. ....Family LEPTINIDAE

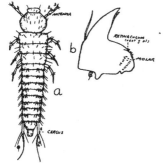

This is a very small family. Its habits are practically unknown but they
have been found in rotten wood, in the
nests of birds and of field mice.

Fig 188 a, **Leptinus testaceus**
Mull, b, Mandible

20b. Mandible with distinct retinaculum or prostheca, or both.
    Fig. 189. ... .Subfamily Anistominae, SILPHIDAE

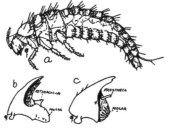

They are found among damp herbage, in fungi, under bark, etc. They
are fairly abundant but their very
small size results in their being
rather poorly known.

Fig 189 a, **Prionochaeta opaca**
Say; b, Mandible with retinaculum;
c, Mandible with prostheca.

21a. Mala (lacinia and galea) and stipes fused.
   Fig. 190. 22

Fig 190 Maxilla

21b. Mala segment-like, movable. Fig. 191. . .Family STAPHYLINIDAE

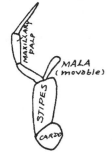

This is one of the largest family of insects and including more than 20,000 species. The adults are called rove beetles. The larvae are typically campodeiform and often closely resemble the Carabidae. The larvae of certain species are definitely known to be carnivorous and predacious. Certain larvae are pupal parasites of cyclorrhaphous Diptera and undergo hypermetamorphosis.

Fig 191 Maxilla

22a. Mandible with apex simple, recurved and bent away from the sagittal plane of the larva.
   Fig. 192. . . . . .Family PLATYPSYLLIDAE

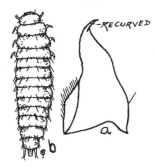

The family consists of a single species, the beaver beetle, *Platypsyllus castoris* Rits., which is an ectoparasite of the beaver in Europe and America. The biology of the immature stages is not known.

Fig 192 a, Mandible, b,
Platypsyllus castoris Rits

22b. Mandible with apex differently shaped, never recurved. 23

23a. Galea present, often developed as a small, hairy lobe on top of lacinia. Fig. 193. . . .24

23b. Galea and lacinia fused. 25

Fig. 193 Maxilla —

24a. Lacinia with entire surface asperate; terminal segment of maxillary palpus subulate; ligula trilobed.

Fig. 194. ....Family SCAPHIDIIDAE

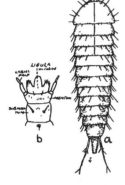

The members of this family are fungivorous or occur in rotting wood both as larvae and adults. Less than 100 species are known in North America although some species are very common.

Fig 194 a, **Scaphisoma convexum** Say, b, Ventral aspect. of labium.

24b. Lacinia not asperate, or only along posterior margin; terminal segment of maxillary palpus not subulate; ligula bilobed.

Fig. 195. ....Family SILPHIDAE

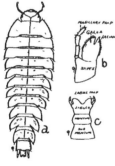

The carrion beetles, burying beetles and sexton beetles are the common names of the adult members of this family which include about 1,600 described species. The eggs are laid in dead animal bodies and their larvae lead a saprozoic life, However, some are predacious and feeding upon snails or other insects; others are found among plants and fungi.

Fig 195 a, **Silpha** sp.; b, Mandible, c, Labium

25a. Ligula either deeply bilobed anteriorly, or absent; labrum fused to become nasale.

Fig. 196. 26

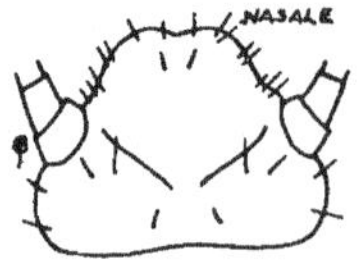

Fig. 196. Dorsal aspect of head.

25b. Anterior margin of ligula entire; labrum distinct, often movable. Fig. 197. ....most STAPHYLINIDAE

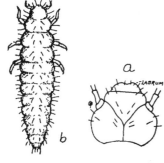

The short elytra of the adult staphylinids result in the larva and adults often resembling each other rather closely. The many species range rather widely in size.

Fig 197. a, Dorsal aspect of head, b, **Oligota oviformis** Casey.

26a. Cerci long and 2-segmented; antennae more than twice as long as head; ligula bilobed; 6 ocelli on each side. Fig. 198. . ... Subfamily Steninae, STAPHYLINIDAE

The members of this subfamily are rather short and thick as compared with most staphylinids. They live in sand and debris at the edge of water courses and seem to be predacious.

Fig 198. **Stenus sp.**

26b. Cerci absent or small and immovable; antennae not longer than head; ligula absent; less than 6 ocelli on each side, sometimes no ocelli. 27

27a. Terga expanded laterally; body oval; antenna club-shaped.
Fig. 199. ....Family SCYDMAENIDAE

It includes more than 1,200 species of small insects. They mostly occur in moss, under bark or in ants' nests. Scarcely anything appears to be known of the biology of the family.

Fig 199 A scydmaenid larva

27b. Terga not expanded; antenna not club-shaped.
Fig. 200. ....Family PSELAPHIDAE

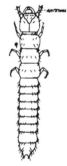

The species mostly live in ants' nests and the adult bears a resemblance to ants. The biology of the larvae is little known. More than 3,000 species have been described. Their size is small.

Fig 200 **Euplectus confluens** Lec

28a. Hypermetamorphosis present; mandible without molar part; maxillary mala short, thick, almost vestigial; gular area present; cerci absent. Fig. 201. 29

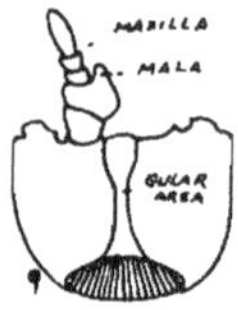

Hypermetamorphosis is a condition that prevails among a relative small percentage of insect species. Some of the instars are radically different from each other in habits and form or in some cases additional instars occur between the full grown larva and the adult.

Fig 201 Ventral aspect of head

28b. No hypermetamorphosis; different combination of characters than in 28a. 31

29a. Gula well developed; maxillae inserted at a considerable distance in from anterior margin of prosternum: labial palpi 2-segmented. Fig. 202. ....Family MELOIDAE

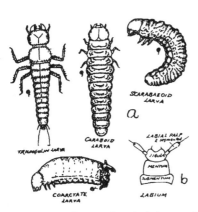

Fig 202 a, Forms of meloid larvae; b, Ventral aspect of labium.

This family comprises no less than 2,500 species. The adults are called blister beetles. Eggs are laid in masses in the soil. The newly hatched larvae called triungulins or primary larvae, are campodeiform. They are active and feed on egg masses of other insects in the soil, or they may attach themselves to certain adult hosts and ride to the nests and feed upon the food or devour the young. Then they transform into scarabaeoid type of larvae, and some into still a third type of larvae. A prepupa stage is followed by the pupa and then the adult.

29b. Gula area short; maxillae extending posteriorly to near the anterior margin of prosternum; labial palpi not segmented, reduced to warts, or entirely absent. Fig. 203. 30

Fig 203. Ventral aspect of head and prothorax of **Rhipiphorus solidaginia** Pierce

30a. 1 ocellus on each side of head.
Fig. 204. ..Genus *Tetraonyx*, MELOIDAE

The larvae of this genus seem so different from other Meloids that some systematists would errect a family (Tetraonycidae) for the few members of the genus.

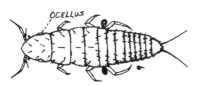

Fig 204 **Tetraonyx quadrimaculata** F 1st instar.

30b. Several ocelli placed together on each side of head.
Fig. 205. . . . .   Family RHIPIPHORIDAE

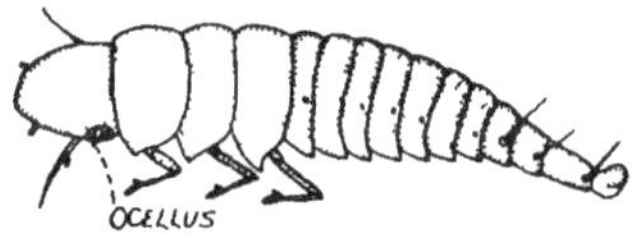

Fig 205 **Rhipiphorus solidaginis**
Pierce

The larvae of this family are of great interest on account of their parasitic habits. *Metaecus paradoxus* is a parasite in nests of *Vespa*, but the eggs are laid in old wood. The larva becomes an endoparasite and then changes to ectoparasite. Pupation takes place in the cell of the host.

31a. Mandible bearing an accessory ventral condyle; with either a free galea well separated from a distinct lacinia or with cribriform spiracles, or with both characters. Fig. 306.   .32

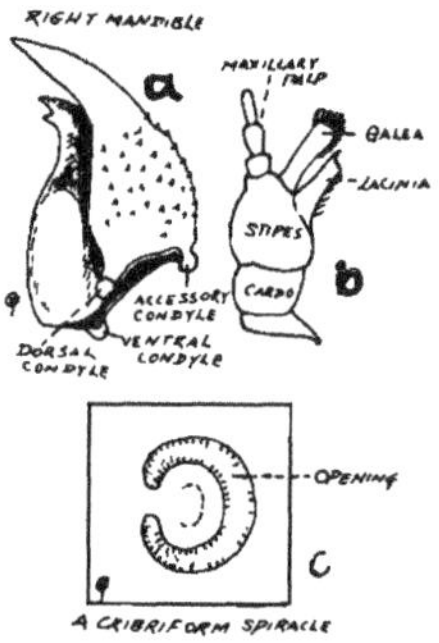

Fig 206 a, A right mandible, b, A maxilla, c, A cribriform spiracle

31b. Characters not so combined. 40

32a. Median epicranial suture present; 10th abdominal segment well developed, usually about as large or larger than the well developed 9th abdominal segment, sometimes fused with it dorsally, when shorter than 9th abdominal segment, then provided with a pair of large anal pads. 33

32b. Median epicranial suture absent; 10th abdominal segment much smaller than the well developed 9th abdominal segment and always without anal pads, or both 9th and 10th abdominal segments vestigial. 37

33a. Stridulating organ present on mesothoracic leg; abdominal terga not plicate. Fig. 207. 34

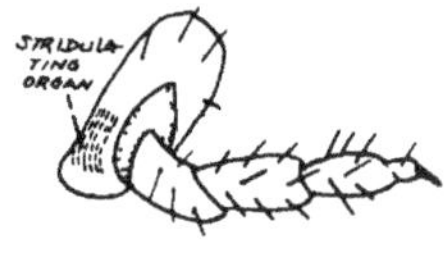

Fig 207 A mesothoracic leg

33b. Stridulating organ absent, or present as teeth on dorsal inner margin of maxillary stipites, usually working against a granulate or striped area on ventral side of mandibles; abdominal terga plicate. Fig. 208. 35

Fig. 208. A mesothoracic leg

34a. Anus longitudinal between 2 large oval, often sclerotized pads at end of body; metathoracic legs normal. Fig. 209. ....Family LUCANIDAE

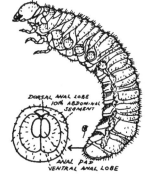

DORSAL ANAL LOBE
10th ABDOMINAL SEGMENT
ANAL PAD
VENTRAL ANAL LOBE

Fig. 209 **Sinodendron cylindricum.**

The family consists of around 900 species. The adults are called stag beetles. Their larvae live largely in decaying wood. The larval stage lasts 4 to 6 years to complete their development. Pupation takes place in a cell formed of gnawed wood fragments. Some species are very large.

34b. Anus transverse; end of body different; metathoracic legs reduced and much shorter than mesothoracic legs. Fig. 210. ....Family PASSALIDAE

META-THORACIC LEG

About 300 species have been described. It was reported that the parent beetles stay with the larvae and chew wood into a condition suitable for their progeny. The metathoracic legs of the larvae are greatly modified and adapted to form an organ which works across a striated area on the mesocoxa, thus producing a squeaking noise.

Fig 210. **Passalus** sp.

35a. Lacinia and galea separate. Fig. 211. 36

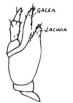

Fig 211. Maxilla.

35b. Lacinia and galea fused. Fig. 212. . . . .Family SCARABAEIDAE

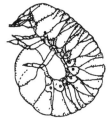

Fig 212 **Anomala kansanas** Hayes & McColloch.

About 15,000 species are known in this very large family. The larvae are typically scarabaeoid type, living mostly in the soil and feeding upon plant tissues, but some forms are recorded as being myrmecophilous. The white grubs are best known larval pests while the Japanese beetle, June beetle and rose chafer are the serious adult pests. The world's largest beetles belong here, and of course the largest grubs.

One fairly large and widely represented group within this family, the Tumble bugs, are unique in their method of providing for their young. A pair of beetles make a large ball of mammalian dung which they roll, often for a considerable distance, and bury in an excavation which they prepare. An egg is laid in the ball and the grub makes its entire growth within the ball.

36a. Stridulating organs absent. Fig. 213. . . . . .Family TROGIDAE

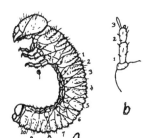

It is a small family composed of three genera and about 160 species. They mostly live in dried decomposing animal matter, and may be found in carrion.

Fig 213 a, **Trox scaber** L, b, Antenna

36b. At least maxillary stridulating teeth present.
Fig. 214. ....Family SCARABAEIDAE

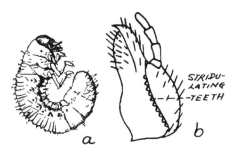

Fig 214 a, White grub, b, Maxilla.

The larvae of many Scarabaeids live in dung or other decaying organic matter and are of little consequence except to act as scavengers. Many others feed on the roots of growing plants and are highly destructive.

37a. 8th abdominal segment of normal form and not terminal; 9th abdominal segment large. (See Fig. 215). 38

37b. 8th abdominal segment large and terminal; 9th abdominal segment vestigial. (See Fig. 217)................................39

38a. 10th abdominal segment almost obliterated and without soft, terminal prolongation; ocelli absent.
Fig. 215. ....Family DASCILLIDAE

Fig 215 **Dascillus davidsoni** Lec

This is a group of small to medium terrestrial and aquatic beetles. The larvae have been found in pasture land. Some 500 species are known.

38b. 10th abdominal segment well developed, with soft terminal unpaired, 2-segmented and retractile prolongation; 5 ocelli on each side. Fig. 216. ....Family HETEROCERIDAE

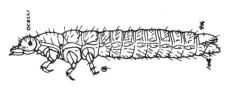

Fig 216 **Heterocercus ventralis** Meish

The family is very widely distributed and about 100 species are known. The larvae live in galleries which they excavate in the mud bordering pools and streams.

39a. 3 terminal tufts of gills retractile into a pocket; antenna long and multisegmented; one large ocellus and one small ocellus on each side of head. Fig. 217. . . . . .Family HELODIDAE

It is a small family. Their larvae are aquatic. They are all of small size.

Fig 217. **Prionocyphon discoideus** Say.

39b. Gills absent; antenna 3-segmented; 5 ocelli on each side of head. Fig. 218. . . . . .Subfamily Nosodendrinae, BYRRHIDAE

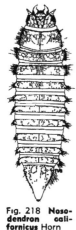

The single genus *Nosodendron* contains 3 described species, 2 from North America and 1 from Europe. The larvae have been taken in fungi, under bark and around the flowing sap of trees. They are thought to be predators on dipterous larvae. No information concerning the pupae is available.

Fig. 218 **Noso-dendron cali-fornicus** Horn

40a. Gular region or median gular suture present or absent; when absent, with mandibles having mola or prostheca or extraordinary structures except a pseudomola. Fig. 219. 41

Fig 219 a, Ventral aspect of head; b, Mandible.

40b. Gular region or gular suture absent; mandibles with pseudomola or no mola. 118

41a. Maxillary articulating area either large or indistinct; when indistinct, mandibles with mola (except in Catogenidae, Epilachninae and Laminae). Fig. 220. 42

Fig. 220. Maxiilla.

41b. Maxillary articulating area absent, or very small, or concealed by mentum, not large and cushioned; mandible without molar part. 43

42a. Maxillary mala divided into a well developed lacinia and a finger-shaped, 1 or 2-segmented galea; mandible without a distinct molar part but with a longitudinal series of hairs at the base. Fig. 221. . . . . .Family BYRRHIDAE

The family has about 500 species. The adults are called pill beetles. Their life histories are in need of study. The larvae of *Byrrhus pilula* are found beneath turf or moss. The larvae of *Amphicyrta dentipes* are often injurious to wild and cultivated plants.

Fig 221. a, **Byrrhus fasciatus** Forst.; b, Mandible.

42b. Mala simple, or division either indicated by distal notch or present with lobe-like galea; mandibles with or without a molar part but without a longitudinal series of hairs at the base. 66

43a. Either with exposed gills below the entire abdomen, or with movable 10th abdominal segment usually covering retractile gills at the end of the body, or with mamillaeform appendices from the 10th abdominal segment; mandibles never perforate or deeply cleft. Fig. 222. 44

Fig. 223. Tip of abdomen.

43b. Gills or anal appendices usually absent; when present, then mandible either perforate or deeply cleft longitudinally. 48

44a. Movable 10th abdominal segment absent. 45

44b. Movable 10th abdominal segment present below 9th abdominal tergum. Fig. 223. 47

45a. Body cylindrical, without ventral gills. 46

Fig 222. Tip of abdomen.

45b. Body flat, broadly oval; with ventral gills freely exposed from
2nd to 6th abdominal segments.
Fig. 224. ....Family PSEPHENIDAE

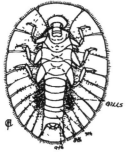

The larvae are aquatic and attach to
stones in swift-flowing streams, rapids,
cascades and waterfalls. They are flattened and disc-like. Their pupae are submerged and firmly attached to stones.

Fig 224 **Psephenus le-
contei** Lec

46a. Antennae comparatively long; 10th abdominal segment with a pair
of large lobes usually carrying spinose diverticles.
Fig. 225. ....Subfamily Ptilodactylinae, HELODIDAE

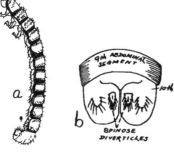

The biology of this subfamily
needs to be investigated. The larvae
of *Ptilodactyla serricollis* Say are found
in the damp soil of forests. Only a
few species are known in North
America. Some systematists believe
that this subfamily belongs else-
where or as a separate family.

Fig 225 a, **Ptilodactyla serricollis** Say; b, 9th and 10th abdominal segments

92

46b. Antennae short; 10th abdominal segment without diverticles.
Fig. 226. .... Genus *Eurypogon*, DASCILLIDAE

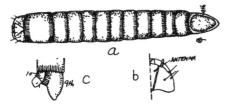

Fig 226 a, **Eurypogon niger** Melsh; b, Half aspect of head, c, 9th and 10th abdominal segments

Some 500 rather widely distributed s p e c i e s a r e known for this family. They are found in damp places and are small sized. The adults are dull colored and of rather soft texture.

47a. 8 pairs of abdominal spiracles, all projecting, either cribiform or biforous but of a deviating sinuous type.
Fig. 227. .... Family CHELONARIIDAE

Only one species of this small family is known in the United States.

Fig. 227 **Chelonarium** sp.

47b. Abdominal spiracles vary from 1 to 8 pairs, either annuliform or regularly biforous, never sinuous.
Fig. 228. .... Family DRYOPIDAE

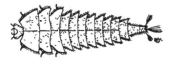

Fig 228 **Helmis aeneus** Muller.

The larvae of *Dryops* is stated to live in damp earth beneath stones. The larva of one species of *Psephenus* is said to resemble a trilobite except that its lateral margins are notched. More than 400 species are known. The adults are named "long-toed water beetles."

48a. 9th abdominal segment operculate, vertical and terminal.
Fig. 229. .... Family RHIPICERIDAE

Fig 229 **Zenoa picea** Beauv

This small family of "cedar beetles" are dull colored and of medium to large size. Their life history is not well known.

48b. 9th abdominal segment otherwise. **49**

49a. Spiracles cribriform; 10th abdominal segment terminal; prothorax large and more or less depressed, usually covered with a plate both dorsally and ventrally.
Fig. 230. . . . . .Family **BUPRESTIDAE**

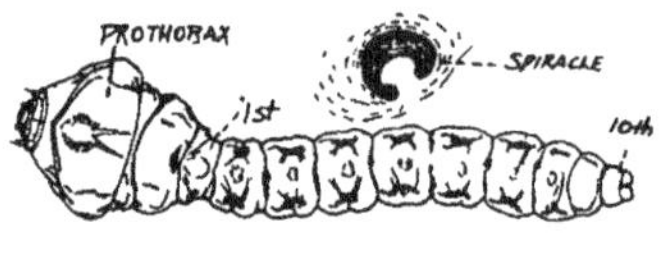

Fig 230 Western cedar borer, **Trachykele blondeli** Mars

The flat-headed borers are a large family which consists of about 8,000 described species. The larvae are blind and legless but capable of excavating in all kinds of dry and moist wood. They live in the trunks, limbs and roots of trees. A few are leaf miners and gallmakers; some are highly destructive to fruit and forest trees.

49b. Not so. **50**

50a. Labrum present. Fig. 231. . . . .**60**

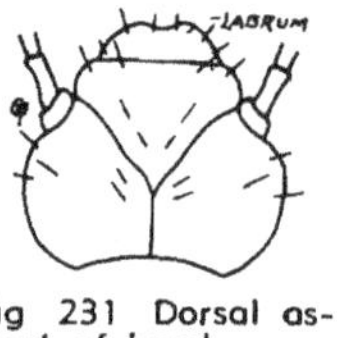

Fig 231 Dorsal aspect of head

50b. Labrum fused. Fig. 232. . . . .**51**

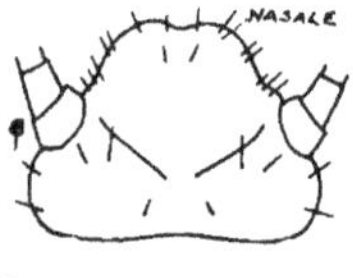

Fig 232 Dorsal aspect of head

51a. Frontal sutures present (except in Throscidae and Eucnemidae the head capsule and mouth parts are reduced or much specialized). **52**

51b. Frontal sutures absent (except in Brachypsectrini and Lampyridae, both of which have piercing mandibles). **56**

52a. Head capsule and mouth parts very much reduced or extremely specialized. (See Fig. 233). **53**

52b. Head capsule and mouth parts slightly reduced or entirely normal. **54**

53a. Legs short but with normal segments.
Fig. 233. ....Family THROSCIDAE

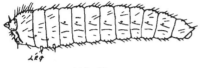

Fig 233 **Throscus** sp

The members of this small family are of small size and are known as "pseudo click beetles". The adults are found on flowers but not much is known about the habits of the larvae.

53b. Legs vestigial or absent. Fig. 234. ....Family EUCNEMIDAE

Fig 234 **Melasis rufipennis** Horn

Less than 100 species are known for North America. The larvae have the head parts enlarged and closely resemble the buprestid larvae.   They bore in wood usually that is just beginning to decay and are fairly common.

54a. Gular area well developed and quadrate.
Fig. 235. 55

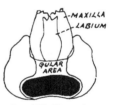

Fig 235 Ventral aspect of head

54b. Gular area small and indistinct, or represented only by a median gular suture. Fig. 236. ....Family ELATERIDAE

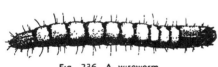

Fig 236 A wireworm

This family is a large one with about 8,000 known species. The larvae are called wireworms and are well known pests of farm and garden. They are mostly subterranean and phytophagous. Some are predacious upon white grubs and a number of species inhabit decaying wood and prey upon the xylophagous larvae.

55a. Larva strongly sclerotized; dorsal and ventral prothoracic scler-
omes united into a solid cylinder; cervical membrane very large
and eversible forming a balloon-shaped sack below the head
when raised. Fig. 237. .... Family CEBRIONIDAE

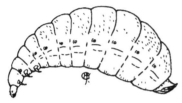

Fig 237 **Cebrio antennatus** Schfr.

This small family is
related to the wire
worms. As for the Uni-
ted States our species
are southern or west-
ern.

55b. Larva white and soft-skinned; dorsal and ventral prothoracic
parts not forming a cylinder; cervical membrane not eversible.
Fig. 238. .... Genus *Sandalus*, RHIPICERIDAE

Fig 238 **Sandalus niger** Knoch

The information available regarding the habits of this genus
is very limited. It is reported
that a mature larva of *Sandalus
niger* Knoch was taken from the
nymph of a Cicada, having developed as a parasite.

56a. 9th abdominal segment with an unpaired pointed prolongation, or
paired cerci; body with feather-like or spinose processes.
Fig. 239. .... Group Brachypsecti, DASCILLIDAE

This group has but one known North American
species.

This family of Soft-bodied Plant Beetles, has less
than a thousand known species. The most frequent
habitat is in proximity to water but only a comparatively small percentage of larvae and adults are
aquatic as with the species here pictured.

Fig 239 **Bra-
chypsectra ful-
va** Lec.

56b. 9th abdominal segment without prolongation or cerci; body without conspicuous processes. 57

57a. Epicranial halves meeting ventrally forming a transverse bridge. Fig. 240. ....Family **CANTHARIDAE**

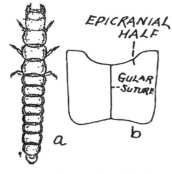

Fig. 240. a, **Cantharis** sp.; b, Ventral aspect of head (appendages omitted).

The family is composed of 1,300 described species. Their adults are commonly called soldier beetles. The eggs are deposited in masses in the soil. The newly hatched larvae of some species are feebly developed and are called "prolarvae". The larvae are primarily carnivorous and have a velvety appearance due to a covering of fine hairs. Pupation takes place in cells in the soil.

57b. Epicranial halves not meeting ventrally. 58

58a. Frontal sutures present. Fig. 241. ....Family **LAMPYRIDAE**

Fig. 241. **Photinus** sp.

There are about 2,000 described species. The adults are known as fireflies and glowworms. The eggs, larvae and pupae are also sometimes luminous. The larvae are predacious and feed upon small animals including earthworms, snails, crustaceans and insects. They are subterranean but several Asiatic species are reported to be aquatic. Pupation usually takes place in a soil cell beneath rubbish or on the surface in moist situations.

58b. Frontal sutures absent. 59

59a. Antenna 3-segmented with apical segment and a disk-shaped appendix; stipes and mentum separate; cardo present; galea 2-segmented. Fig. 242. ....Family PHENGODIDAE

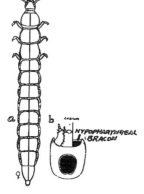

It is reported that the species of *Phengodes* prey upon myriapods. Some larvae have light-producing organs, and are very attractive, sometimes displaying two or more colors of lights. The adult females of some species resemble the larvae.

Fig 242. a, **Phengodes** sp.;
b, Ventral aspect of head.

59b. Antenna 1 or 2-segmented, distally covered with a large dome-shaped appendix; stipes and mentum fused; cardo vestigial or absent; galea 1-segmented. Fig. 243. ....Family LYCIDAE

Fig. 243. **Calopteron reticula-tum** F.

They are similar to the lampyrids to which they are related. The adults fly by day, and are not luminous. Less than 100 species are known for North America.

60a. Frontal sutures present. 61

60b. Frontal sutures absent. 65

61a. Lacinia distally armed with 1 or more spurs. Fig. 244. ....Family DERMESTIDAE

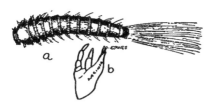

The family consists of about 550 described species. The larvae are covered with long or short hairs and feed upon dead animal and plant materials including skins, horn, hair, wool, tallow, cured meats, cheese, museum specimens and cereal products. Some very serious household pests belong to this family.

Fig. 244. a, Carpet beetle; b, Maxilla.

Fig 245 Ventral aspect of the left half of head

61b. Lacinia without spurs. 62

62a. Ventral mouth parts deeply retracted; cardo much smaller than stipes. Fig. 245. 63

62b. Ventral mouth parts inserted in a rather shallow emargination of the front margin of the head; cardo at least as large as stipes. Fig. 246. .... Family CLERIDAE

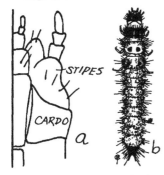

Fig. 246 a, Ventral half of the head, b, **Callimerus ar-cufer** Chapin

This family consists of about 2,500 described species. The larvae are predacious and may be found in the soil, frequently in the nests of bees and wasps above ground, and also in the burrows of woodboring insects. The adults are known as checkered beetles and are attractively marked and colored.

63a. Mandible with a long, stiff prosthecal process near the middle or at the base of the inner margin; epicranial suture well developed. Fig. 247. .... Family MELYRIDAE

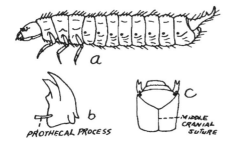

PROTHECAL PROCESS

MIDDLE CRANIAL SUTURE

Fig. 247. a, **Collops nigriceps** Say; b, Mandible; c, Dorsal aspect of head.

At least some of the larvae of these soft winged flower beetles are predacious. Some species of adults are very common on green plants. Around 1,500 species have been described.

63b Mandible with a short or no prothecal process; median epicranial suture usually not well developed, or entirely absent. 64

64a. Antenna with the sensory appendix longer than the distal segment. Fig. 248. ....Family CISIDAE

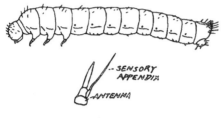

Fig. 248. Enneearthron sp.

This is a widely distributed family comprising probably over 300 species which are found in old wood or fungi. Some of the grubs eat paper and are known as "bookworms"; other species are pests where grain feed is stored.

64b. Antenna with the sensory appendix shorter than the distal segment or absent. Fig. 249. ....Family OSTOMIDAE

Fig. 249 Airora cylindrica Serv.

The well-known cadelle, Tenebroides mauritanicus L., feeds primarily upon grain and grain products, but sometimes also preys on other insects which live in the same medium. They are whitish grubs and noticably flattened.

65a. Antenna without sensory appendix; ventral mouth parts apparently protracted. Fig. 250. ....Family CUCUJIDAE

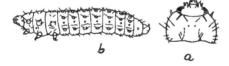

b

a

Fig. 250 a, Ventral aspect of head, showing the protracted mouth parts; b, Scalidia linearis Lec.

This family of flat bark beetles contains less than 1,000 known species but they are so variable that the family appears at several places in our key.

65b. Antenna with dilated sensory appendix; ventral mouth parts retracted. Fig. 251. ....Group Bothriderini, COLYDIIDAE

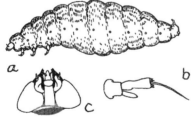

a

b

c

Fig 251 a, Deretaphrus oregonensis Horn; b, Antenna, c, Ventral aspect of head, showing the retracted mouth parts.

Some species of this group are phytophagous, some are predacious upon wood boring insects, and a few are parasitic. Look for them on leaves or under the bark of trees.

100

66a. Ventral mouth parts retracted. (See Fig. 251c). 67

66b. Ventral mouth parts protracted. (See Fig. 250).
Fig. 252. ....Family CERAMBYCIDAE

Fig 252 Roundheaded apple tree borer, **Saperda candida** Fab.

The family is about sixth in size in the order and contains about 20,000 described species. Because of the large thorax the larvae are called roundheaded borers. The eggs are laid on or in the host plants and the female beetle sometimes girdles a limb so that the larvae may feed on the dying wood. The larvae feed as borers on both living and dead plants, and are very destructive. Some of these larvae are known to live for many years.

67a. (a) The back of the mandible either with 2 long flagellate setae distally, and the body of the mandible partially fleshy or fully sclerotized; or (b) the back of the mandible without long setae distally, and the body of the mandible always fleshy, only with the base, or the tip and the base sclerotized.
Fig. 253. ....most LATHRIDIIDAE

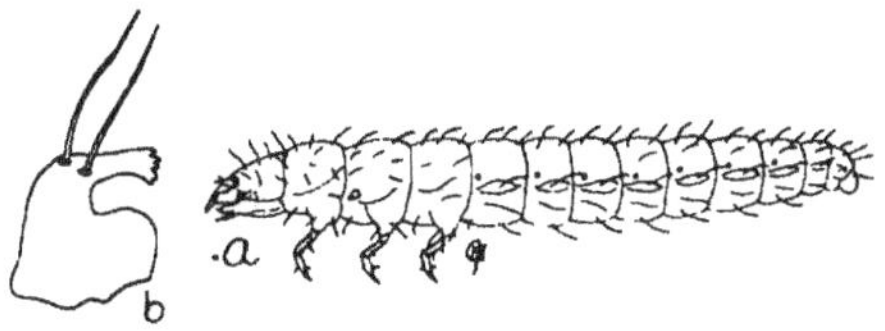

Fig. 253. a, **Cartodere costulata** Reit.; b, Mandible.

The members of this family number more than 700 species and are found in moss, decaying wood and fungi. A few have occured in herbaria, dried carcasses and in ants' nests.

67b. The back of the mandible without long flagellate setae distally, and the body of the mandible completely sclerotized. 68

68a. Maxillary mala with distinguishable lacinia and galea. Fig. 254. 69

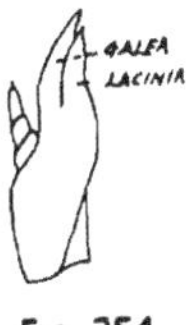

Fig. 254
Maxilla.

68b. Maxillary mala entire, sometimes bilobed anteriorly. Fig. 255. 71

Fig. 255.
Maxilla.

69a. 2nd antennal segment more than 4 times as long as the basal segment. Fig. 256. ....Family LATHRIDIIDAE

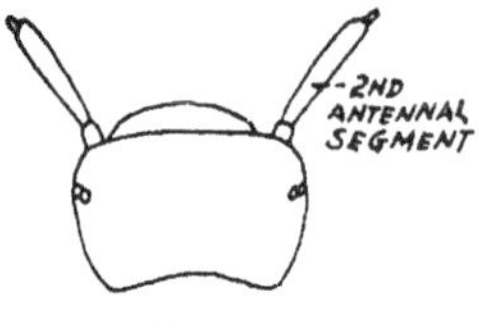

Fig. 256. Dorsal aspect of head.

These "minute brown scavenger beetles" are very small. Some are pests in drugs and other commercial products. Both larvae and adults are so small that they often escape detection.

69b. 2nd antennal segment subcylindrical, 3 times or less, as long as the basal segment. 70

70a. Spiracles annular, not on tube; cerci not distinct. Fig. 257. ....Subfamily Eucinetinae, DASCILLIDAE

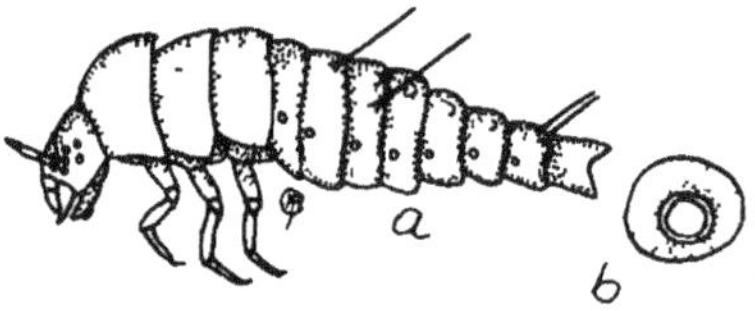

Fig. 257. a, Eucinetus sp.; b, A spiracle.

This subfamily contains only a few small beetles. Their larvae are not well known.

70b. Spiracles biforous, on tubes; cerci strong. Fig. 258. .. ..Family DERODONTIDAE

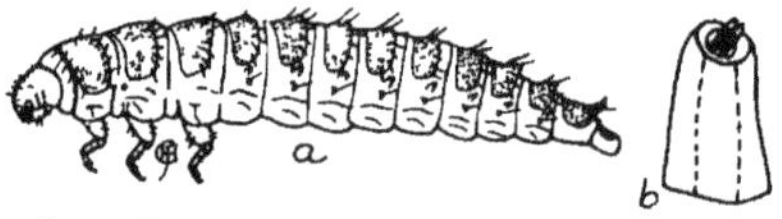

Fig 258 a, Derodontus maculatus Melsh; b, A spiracle on tube.

The members of this small family live in fungi. They are known as the "Tooth necked" fungus beetles.

71a. Mala falciform. Fig. 259. 72

Fig 259 Maxilla.

71b. Mala obtuse, or with inner margin irregularly toothed or notched. Fig. 260. ... ... .78

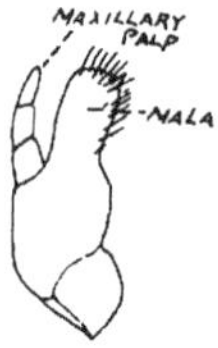

Fig 260. Maxilla

72a. Spiracles biforous. Fig. 261. 73

The spiracles, openings along the sides of the thorax and abdomen of both immature and adult insects which function in respiration take various forms and numbers in different species.

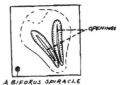

Fig 261 A biforus spiracle

72b. Spiracles annular. Fig. 262. 77

Fig 262 An annular spiracle.

73a. Spiracles at least some borne on tubes; cerci terminating abruptly with 2 or 3 conical processes. (See Fig. 263). 74

73b. Spiracles not at all on tubes; cerci terminally pointed and simple, or cerci absent. (See Fig. 265). 75

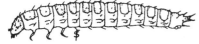

Fig 263 **Hesperobaenus** sp.

74a. Labial palpus 1-segmented. Fig. 263. . .Family MONOTOMIDAE

74b. Labial palpus 2-segmented. Fig. 264. . . ..Famly RHIZOPHAGIDAE

Very little is known regarding the habits of the family. The larvae of *Rhizophagus* are predacious upon xylophagous insects. Less than 20 species are known for North America.

Fig. 264 **Rhizophagus grandis** Gyll

75a. Body cylindrical; mandible with 3 apical teeth. Fig. 265. ....Subfamily Languriinae, EROTYLIDAE

This subfamily does not contain many American species, but a few of them are rather important as plant pests. The larvae are slim whitish "worms" which bore in the stems of clover and other plants.

Fig 265 **Languria angustata** Beauv

75b. Body fusiform; mandible with 2 apical teeth. 76

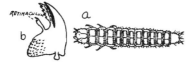

Fig 266 a, **Pharaxonotha kirshi** Reit,
b, Mandible.

76a. Cutting edge of mandible behind the apical teeth with a single rounded projection; retinaculum short and broad. Fig. 266. .Subfamily Clado-xeninae, EROTYLIDAE

76b. Cutting edge of mandible behind the apical teeth multiserrate; retinaculum long and slender. Fig. 267. ....Family CRYPTOPHAGIDAE

Fig 267 a, **Cryptophagus saginatus** Sturm, b, Mandible

About 800 species are described. They are found on fungi and decaying organic matter. A few are found in the nests of ants and wasps where they are thought to be predators or scavengers.

77a. Cerci absent. Fig. 268. ....Group Silvanini, CUCUJIDAE

Fig 268 Saw-toothed grain beetle, **Oryzaephilus surinamensis** (L.)

The genus *Silvanus* contains 55 known species. The larvae of some of the species are very destructive to stored grain products, dried fruit, etc. Their small size often permits them to get a good start before being detected.

77b. Cerci present. Fig. 269. ....Family CUCUJIDAE

Fig 269 **Cucujus clavipes** Fab

This family consists of about 1,000 species. The development of many species takes place in grain and grain products. A few are predacious upon wood-boring insects and also on termites.

78a. Mentum with only apex free, or small, or indistinct by fusion with other areas (except in Sphindidae, mentum free to base and distinct, but appearing together with a mandible provided with retinaculum and a 9th abdominal segment without cerci). Fig. 270. 79

Fig 270 Mentum and maxilla

78b. Mentum with more than apex free, often free to base, always well developed and distinct. 93

79a. Head swollen laterally, and much broader than thorax; cardo of normal shape and position; maxillary articulating area round and well developed; hypostomal inner margin concave between fossa for mandible and posterior end of cardo.

Fig. 271. . . . . .Genera *Prostomis* and *Dryocora,* CUCUJIDAE

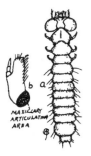

Prostomis mandibularis, here figured is almost cosmopolitan in its distribution. The group is a relatively small one.

The family Cucujidae has about a thousand known species of rather widely diversified forms. Both the larvae and the adults are often serious pests of stored food products and as such have been distributed world wide. Many of the species live under the bark of trees, some being plant feeders and others feeding upon the small animal forms they find associated with them. The larvae are usually elongate and flattened.

Fig 271 a, Pros-
tomis mandibularis
Fab ; b, Maxilla

79b. Different development of some, or all, of the 4 characters. . . . 80

80a. Maxillae appearing protracted in front of the mandiblular articulations by a complete or partial elimination of the cardines.
Fig. 272. 81

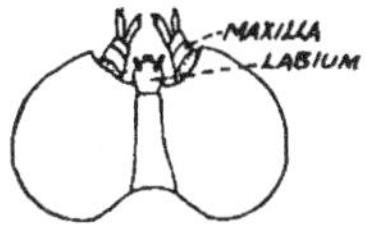

Fig 272 Ventral aspect of head.

80b. Maxillae deeply retracted. Fig. 273. 85

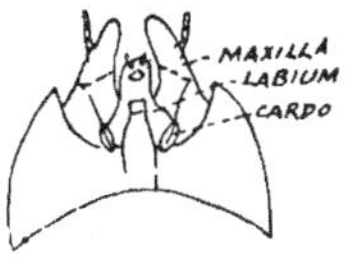

Fig. 273. Ventral aspect of head.

81a. Cerci present; terga without glandular openings. 82

81b. Cerci absent; terga with paired glandular openings.
Fig. 274. . . ..Family ORTHOPERIDAE

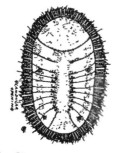

These are the "fringe-winged fungus beetles". They are small but quite abundant. As the name indicates they live in fungi.

Fig. 274. **Corylophodes marginicollis** Lec.

82a. 8th abdominal segment distinctly longer than 7th.
Fig. 275. . . ..Family CUCUJIDAE

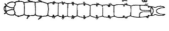

Fig 275 **Laemophloeus biguttotus** Say

The genus *Laemophloeus* contains more than 320 species which occur under bark and some are destructive to dried fruit and cereals.

82b. 8th abdominal segment about as long as seventh or shorter....83

83a. Larvae parasitic, having a swollen abdomen, slightly sclerotized; head and body white.
Fig. 276. ....Genera *Scalidia* and *Catogenus*, CUCUJIDAE

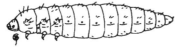

Fig 276. **Scalidia linearis** Lec.

The species here pictured is found in our southern states. Only a few species of these two genera are known to America.

83b. Larvae not parasitic and abdomen not swollen; head and body normally sclerotized. 84

84a. Apical segment of labial palpus normal; hypostomal rods diverging posteriorly. Fig. 277. ....Family PHALACRIDAE

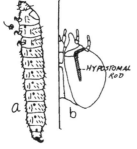

The larvae of *Olibrus* bore into stems and pupate underground. *Eustilbus apicalis* Melsh. is a predator upon the pea aphids. There are some 500 species of these "shining flower beetles".

Fig. 277. a, **Phalacrus** sp.; b, Ventral aspect of a half head

84b. Apical segment of labial palpus minute; hypostomal rods parallel. Fig. 278. ....Subfamily Smicripinae, MONOTOMIDAE

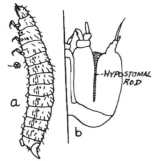

-HYPOSTOMAL ROD

Only two species of this interesting subfamily are known for North America. They are southern in their range.

Fig. 278. a, **Smicrips palmicola** Lec; b, Ventral aspect of a half head.

85a. Cardo (a) comparative small, narrow, often spindle-shaped and longitudinally directed; or (b) large, about as long or longer than stipes, triangular, and immovable, without posterior condyle. Fig. 279. ....Family NITIDULIDAE

The family comprises some 2,500 species. The larvae are mostly saprophagous. They are found in fruit and garbage dumps, in cereals, under bark of dead trees, in galleries of woodboring beetles and in ants' nests. Several genera are predacious upon aphids and scale-insects. Pupation takes place in a cell in the soil.

Fig. 279 a, **Glischrochilus obtusus** Say; b, Ventral aspect of head.

85b. Cardo (a) moderate size, subtriangular, much shorter than stipes and obliquely directed; or (b) fused with stipes to a large, movable structure with a posterior condyle. 86

86a. Mentum well developed and free to base. Fig. 280. ....Family SPHINDIDAE

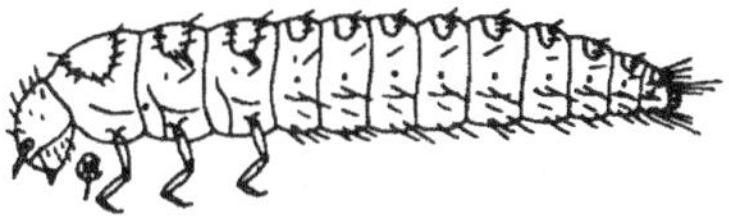

Present day knowledge of this family is quite limited. The larvae are found under bark and in fungi. Only a few species are recorded for North America.

Fig 280 **Sphindus americanus** Lec

86b. Mentum not well developed, often fused with submentum, only free apically. Fig. 281. 87

- PREMENTUM

- MENTUM & SUBMENTUM

Fig. 281. Labium.

107

87a. Mandible with large, multituberculate or multicarinate molar structure; cardo proper distinct
and subtriangular. Fig. 282. 88

Fig. 282
Mandible

87b. Mandible not so. 89

88a. Body shape similar to a scale-insect; along the sides with flat
projections carrying spinulose setae.
Fig. 283. ....Family MURMIDIIDAE

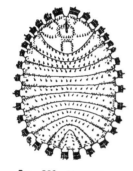

The species here pictured is widely scattered in both hemispheres. Only a few other
species are known for America.

Fig 283 **Murmidius
ovalis** Beck

88b. Body different. Fig. 284. ....Family ENDOMYCHIDAE

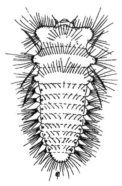

The family has about 950 known species.
Their adults are commonly called fungus
beetles. The larvae feed upon fungi, dead
wood and vegetable refuse.

Fig 284 **Rhymbus
ulkei** Cr

108

89a. Mandible with reduced, smooth, and usually condyliform molar structure; distinct hypopharyngeal sclerome present.

Fig. 285. ... .Subfamily Coccinellinae, COCCINELLIDAE

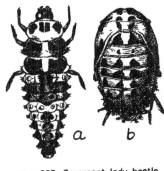

The family is a fairly large one consisting of about 3,000 species. The adults are called ladybird beetles. Both the adults and the larvae have the same food habits. Among the few phytophagous species the genus *Ephilachna* are very serious pests of agricultural crops. Most of them are predacious and feed upon aphids, scale-insects, mites and other small insects. They have been utilized effectively in the biological control of crop pests. The larvae and adults may produce a kind of protective fluid from the joints of the legs.

Fig 285 Covergent lady beetle, **Hippodamia convergens** Guerin: a, pupa, b, larva. (U S D A)

89b. Mandible without molar structure; hypopharyngeal sclerome weak or absent. 90

90a. Body armed with many long, often branched, setiferous dorsal and lateral processes. 91

90b. Body without long setiferous dorsal and lateral processes. 92

91a. 3 ocelli on each side, cerci absent.

Fig. 286. ....Subfamily Ephilachninae, COCCINELLIDAE

The "black sheep" of this otherwise quite helpful family fall in this subfamily. Larvae and adults unite to destroy as many bean, squash and similar plants as possible.

Fig. 286. Mexican bean beetle, **Epilachna varivestris** Mulsant.

91b. 5 ocelli on each side; cerci well developed.
　　Fig. 287. ....Family EROTYLIDAE

Fig 287. Clover stem borer, **Languria mozardi** Latr.

It has about 2,600 described species. The larvae live in the soil, in stems of plants and on fungi. Some species are fairly large and many of the adults are brightly colored.

92a. Mentum and submentum distinct.
　　Fig. 288. ....Group Dacnini, EROTYLIDAE

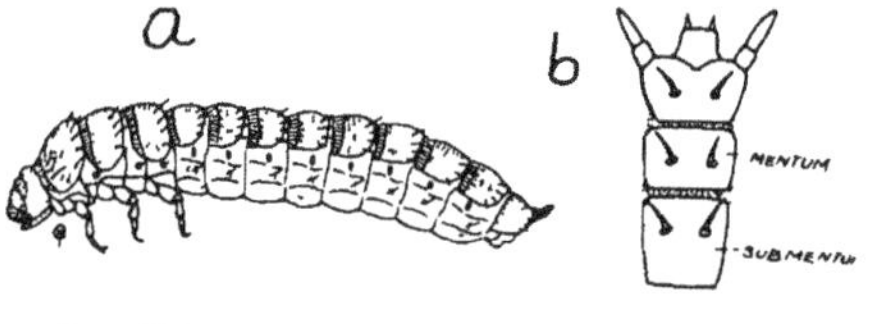

Fig 288 a, **Penthe pimelia** Fab , b Labium

The larvae have been found in herbaceous plants. They live in decaying wood and are of little importance economically.

92b. Mentum and submentum fused.
　　Fig. 289. ....Family MELANDRYIDAE

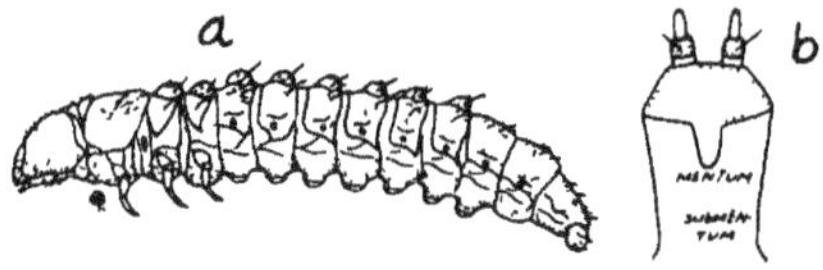

Fig 289 a, **Melandrya striata** Say, b, Labium.

They occur in dry wood and fungi or sometimes under bark. The larvae are slender and cylindrical and may often be found with the adults.

93a. Body terminating in a deciduous ovate appendix.
　　Fig. 290. ....Group Scraptini, MELANDRYIDAE

Fig 290 **Scraptia sericea** Melsh

The species of *Scraptia* occur in rotten wood, fungi, etc. This is a small group with but two genera and only a few species in America.

93b. Not so. 94

94a. Mandible with a tail-like, hairy appendix or a fleshy, hairy lobe behind the base of mola.
　　Fig. 291. 95

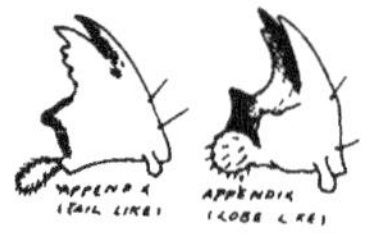

Fig 291 Two mandibles

94b. Mandible not so. . ..　　 . .　 . ... 　 .... 　96

110

95a. 3 large and 2 or 3 small ocelli on each side of head; appendix of mandible tail-shaped.
Fig. 292. ....Subfamily Byturinae, DERMESTIDAE

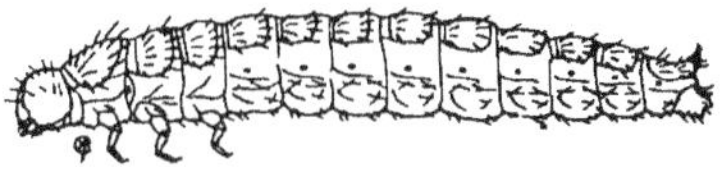

Fig 292 **Byturus unicolor** Say

It includes a single genus *Byturus* with few species. Both adults and larvae are injurious to raspberries.

95b. 1 ocellus on each side of head; appendix of mandible lobe-like.
Fig. 293. ....Family ANTHICIDAE

Fig 293 **Anthicus heroicus** Csy

Well over 1,000 species of these rather small beetles have been described. They are widely scattered and often very numerous.

96a. Abdominal spiracles located in disk-like sclerites.
Fig. 294. ....Family EURYSTETHIDAE

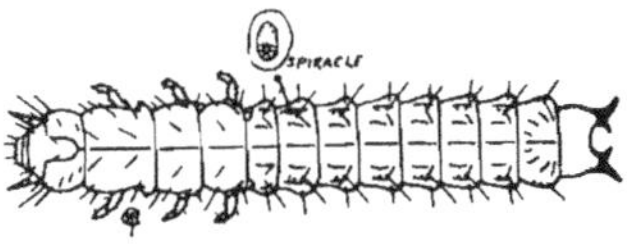

Fig 294 **Eurystethus californicus** Melsh

Only a few species are recorded in America for this family. All of them are on the west coast.

96b. Abdominal spiracles not located in disk-like sclerites. 97
97a. Mandible without molar structure; larvae parasitic with swollen abdomen. Fig. 295. ....Group· Bothriderini, COLYDIIDAE

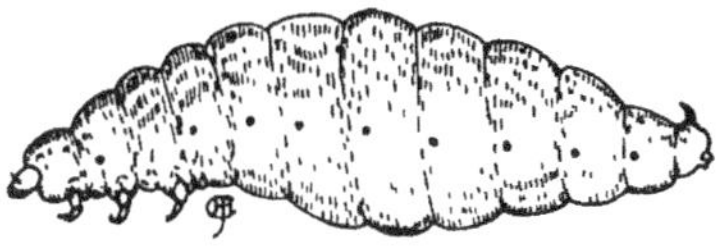

Fig 295 **Deratophrus oregonensis** Horn.

The larvae of several species of *Bothrideres* have been noted to be ectoparasites or predators of other coleopterous larvae.

97b. Mandible with molar structure.
Fig. 296. 98

Fig 296 Mandible

98a. Body elongate, cylindrical or subcylindrical, or more fusiform..99

98b. Body elongate and strongly depressed with parallel sides. 107

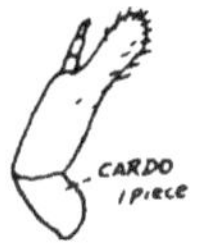

Fig. 297.
Maxilla.

99a. Cardo simple. Fig. 297. 100

99b. Cardo divided into 2 parts. Fig. 298. 102

Fig 298
Maxilla

100a. Mandible symmetrical. Fig. 299. ....Family COLYDIIDAE

Fig 299 Aulonium tuberculatum
Lec

Some species are known to feed upon decaying vegetable matter, a number of them are predacious upon larvae or pupae of several Cerambycidae.

100b. Mandible asymmetrical. 101

101a. Mola of mandible depressed, with a grinding surface on the ventral or dorsal side or both. Fig. 300. ....Family MYCETOPHAGIDAE

Fig 300 a, Mycetophagus punctatus Say;
b, Mandible

The members of this family chiefly live in rotting wood or under bark, associated with fungi. The larvae of Berginus maindroni Grouv. are reported to feed upon lac and the lac insects in India.

101b. Mola not depressed. 111

102a. Cerci present. .... , ... 103

102b. Cerci absent. ....Subfamily Oedemerinae, OEDEMERIDAE

Most of the members of this interesting family fall here. They are small to medium size. The known larvae live largely in decaying wood.

103a. Ambulatorial warts present ventrally on 2nd to 5th abdominal
segments. Fig. 301......Subfamily Calopodinae, OEDEMERIDAE

Fig. 301. **Calopus angustus** Lec.

The larvae have been found in
old wood or under bark. It is a
very small subfamily.

103b. Ambulatorial warts absent. 104

104a. 9th abdominal venter simple, without conical points. 105

104b. 9th abdominal venter with a conical point on each
side. Fig. 302. 103

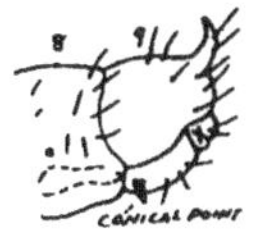

Fig. 302. 8th
and 9th ab-
dominal seg-
ments.

105a. Submentum and galea fused and heavily sclerotized.
Fig. 303. ....Family CEPHALOIDAE

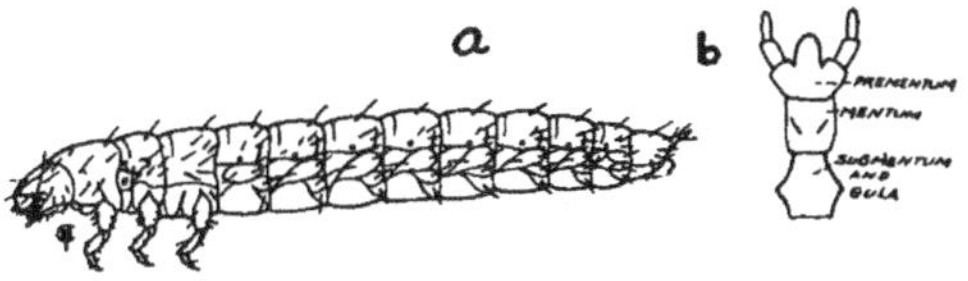

Fig. 303. a, **Cephaloon
lepturides** Newn , b, Labium.

Only a few genera and
not many species are
known for this small fa-
mily. They are mostly
western species.

105b. Submentum and galea fleshy.
Fig. 304. ....Group Nosodermini, TENEBRIONIDAE

Fig. 304. **Phellopsis obcordata** Kby.

This is a small group of mostly western beetles although the
species pictured is found in the
East.

106a. Cerci simple, corniform and curved upward.
Fig. 305. ....Group Sychroini, MELANDRYIDAE

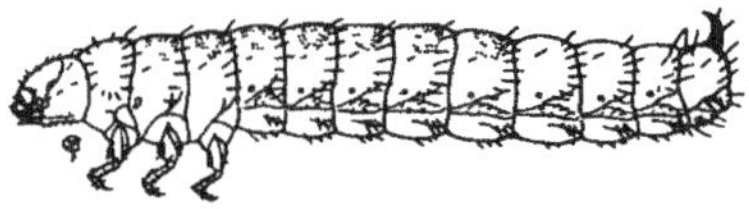

Fig. 305 **Synchroa punctata** Nwn

The one North American species of this group is here pictured. The adult is brown and of
medium size. Both adults and
larvae live under dead bark of
trees.

106b. Cerci with a branch at base. Fig. 306. ......Family PEDILIDAE

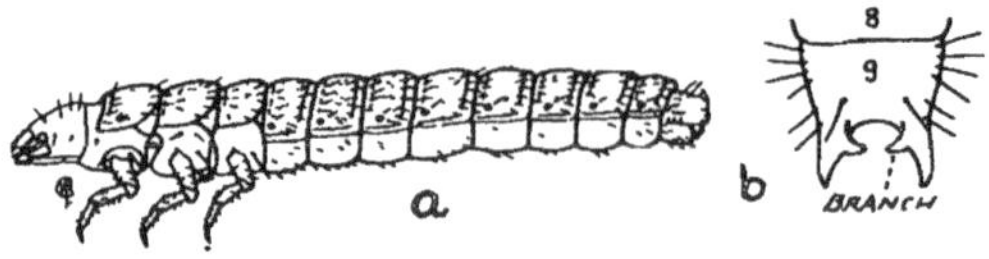

Fig. 306 a, **Eurygenius campanulatus** Lec ; b, 9th abdominal segment with cerci.

This is a small family of some 50 North American species. The one pictured is western. Members of the genus *Pedilus* are more frequent.

107a. Venter of 9th abdominal segment with transverse row of asperities, or small plates. Fig. 307. 108

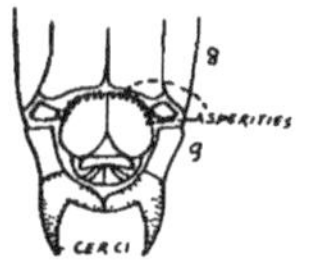

Fig. 307 Ventral aspect of 8th and 9th abdominal segments

107b. Venter of 9th abdominal segment not so armed. Fig. 308. ....Family PYTHIDAE

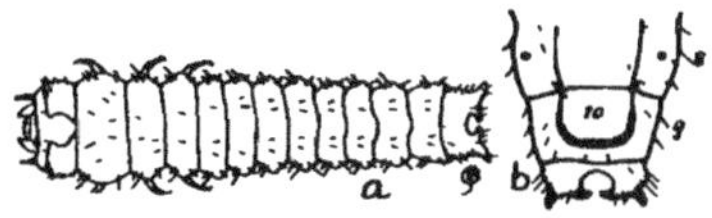

Fig. 308. a, **Rhinosimus ruficollis** L.; b, Ventral aspect of 8th and 9th abdominal segments.

This little family of bark beetles boasts less than 25 North American species. Adults and larvae are found under bark of pine trees and occasionally other species.

108a. 8th abdominal segment at least twice as long as 9th, cerci excluded; a pair of pits in margin between cerci. (See Figs. 309 and 310). 109

108b. 8th and 9th abdominal segments subequal, cerci excluded; a single pit present in margin between cerci. (See Figs. 311 and 312). 110

109a. 9th abdominal venter bearing asperities arranged in a continuous arch. Fig. 309. ....Family PYROCHROIDAE

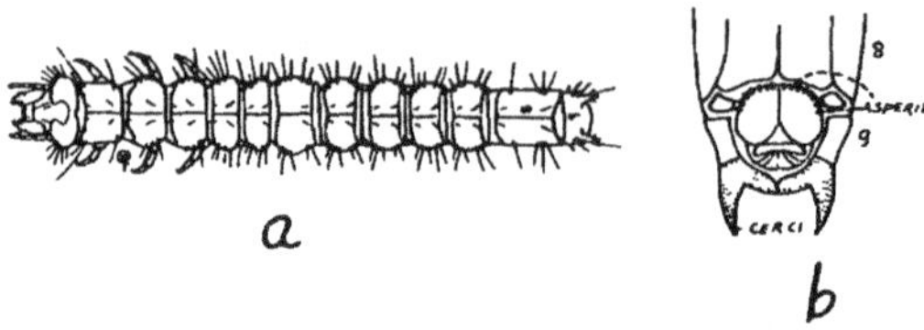

Fig. 309. **Neopyrochroa femoralis** Lec.; b, Ventral aspect of 8th and 9th abdominal segments.

The larvae are found under bark or in wood. Adults have areas of brilliant yellow or red and are known as "fire-colored beetles".

109b. 9th abdominal venter bearing small plates in place of asperities. Fig. 310. ....Genus *Boros,* TENEBRIONIDAE

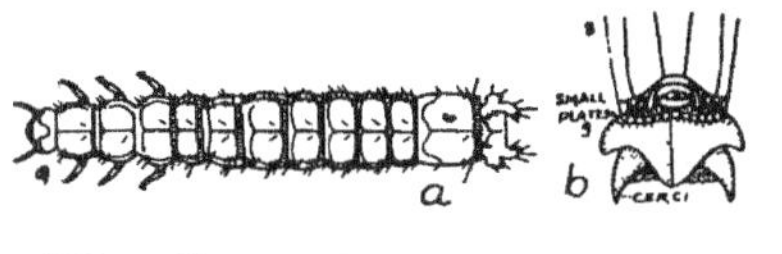

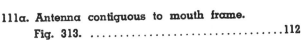

Fig 310. a, **Boros unicolor** Say; b, Ventral aspect of 8th and 9th abdominal segments.

The species pictured is a medium sized beetle, both adults and larvae being found under bark of dead pine trees. Some systematists wish to make a new family Boridae.

110a. 9th abdominal segment dorsally with a continuous row of small dark tubercles on the cerci and on the space between them. Fig. 311. ....Family PYTHIDAE

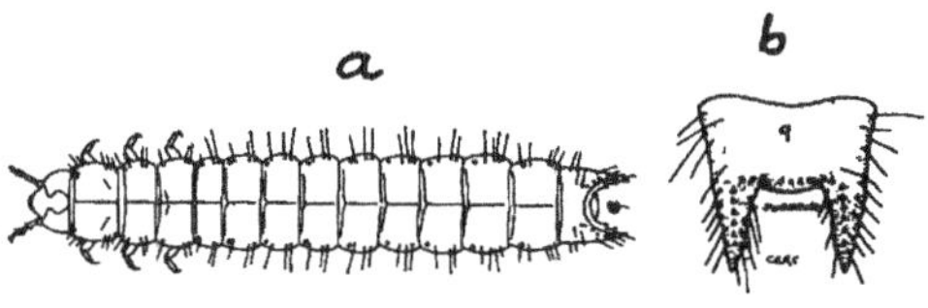

Fig. 311. a, **Pytho niger** Kby.; b, Dorsal aspect of 9th abdominal segment with cerci.

Look under bark for all stages of these small beetles. The species pictured ranges from Labrador through the New England states.

110b. 9th abdominal segment only with 2 small tubercles proximally on dorsal side of each cercus. Fig. 312. ....Family OTHNIIDAE

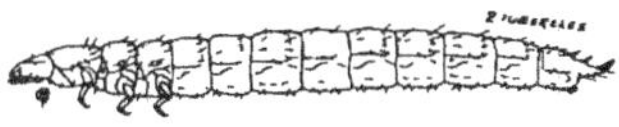

Fig 312 **Othnius umbrosus** Lec.

The species pictured is found in the Middle West. This small family has only this one genus and but a few species.

111a. Antenna contiguous to mouth frame. Fig. 313. 112

Fig. 313 Dorsal aspect of head.

111b. Antenna inserted some distance in from mouth frame. Fig. 314. 113

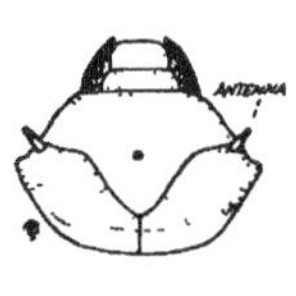

Fig. 314. Dorsal aspect of head.

112a. Back of mandible opposite the cutting edge with sharp margin; opposite the mola, excavate and without a spinose setose elevation. Fig. 315. ....Family ALLECULIDAE

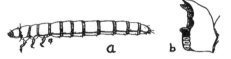

These are the "comb-clawed bark beetles". They are closely related to the tenebrionids. T h e larvae look like wireworms and live in rotten wood

Fig. 315. a, **Capnochroa fuliginosa** Melsh; b, Mandible.

112b. Back of mandible not as described above. Fig. 316. ....Family TENEBRIONIDAE

One of the largest family of Coleoptera comprising more than 10,000 species. The larvae bear a close resemblance to those of the Elateridae, but the labrum is distinct. The majority of the species are scavengers, some feed upon grain or grain products and) a few are found in association with bark and wood borers. The well-known mealworm, *Tenebrio molitor* L., and the confused flour beetle, *Tribolium confusum* Duval, are pests in mills and storehouses.

Fig 316 **Alobates pennsylvanica** DeGeer

113a. Molar part of mandible with the grinding surface transversely multicarinate; antenna short and 2-segmented. Fig. 317. ....Family NILIONIDAE

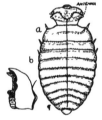

The members of this exotic family are found in South America.

Fig 317. a, **Leio-chrodes** sp ; b, Mandible.

113b. Molar part of mandible with the grinding surface either smooth, or bearing obtuse tubercles; antenna elongate and 2 or 3-segmented, distal segment minute or absent. Fig. 318. ....Family LAGRIIDAE

This is still another family of bark beetles. The larva often feed on leaves. They are elongate and cylindrical.

Fig. 318 a, **Lagria** sp., b, Mandible

116

114a. 9 complete abdominal segments; 10th small.
(See Fig. 319). 115

114b. 8 complete abdominal segments; 9th and 10th reduced.
(See Fig. 321). 116

115a. No ocelli or but 1; cardo fused with stipes; coxae small and
widely separated. Fig. 319. . . . . .Family HISTERIDAE

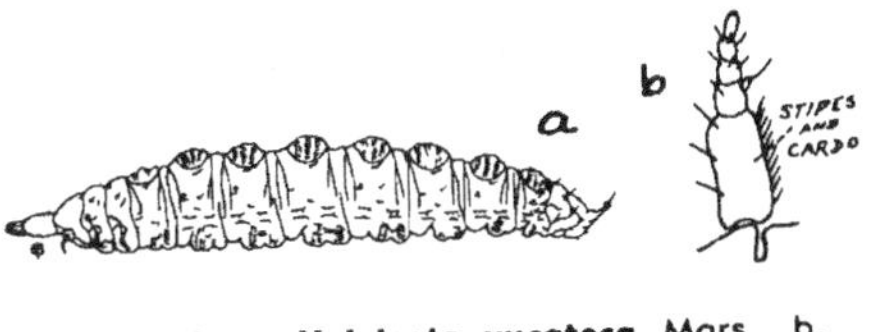

This family consists of about 3,000 known species. Many of the larvae are predacious upon coleopterous and dipterous larvae and a few species attack immature stages of Chrysomelidae and Lepidoptera. A number of them are myrmecophilous in habitat.

Fig 319 a, **Hololepta yucateca** Mars , b,
Maxilla

115b. 6 ocelli; cardo distinct;
coxae large, approximate.
Fig. 320. Subfamily
Helophorinae, HYDRO-
PHILIDAE

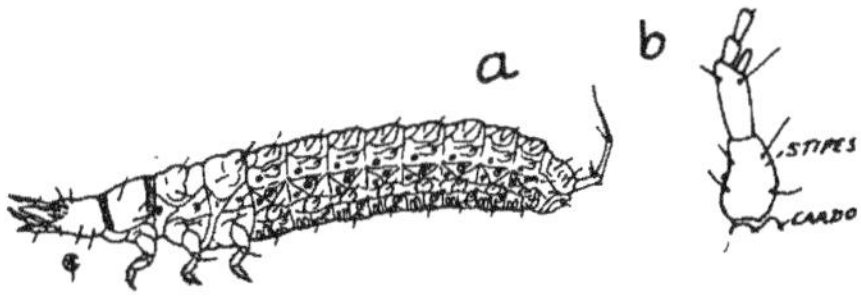

Fig 320 a, **Helophorus aquaticus** L (Redrawn from Boving & Craighead), b, Maxilla.

116a. Head elevated; antenna inserted farther from the lateral
margin of the head than is the mandible.
Fig. 321 . . . . .Family HYDROPHILIDAE

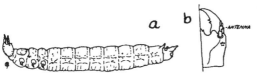

Fig. 321. a, **Chaetartria seminulum** Herbst. (Redrawn from Boving & Craighead); b, Dorsal aspect of a half head.

This family comprises about 1,700 species. The eggs of several genera are enclosed in silken cases and attached to grass or floating objects, but *Helochares* a n d *Spercheus* fasten them on their own bodies. The larvae are chiefly vegetable scavengers, but a few species are predacious. The majority of species are aquatic or semiaquatic, but a number of the subfamily Sphaeridiinae are known to be terrestrial.

116b. Head slightly inclined; antenna inserted near the lateral
margin of the head than is the mandible. 117

117a. Abdominal segments soft, with short conical gills; last 3 ab-
dominal·segments attenuate, not forming a breathing pocket.
Fig. 322. ....Subfamily Spercheinae, HYDROPHILIDAE

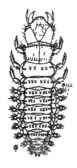

The hydrophilids include many species of rather widely diversified forms
and habits. The species of this subfamily are exotic.

Fig 322 **Spercheus emar-
ginatus** Schall (Redrawn
from Boving & Craighead)

117b. Abdominal segments with well developed plates; last 3 abdominal segments forming a breathing pocket.
Fig. 323. ... .Subfamily Hydrochinae, HYDROPHILIDAE

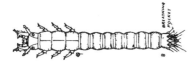

The members of this subfamily are
small and in consequence frequently
overlooked. The species pictured is
known from the Great Lakes area.

Fig 323 **Hydrochus squamifer**
Lec.

118a. Hypopharyngeal sclerome absent; mandible without a real molar
structure. 119

118b. Hypopharyngeal sclerome present;
mandible with a definite molar structure. Fig. 324. 142

Fig 324 a, Mandible; b,
Dorsal aspect of labium

119a. 9th abdominal tergum armed with a pair of cerci or an unpaired spine. Fig. 325. ....Family MORDELLIDAE

There are about 800 known species. Some larvae are found in termite nests and the burrows of stem
and wood-boring insects. They are
possibly predacious, but that has
been questioned.

Fig 325 **Tomoxia bidentata**
Say.

119b. 9th abdominal tergum without a pair of cerci and without an unpaired spine. 120

120a. 10th abdominal segment in front of anus provided with a pair of cushioned and adjacent lobes separated by a median, longitudinal groove often marked at the anterior end by a small transverse sclerome. (See Figs. 326 and 330). 121

120b. 10th abdominal segment in front of anus without a pair of soft, oval lobes separated by a longitudinal groove. (See Fig. 333). 125

121a. Head protracted; mandible dentate. ....·...122

121b. Head retracted; mandible not dentate. 123

122a. Thoracic spiracle pushed forward to the anterior margin of prothorax. Fig. 326. ....Family PTINIDAE

Fig. 326. **Niptus** sp.

About 550 species have been described. The larvae are scarabaeoid form and feed upon dead and dried animal and vegetable matter. The storehouse beetle, *Gibbium psylloides* (Czempinski), is a most destructive species to stored products. Several species are reported as inguilines in ants' nests.

122b. Thoracic spiracle not reaching anterior margin of prothorax. Fig. 327. ....Family ANOBIIDAE

Fig 327 **Nevermannia dorcatomoides** Fisher (Redrawn from Boving & Craighead)

There are around 1,200 described species. The larvae are scarabaeoid form, very small, and living in dead and usually well-seasoned hard woods. Many feed on animal and plant products. The furniture beetle, *Anobium striatum* Olivier, the cigarette beetle, *Lasioderma serricorne* (Fab.) and the drugstore beetle, *Stegobium paniceum* (L.) are serious pests.

119

123a. Mandible without a dorsal, molar-like process; epipharynx without a large sclerome; lacinia mandibulae absent.
Fig. 328. ... . .Family BOSTRICHIDAE

There are about 400 known species. They are known as branch and limb borers. The larvae are scarabaeoid in form, feed in dead wood and may be injurious to furniture and building materials. The very interesting lead cable borer, or short-circuit beetle, *Scobicia declivis* (Lec.) here shown, bores holes into the aerial lead telephone cables causing the linemen frequent trouble.

Fig. 328 Lead cable borer, **Scobicia dec-livis** (Lec)

123b. Mandible with a dorsal, molar-like process, grinding against a large sclerome in epipharynx; lacinia mandibulae present and fleshy. Fig. 329. 124

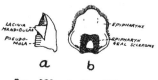

Fig 329 a, Mandible, b, Epipharynx.

124a. Abdominal spiracles subequal in size.

Group Psoini. LYCTIDAE

This small group lives in our western states.

124b. Last abdominal spiracle much larger than the others.
Fig. 330. .... .Family LYCTIDAE

The family consists of 60 species and the adults are known as the powder post beetles. Their larvae scarabaeoid in form with 3- segmented legs, live in dead wood and are particularly destructive to furniture.

Fig. 330. **Lyctus** cavicollis Lec.

125a. Hypopharyngeal bracon absent; usually with segmented legs. 126

125b. Hypopharyngeal bracon present; usually without segmented legs. Fig. 331. 136

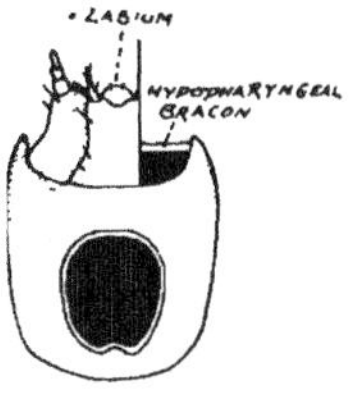

Fig 331. Ventral aspect of head, showing the hypopharyngeal bracon.

126a. Mandible simple, distally either with a broad transverse gouge-like cutting edge, or with a simple apex. 127

126b. Mandible dentate, distally with from 2 to 5 teeth. Fig. 332. 129

Fig. 332. Mandible.

127a. Prementum and mentum fused, bearing a common median escutcheon-like sclerome with a pair of light, circular areas anteriorly. Fig. 333. ....Family BRUCIDAE

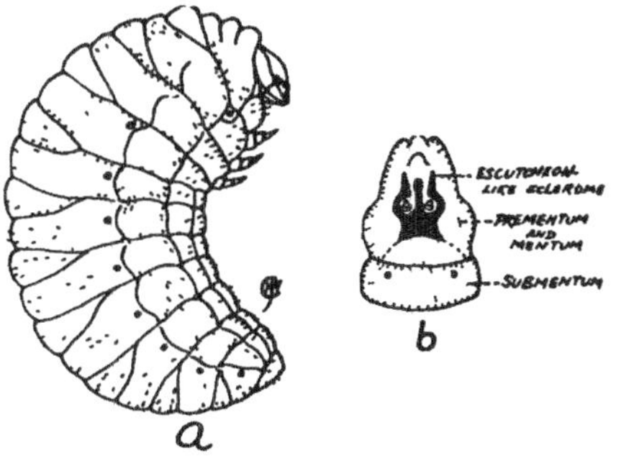

The members of this family number no less than 900 species and they are frequently known as pea and bean "weevils". Their larvae undergo a hypermetamorphosis in which the first instar is more or less carabiform with well-developed legs. The first molt occurs in the host and the body becomes eruciform and mostly apodous and blind. No less than 50 species are of economic importance.

Fig. 333. a, Pea weevil, **Bruchus pisorum** (L.); b, Labium.

127b. Prementum and mentum distinct, without escutcheon-like sclerome. 128

128a. Legs present and fully developed; body curved and plump.
Fig. 334. . . . . .Subfamily Sagrinae*, CHRYSOMELIDAE

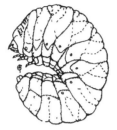

The members of this small subfamily are the most primitive of all the leaf beetles.

Fig 334 **Sagra fe-morata** Jac

128b. Legs absent; body straight.
Fig. 335. . . . . .Subfamily Orsodacninae*, CHRYSOMELIDAE

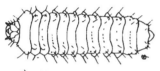

The adults feed on spring buds and are highly variable.

Fig. 335 **Zeugophora scutel-laris** Suffr.

129a. Spiracles on 8th abdominal segment biforous, terminal, and projecting like a pair of spurs.
Fig. 336. . . . . .Subfamily Donaciinae*, CHRYSOMELIDAE

The larvae are aquatic and feed on the roots or in the stems of aquatic plants. The pupae are enclosed in tough cocoons attached to roots of the host plants.

Fig. 336. **Donacia** sp

129b. Spiracles of 8th abdominal segment not projecting like spurs..130

* The family Chrysomelidae is such a large one that some Coleopterists have proposed splitting it up into a number of families. We have chosen to follow Leng and give these ten groups subfamily significance.

130a. Labrum small, or indistinct and fused with front and clypeus. Fig. 337. ....Subfamily Clytrinae*, CHRYSOMELIDAE

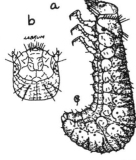

The genus pictured is confined to the Eastern Hemisphere. It is represented in North America by the genus *Antipus.*

Fig. 337. a, **Clytra quadri-punctata** L. (Redrawn from Boving & Craighead); b, Dorsal aspect of head.

130b. Labrum well developed and free. 131

131a. Maxillary palpus 3 or 4-segmented (excluding palpifer); 8th abdominal spiracles present and laterally placed; 9th abdominal segment terminal. Fig. 338. 132

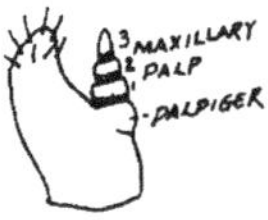

Fig. 338. Maxilla.

131b. Maxillary palpus 2-segmented or less; 8th abdominal spiracles if present, thus dorsally placed, or absent; 8th abdominal segment terminal with free hind margin. 135

132a. Tarsus long, slender, without pulvillus; mandible compressed, with 2 to 3 distal teeth. Fig. 339. ....Subfamily Eumolpinae*, CHRYSOMELIDAE

This is a large and important subfamily. Its members are widely distributed and often highly economic.

Fig. 339. **Chrysochus auratus** Fab.

132b. Tarsus of moderate length, curved, and usually with pulvillus; mandible palmate with 4 to 5 distal teeth. Fig. 340. 133

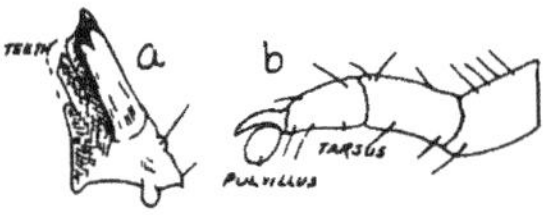

Fig. 340. a, Mandible, b, Leg.

133a. More than 1 ocellus on each side of head, usually 5 or 6 ocelli, antenna 3-segmented. 134

133b. 1 ocellus on each side, or none; antenna 2-segmented or less. Fig. 341. ....Subfamily Galerucinae*, CHRYSOMELIDAE

Fig. 341. Larger elm leaf beetle, **Monocesta coryli** (Say).

Their larval habits are varied, many feed openly on the parenchyma of leaves, others live in roots, and a number are leaf-miners. It is a large and important subfamily.

134a. First 8 abdominal segments with ambulatory warts on ventral region; anal opening dorsal; labial palpus 1-segmented. Fig. 342. ....Subfamily Criocerinae*, CHRYSOMELIDAE

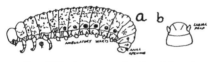

Fig. 342. Asparagus beetle, **Crioceris asparagi** (L.); b, Labium.

Their larvae are fleshy grubs which feed externally on the leaves. Some have the habit of concealing themselves with coverings of excrement. The asparagus beetle, Crioceris asparagi (L.) is familiar to growers of asparagus.

134b. First 8 abdominal segments without any ambulatory warts; anal opening ventral and placed in the middle of the sucking disk of the 10th abdominal segment; labial palpus 2-segmented. Fig. 343. ....Subfamily Chrysomelinae*, CHRYSOMELIDAE

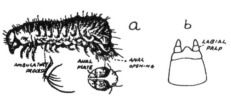

Fig. 343 a, **Myochrous denticolli** Say, b, Labium

This family Chrysomelidae is one of the four largest of the order, comprising more than 25,000 species. The larvae feed on leaves, roots, or live in stems, in galls, in leaf mines, in ants' nests and some are aquatic species. They are most destructive insects to agricultural crops. This subfamily contains some common and very interesting species.

124

135a. 8th abdominal segment terminal, with free hind margin; 8th pair of abdominal spiracles well developed and dorsal. Fig. 344. .... Subfamily Hispinae*. CHRYSOMELIDAE

Fig 344 **Chalepus ater** Weis.

The adults are usually wedge-shaped with engraved elytra. The larvae often feed on the surface of leaves or are leaf-miners. They often conceal themselves with a covering of excrement.

135b. Tergum of 8th abdominal segment often provided with an upright fork bearing the cast skins or the excrement of the larva; 8th pair of abdominal spiracles vestigial. Fig. 345. .... Subfamily Cassidinae*. CHRYSOMELIDAE

Fig 345. **Cassida nebulosa** L.

It includes the tortoise beetles. In certain species the eggs are enclosed in an ootheca. The larvae often cover their bodies with excrement or cast skin for protection and are an odd-looking lot.

136a. Legs present, but small, and usually 2-segmented. Fig. 346. .... Family BRENTIDAE

Fig 346 **Eupsalis minuta** Drury

Around 1,000 species have been described. The immature stages are passed in wood. The rostrum of the female is used for boring holes in which the eggs are laid. The larvae are elongate and slender and provided with thoracic legs.

136b. Legs absent, pedal lobes occupying their place. 137

137a. Head capsule elongate, broadening posteriorly, and with straight sides. Fig. 347. .... Family PROTERHINIDAE

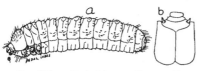

Fig 347 a, **Proterhinus anthracias** Perkins, b, Dorsal aspect of head

This is a very small family consisting of 2 genera. *Aglycyderes* occurs in the Canary Islands and New Zealand and *Protherhinus* inhabits the Hawaiian and other Pacific Islands.

125

137b. Head capsule narrowing posteriorly and with curved sides...138

138a. Abdominal hypopleuron subdivided into at least 2 lobes.
(See Fig. 352). 141

138b. Abdominal hypopleuron not subdivided. 139

139a. Abdominal segments with no more than 2 transverse dorsal
plicae. (See Fig. 350). 140

139b. Abdominal segments with 3 or 4 transverse dorsal plicae.
Fig. 348 and 349. ...Families CURCULIONIDAE and SCOLYTIDAE

TRANSVERSE DORSAL PLICAE

These two families are not separable by larval characters. The Curculionidae is probably the largest family of insects, it includes about 40,000 known species.

Fig 348 **Tychius pici-rostris** (Fab) (Cucur-lionidae)

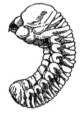

The larvae feed on roots, fruits, leaves, seeds and also live as borers and leaf miners. No truly aquatic forms are known although the larvae of many species live in the roots of plants growing in bogs and marshes. The female usually uses her snout to make a hole in the plant tissue into which the eggs are thrust.

Fig. 349 Shot-hole borer, **Sco-lytus rugulosus** (Ratz) (Sco-lytidae (

The Scolytidae is also a large family comprising about 2,000 known species. The adults are called bark beetles or engraver beetles. Their larvae live in galleries in dead or healthy shrubs and trees. They attack all parts of the plants. In the United States alone the annual losses in destruction of timber has been estimated at about $100,000,000.

140a. More than 2 ocelli on each side; head retracted.
Fig. 350. . . . . .Subfamily Rhynchitinae, CURCULIONIDAE

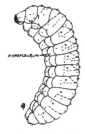

The larvae of *Rhynchites* and *Attelabus* live in tunnels formed of rolled leaves constructed by the adults.

The larvae of the species pictured live in *Helianthus*. *R. bicolor*, a very common species, develops within the hips of wild and cultivated roses.

Fig 350 **Rhychites aeneus** Boh.

140b. 1 ocellus on each side; head protracted.
Fig. 351. . . . . .Subfamily Apioninae, CURCULIONIDAE

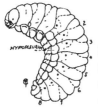

This small subfamily is cosmopolitan in its distribution. The species here pictured makes galls on the scrub pine. The larvae of *Apion*, a rather large genus, live principally within the seeds of legumes and other plants. Some are gall makers.

Fig 351 Pine gall weevil, **Podapion gallicola** Riley.

141a. Maxillary palpus 2-segmented.
Fig. 352. . . . . .Subfamily Calendrinae, CURCULIONIDAE

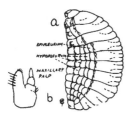

Many of our most destructive "bill-bug" larvae belong here. The larvae of the larger species bore into the stems of plants, principally corn and grasses while the smaller ones give their attention to seeds and grain.

Fig 352. a, Granary weevil, **Sitophilus granarius** (L.); b, Maxilla.

127

141b. Maxillary palpus 1-segmented. Fig. 353. Family PLATYPODIDAE

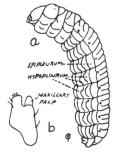

The eggs are laid in the primary galleries which are made by the adults. The larvae then make new tunnels. Often the burrows form definite patterns which are characteristic of the species. The ambrosia beetles live in dead wood and cultivate fungi to feed their young.

Fig 353. a, **Platypus compositus** Say, b, Maxilla

142a. **Legs vestigial, without pointed tarsal segment, or absent; body curved, fleshy, and with dorsal transverse plicae; 10th abdominal segment small, in continuation of 9th.**
Fig. 354. .... Family PLATYSTOMIDAE

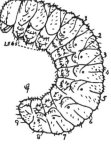

Certain species of *Brachytarsus* are predacious upon scale-insects. The larvae of *B. niveovariegatus* Roel. attack the Chinese wax scale, *Ericerus pela* Chev.

Fig. 354. **Euparius marmorius** Oliv.

142b. **Legs normal, with strong tarsus; body elongate, cylindrical, covered with tergal shields; 10th abdominal segment well developed, asperate, and placed below base of large 9th segment.**
Fig. 355. ...Family LYMEXYLIDAE

Fig 355 Chestnut timberworm, **Melittomma sericeum** (Harris)

128

ORDER HEMIPTERA

5a. Back swimmers; fore tarsi with 2 claws.
Fig. 356. ....Family NOTONECTIDAE

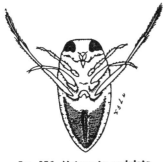

The family is composed of more than 200 species. They are known as back swimmers because they swim on their back with oar-like hind legs. They are common around edges of fresh water ponds, lakes and streams. They feed upon small animals. Eggs are laid on or in the tissues of aquatic plants.

Fig 356. **Notonecta undulata** Say, 3rd instar.

5b. Fore tarsi flattened, without claws. Fig. 357. ...Family CORIXIDAE

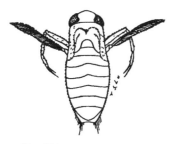

About 300 species have been described. The common name is water boatman. They live in fresh and brackish water. Eggs are laid on aquatic plants and other objects. Their food consists of all kinds of organic ooze.

Fig. 357. **Arctocorixa alternata** Say, 5th instar.

6a. Tarsi 2-segmented apical appendages of abdomen short and flat.
Fig. 358. ....Family BELOSTOMATIDAE

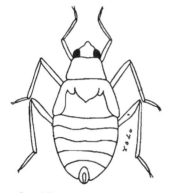

The family consists of about 150 described species. They are commonly called giant water bugs or electric light bugs. The fore legs are short and raptorial; the middle and hind legs are for swimming. They live in fresh water where they feed on small aquatic animals.

Fig. 358. **Belostoma flumineum** Say, 5th instar.

6b. Tarsi 1-segmented; apical appendages of abdomen long and slender. Fig. 359. ....Family NEPIDAE

About 200 species have been described. They are called water scorpions. The fore legs are raptorial, the middle and hind legs are long and linear. They swim slowly, often crawling on objects in the water. They are predacious and usually awaiting for prey. They come to the surface for air and often hide under stones near water.

Fig. 359. Water scorpion, **Rana-tra fusca** Palisot-Beauvois.

7a. Body toad-shaped; fore legs raptorial.
Fig. 360. ....Family GELASTOCORIDAE

They resemble toads both in shape and in method of crawling and hopping, which facts have given the name "toad bugs". About 60 species have been described.

Fig. 360. Cephalic view of a toad bug, Gelastocoris oculatus (Fabr.)

7b. Body not toad-shaped; fore legs similar to middle legs.
....Family OCHTERIDAE

These are shore-inhabiting bugs. The family includes only a single genus, *Ochterus* and only three species have been described in the United States. They are all predacious.

8a. Head as long as entire thorax. Fig. 361. Family HYDROMETRIDAE

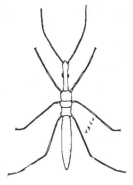

The members of this family are called water-measurers because they creep slowly upon the water surface. The body is very slender and the head is as long as the entire thorax. Only three species have been described in the United States.

Fig 361 **Hydrometra martini** Kirk, 4th in-star.

8b. Head shorter than thorax. 9

9a. Beak 4-segmented; hind femur extending much beyond the apex of abdomen. Fig. 362. ....Family GERRIDAE

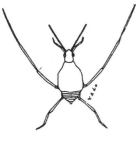

The water-striders skim rapidly over the water surface and often congregate in large numbers. They are predacious and feed upon insects that fall into the water or they sometimes jump to capture their preys. Only about 20 species have been described in the United States as belonging to the genus *Gerris*. A few live on salt water and are truly marine.

Fig. 362. **Gerris remigis** Say, 1st instar.

9b. Beak 3-segmented; hind femur not extending much beyond the apex of abdomen. Fig. 363. ....Family VELIIDAE

The broad-shouldered water-striders are closely allied to the Gerridae. The distal segment of the tarsi, at least of the fore leg is bifid and the claws are inserted before the apex. They are predacious and live on the water surface. About 20 species have been described in the United States.

Fig. 363. **Mesovelia mulsanti** White.

10a. Beak 3-segmented. 11

10b. Beak 4-segmented. 13

11a. Body broad and flat, without wing pads; parasitic. Fig. 364. ....Family CIMICIDAE

These are bedbugs and swallow bugs, about 36 described species. Among them, 2 species attack humans: the bedbug, *Cimex lectularius* L. in temperate and subtropical regions; *Cimex rotundatus* Signoret in tropical Africa and Asia. The former has a straight posterior margin of the prothorax while the latter is rounded.

Fig. 364. Bed bug **Cimex lectularius** L, newly hatched.

11b. With wing pads; not parasitic. 12

12a. Fore legs with greatly thickened femora. Fig. 365. ....Family PHYMATIDAE

Fig. 365. a, Ambush bug, **Phymata erosa fasciata** (Gray), b, fore leg.

This family of "ambush bugs" contains about 150 described species. They feed upon many kinds of insects including honey bees.

12b. Fore legs somewhat thickened. Fig. 366. ....Family REDUVIIDAE

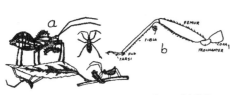

Fig 366 a, Wheel bug, **Arilus cristatus**
(L.) (From Glover), b, Fore leg

About 2,500 species of the assassin bugs have been described. They are predacious and feed upon insects. Some species invade habitations in search of insects and other household pests, but often inflict wounds on humans. A few species which suck blood from rodents and other animals including man are carriers of trypanosomes.

13a. Dorsal scent glands prominent. (See Fig. 367). 14

13b. Dorsal scent glands not prominent. 16

14a. Body broad and oval, with more than 3 dorsal abdominal segments with scent glands.
    Fig. 367. ....Family PENTATOMIDAE

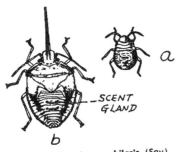

SCENT GLAND

Fig 367. **Acrosternum hilaris** (Say)
a, 1st instar, b, later instar.

They are called stink bugs or shield bugs. About 5,000 species are known. They are often destructive to orchards and other agricultural crops. The members of the subfamily Asopinae are predacious upon other insects and in consequence are counted as helpful.

14b. Body elongate, with less than 3 dorsal scent glands. 15

15a. Antennae inserted high on side of head, about the position of the upper half of the eye. Fig. 368. . . . . Family LYGAEIDAE

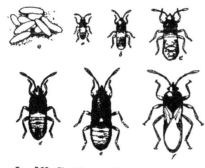

About 2,000 species are described. Most of them are destructive to crops: the chinch bug, *Blissus leucopterous* (Say), and the false chinch bugs, *Nysius* spp. are serious pests. Some species belonging to the genus, *Geocoris* are predacious on other injurious insects.

Fig. 368. Chinch bug, **Blissus leucopterous** (Say). a-e, 1st to 5th instars, f, adult; g, eggs.

15b. Antennae inserted low on side of head, about the position of the lower half of the eyes. Fig. 369. . . . . Family COREIDAE

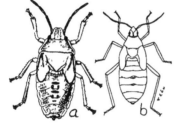

About 1,000 species have been described. They are destructive to crops. The squash bug, *Anasa tristis* (DeGeer) is very injurious to pumpkins, melons, gourds and squashes. The nymphs are often associated with the adults.

Fig 369 a, **Leptocorixa varicornis** Fab, 5th (last) instar; b, Squash bug, **Anasa tristis** (De Geer).

16a. Body spinous; meso- and metapleuron fused into a single piece. Fig. 370. . . . . Family TINGITIDAE

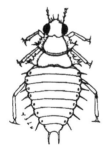

About 700 species of lace bugs have been described. They are plant feeders. The eggs are laid in the plant tissues and the young are spinous. Look on the underside of leaves for them.

Fig 370 **Corythucha arcuata** (Say)

16b. Body not spinous, meso- and metapleuron distinct.
Fig. 371. ....Family MIRIDAE

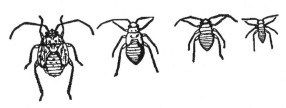

Fig. 371. Tarnish plant bug, **Lygus oblineatus** (Say).

They are called plant bugs or leaf bugs. About 5,000 species have been described. They are mostly plant feeders, but some are predacious. The tarnished plant bug, *L y g u s oblineatus* (Say) and *Creontiades pallidus* Rambur carry p l a n t diseases.

ORDER HOMOPTERA

1a. Beak evidently arising from the head; tarsi 3-segmented. Fig. 372...2

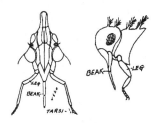

Fig 372 Cephalic aspect (a) and lateral aspect (b) of head and legs

1b. Beak evidently arising between the fore legs; tarsi 1 or 2-segmented; insects usually live in colonies. Fig. 373. 6

Fig 373 Beak (a) arising between the fore legs.

2a. Large insects, live underground in nymph stage; fore legs enlarged and adapted for digging. Fig. 374. . . . . .Family CICADIDAE

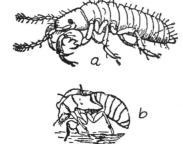

Fig 374 Periodical cicada, **Magicicada septendecim** (L.) a, nymph, b, nymphal skin

About 1,500 species of cicadas have been described. Eggs are laid in stems, twigs, etc. A few weeks after hatching, the nymphs crawl into the ground and feed upon the roots of plants for a long period. The 17-year cicada, *Magicicada septendecim* (L.) spends almost the full 17 years of its life cycle in the nymph stage. A strain living in the southern states completes its life cycle in 13 years.

2b. Smaller insects, seldom over half an inch long; live on plants; fore legs not adapted for digging. 3

3a. Antennae inserted on the sides of the checks beneath the eyes. Fig. 375. . . . . .Family FULGORIDAE

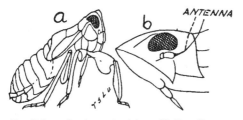

Fig 375. a, Cranberry toad bug, **Phylloscelis atra** Germar, b, Lateral aspect of head.

This family is represented in the United States by about 400 known species. They are called lanternflies and all are plant feeders. Certain tropical forms are luminous. Some species secrete large quantities of wax.

3b. Antennae inserted in front of and between the eyes. Fig. 376. 4

Fig. 376 Front aspect of head.

4a. Thorax with tubercles or spines.
Fig. 377. ....Family MEMBRACIDAE

About 200 known species of treehoppers are represented in North America. They are plant feeders. Eggs are laid in groups arranged in two parallel slits in twigs of trees or shrubs. The nymphs are different from their adults in the absence of the pronotal process, but filaments or spinose projections are often developed on the tergites.

Fig. 377 Stic-
tocephala sp
a, 4th instar,
b, 5th instar

4b. Thorax without tubercles or spines. 5

5a. Hind tibiae with 1 or 2 stout teeth, and crowned with short, stout spines at the tip. Fig. 378. ....Family CERCOPIDAE

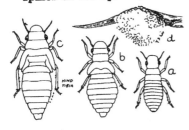

They are called froghoppers on account of the frog-like appearance of both the young and the adults. They are also known as spittle-bugs since the numphs of some genera hide in a mass of white froth. The frothing is the result of a fluid issuing from the anus becoming blown into bubbles by the anus.

Fig. 378. a, b, c, **Philaenus spumarius** (L.) (1st intermediate and last instars); d, A spittle mass of the lined spittle-bug, **Philaenus lineatus** (L.)

5b. Hind tibiae with a row of spines.
Fig. 379. ....Family CICADELLIDAE

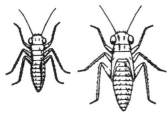

There are more than 700 species of leafhoppers known in the United States. They are able to leap powerfully and feed on many different kinds of plants. The leafhoppers not only cause damage to cultivated plants but also transfer plant diseases.

Fig 379 The potato leaf-
hopper, **Empoasca fabae**
(Harris) 2nd and 4th in-
stars.

6a. Tarsi with but 1 claw and 1 segment.
  Fig. 380. ....Family COCCIDAE

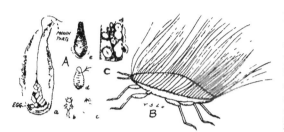

The members of this family are scale-insects, mealy-bugs and others. They live on the stems, leaves, roots and are the most serious pests of horticulturists. However, there are some useful species: shellac is prepared from the lac-insects, *Laccifer lacca* Kerr in India. The wax is produced by *Ericerus pe-la* Chavannes in China; and the cochineal is composed of dried bodies of *Coccus cacti* L.

Fig 380 A, the scale, **Mytilaspis citricola** Packard a, mature stage with eggs, b, newly hatched nymph, c, same with waxy secretion, d & e, intermediate stages B, **Walkeriana ovilla** Green, 1st instar C, Florida wax scale, **Ceroplastes floridensis** Comstock, different stages.

6b. Tarsi with 2 claws and 2-segmented. 7

7a. Hind legs fitted for leaping. Fig. 381. ....Family CHERMIDAE

The members of this family have the ability to jump and are called jumping plant lice. They are plant feeders and often occur in large numbers. All of them secrete honey dew and a few produce galls on the leaves.

The nymphs are flat and possess large wing pads and often have a marginal fringe surrounding the abdomen. Some are covered with a waxy secretion.

Fig 381. Pear psylla **Psylla pyricola** Foerst.

7b. Hind legs not fitted for leaping. 8

8a. Scale-like insects, with waxy filaments around lateral margins; antennae inconspicuous. Fig. 382. ....Family ALEYRODIDAE

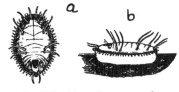

Fig. 382. **Aleyrodes** sp.: a, dorsal aspect; b, lateral aspect.

The common name, whitefly is derived from the covering of whitish powdery wax on the body of the adults. The young produce quantities of honeydew. The greenhouse whitefly, *Trialeurodes vaporariorum* (Westwood) is cosmopolitan and a general feeder.

8b. Not as 8a. 9

9a. Cornicles usually present. Fig. 383. ....Family APHIDIDAE

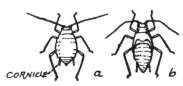

CORNICLE

Fig. 383. Green peach aphid, **Myzus persicae** (Sulzer) · a, 2nd instar; b, 3rd instar.

About 2,000 species have been described. The aphids have a complicated life history which is characterized by an alternation of parthenogenetic generation with a sexual generation. Moreover, they have alternations of winged and wingless forms. The host plants are also changed in different seasons.

9b. Cornicles always wanting. Fig. 384. .....Family PHYLLOXERIDAE

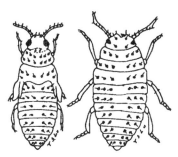

Fig. 384. **Phylloxera** spp., root-inhabiting form.

This family is closely related to the aphids. They are often red, orange or yellow and are frequently covered with wax. The grape phylloxera which feeds on the leaves and roots of some common grapes is a well-known species.

ORDER NEUOPTERA

1a. Mouth parts chewing type. Fig. 385. 2

Fig. 385 Dorsal aspect of head.

1b. Mouth parts mandibulo-suctorial type. Fig. 386. 4

2a. Abdomen with lateral filaments (see Fig. 389). 3

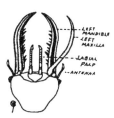

Fig. 386. Mandibulo-suctorial type mouth parts.

2b. Abdomen without lateral filaments. Fig. 387. . . . . .Family RAPHIDIIDAE

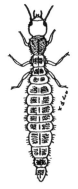

Fig. 387. Raphidia oblita Hagen.

There are 10 species described in the United States, and 12 species in Europe. *Raphidia hermandi* Navas is known in Japan. The adults are called snakeflies. The larvae are found under bark and they are common in California under loose bark of the eucalyptus. They are predacious and believed to be beneficial.

140

3a. Tip of abdomen with a caudal filament; sides of body with 7 pairs of segmented filaments; without anal prolegs.
Fig. 388. ....Family SIALIDAE

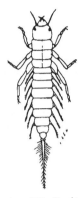

The larvae live in swiftly flowing streams adhering to the lower side of stones and also in trashy places filled with aquatic plants. The full-grown larva leaves the water and transforms in an earthen cell on the banks of the streams or lakes. Two or three weeks later the adult emerges. It is called an alderfly. The larvae are predacious and feed upon different kinds of small animals.

Fig. 388. Smoky alderfly, **Sialis infumata** Newman.

3b. Tip of abdomen without a caudal filament; sides of body with 8 pairs of unsegmented filaments; with a pair of hooked anal prolegs. Fig. 389. ....Subfamily Corydalinae, SIALIDAE

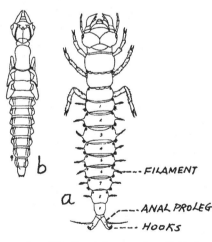

FILAMENT

ANAL PROLEG

HOOKS

About 80 species of dobsonflies have been described. The larvae are found under stones in slow or swift water and are predacious on naiads of dragonflies, stoneflies and Mayflies. These larvae which are known as helgramites are much used for bait in fishing. They are rather readily caught by holding a net down stream below stones in rapids. When the stones are moved the helgramites swim or are washed into the net.

Fig. 389. **Corydalus cornutus** (L.): a, larva; b, pupa.

4a. Aquatic or semiaquatic. 5

4b. Terrestrial. 6

5a. Mandibles and maxillae curved slightly upwards; without abdominal gills but with spiracles; larvae live under stones in or near water. Fig. 390. . . . . .Family OSMYLIDAE

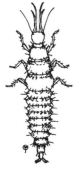

There are about 50 described species but none have been found in North America. The larvae lurk under stones or about moss either in or near the water. Their food consists of dipterous larvae.

Fig. 390 **Osmylus chrysops** (L)

5b. Mandibles and maxillae curved outward; with abdominal gills; larvae live in water and feed on sponges. Fig. 391. . . . . .Family SISYRIDAE

About 20 species have been described. The larvae feed upon fresh-water sponges. Accordingly the adults are called "spongilla-flies." They may be also found on bryozoans and algae. Pupation takes place in an oval loose double cocoon in soil or under stones. Eggs are laid in masses on objects standing in or overhanging fresh-water, and are sometimes covered by a silken web.

Fig 391 **Sisyra umbrata** Ndm

6a. Abdomen more than two times longer than thorax; larvae with hypermetamorphosis. Fig. 392. . . . . .Family MANTISPIDAE

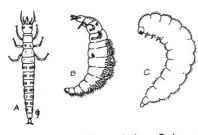

Fig. 392 **Mantispa styriaca** Poda a, newly hatched; b, 1st instar fully fed; c, last instar

The family consists of about 170 known species. The larvae are of two different forms: the first instar is thysanuriform with a squarish head; the second and later instars become robust and eruciform with a small head and weak legs. The fullgrown larvae spin cocoons and pupate within the last larval skin. The habits of larvae are parasitic on eggs of spiders and also in the nests of *Pilybia* wasps.

6b. Not as 6a. 7

7a. Pro- and mesothorax modified into a long and slender neck. Fig. 393. . . . . .Family NEMOPTERIDAE

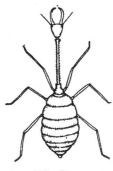

Fig. 393. **Pterocroce storeyi**, Withycombe.

The larvae are predacious and feed upon psocids and other small insects. They cover themselves with dust particles and are found in caves and buildings in semiarid regions and desert. Pupation occurs in a cocoon of silk and debris. They belong to the eastern hemisphere.

7b. Pro- and mesothorax normal. 8

8a. Antennae with long hairs; labial palps long and clavate, extended in front of head; mandibles and maxillae hid underneath the labrum (if long, straight and needle-like).

Fig. 394. ....Family CONIOPTERYGIDAE

This family includes about 50 known species. The adults look like aphids. The structures of their larvae leads us to regard them as Neuroptera. The larvae feed upon aphids, scale-insects and the eggs of red-spiders. When full-grown they make a double cocoon in which pupation takes place.

Fig 394 **Parasemidalis flaviceps** Banks

8b. Not as 8a. 9

9a. Empodium trumpet-shaped. Fig. 395. ......Family CHRYSOPIDAE

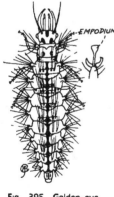

Nearly 500 species of green lacewings have been described. Their larvae are known as aphid-lions and feed on aphids, mites, leaf-hoppers, scale-insects and other small insects. The eggs are laid singly or in group on long slender stalks. In some species the larvae are protected with trash or debris.

Fig. 395 Golden-eye lacewing, **Chrysopa oculata** Say.

9b. Empodium not trumpet-shaped. ... .10

10a. Tarsi and tibia of hind leg fused into a single segment; mandible with teeth. 11

10b. Not as 10a. Fig. 396. ....Family **HEMEROBIIDAE**

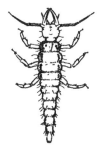

This family consists of about 220 known species. Their adults are called brown lacewings. The larvae resemble the aphid-lions but are smooth without tubercles. Only the 1st instar larvae possess trumpet-shaped empodia which becomes pad-like and greatly reduced in the later instars. They are predacious and feed on aphids, scale-insects, mealybugs, whiteflies, psyllids, etc. The eggs are devoid of pedicels.

Fig 396 **Hemero-bius pacificus** Banks, 1st instar

11a. Sides of thorax and abdomen with projecting filaments; head dilated posteriorly. Fig. 397. ....Family **ASCALAPHIDAE**

About 210 species have been described. The larvae resemble ant-lions in the form of the body, but they have a finger-like appendage on each side of the segment. They live in ambush on the surface of the ground, with the body more or less covered, and wait for small insect prey.

Fig 397. **Ulu-lodes hyalina** Latr.

11b. Sides of thorax and abdomen without projecting filaments; head not dilated posteriorly. Fig. 398. .....Family **MYRMELEONTIDAE**

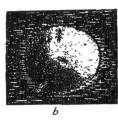

This family consists of about 650 described species. The larvae are known as ant-lions. They make pitfalls in sand to trap the ants and other wingless small animals. However, some species do not make pits but simply hide under sand or debris.

Fig 398 a, Ant-lion, **Myrmeleon** sp.; b, A pitfall.

145

ORDER TRICHOPTERA

(Larval key to some important families, adapted from Ross.)

1a. Either meso- or metanotum or both with sclerotized shield subdivided into separated plates or membranous. Fig. 399. 3

Fig 399. Dorsal aspect of thorax.

1b. Both meso- and metanotum each with a single, sclerotized shield embracing the entire notum. 2

2a. Abdomen with gills. Fig. 400. . . . . .Family HYDROPSYCHIDAE

GILLS---

The larvae are campodeiform, often living gregariously under and about trash, logs, stones, etc. or in running water. They spin loose silken nets. Their food habits are both carnivorous and herbivorous.

Fig 400. Hydropsyche sp.

2b. Abdomen without gills. Fig. 401. . . . . .Family HYDROPTILIDAE

The larvae construct cases which open at both ends. They feed on algae. A modified type of hypermetamorphosis occurs in the larval stage. The early instars of some genera have a slender body fitted for free, active life and have no case.

Fig. 401 Hydroptila waubesiana Betten. (Redrawn from Ross)

3a. Anal legs projecting beyond 10th abdominal segment. Fig. 402. 4

Fig. 402. Apex of abdomen.

Fig. 403. Apex of abdomen.

3b. Anal legs appearing as lateral sclerites of 10th abdominal segment. Fig. 403. 5

4a. Dorsum of 9th abdominal segment with a sclerotized shield. Fig. 404. . . . . .Family RHYACOPHILIDAE

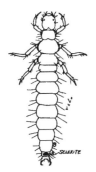

Fig 404 Rhyoco-phila fenestra Ross (Redrawn from Ross)

The larvae of the subfamily Rhyacophilinae are predacious and free-living while the larvae of the subfamily Glossosomatinae are the saddle-case makers.

These are the most primitive of present-day caddisflies. The larvae are campodeiform and possess tracheal gills.

4b. Dorsum of 9th abdominal segment without a sclerotized shield. Fig. 405. . . . . .Family PHILOPOTAMIDAE

Fig 405. Philo-potamus sp. (Redrawn from Ross)

The larvae are campodeiform and live gregariously in swift mountain streams where they construct net-like cases in the form of either cylindrical tubes or broad sacks. Prior to pupating, the larva builds a rough shelter of stone and encloses itself in a cocoon.

147

5a. Claws of hind legs much shorter than those of middle legs.
Fig. 406. . . . . .Family MOLANNIDAE

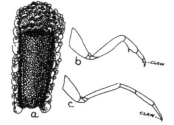

Larvae live on the sandy bottoms of streams and lakes and construct shield-shaped cases consisting of a central cylindrical chamber flanked on each side by an extension.

Fig 406 a, Case of **Molanna uniophila** Vorhies, b, Middle leg; c, Hind leg.

5b. Claws of hind legs as long as those of middle legs. 6

6a. Antennae long, at least 8 times as long as wide.
Fig. 407. . . . . .Family LEPTOCERIDAE

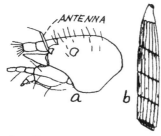

All the larvae make cases using a variety of materials and constructing cases of various shapes. They inhabit a wide variety of streams, ponds, lakes and rivers. The larvae can swim freely with their legs outside the case. They feed on vegetation.

Fig 407 a, Lateral aspect of head, b, **Trianodes flavescense** Banks.

6b. Antennae short, never more than 4 times as long as wide. 7

7a. Mesonotum with sclerotized plates.
Fig. 408. . . . . .Family LIMNEPHILIDAE

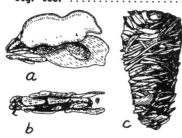

There are about 400 described species in this family. The larvae are eruciform with a prosternal tubercle or horn. They live mostly in quiet water and a few species in swift water. The genus *Enoicyla* live only in damp moss on land. The cases are tubular and ornamented with sticks, tiny shells, sand and small pebbles. They are herbivorous.

Fig. 408. a, Case of **Astenophylax** sp ; b, Larva with case of **Stenophylax** sp ; c, Case of **Limnephilus indivisus** Walker.

7b. Mesonotum submembranous, or with a pair of bar-shaped sclerites. Fig. 409. 8

Fig. 409. Dorsal aspect of meso-thorax.

8a. Mesonotum with a pair of bar-shaped sclerites. Fig. 410. . . . . .Family LEPTOCERIDAE

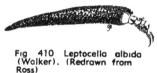

This is a large family of wide distribution. The cases are cylindrical or tapering and may be either straight or curved. They frequent both running streams and quiet water and are good swimmers.

Fig 410 Leptocella albida (Walker). (Redrawn from Ross)

8b. Mesonotum without a pair of bar-shaped sclerites. Fig. 411. . . . . .Family PHRYGANEIDAE

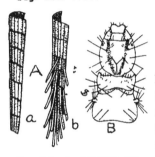

Most of the larval cases are long and built in a spiral. They live in still or slowly running water. In general they favor marshes and lakes for their abodes, but some species are taken in rivers and streams.

Fig. 411 A, **Agrypnia vestita** (Walker) a, larval case, b, young larval case, B, **Ptilostomis ocellifera** (Walker), anterior end of larva.

ORDER LEPIDOPTERA
Key to the LARVAE of the more important families

1a. Thoracic legs present and segmented. 2
1b. Thoracic legs absent or reduced to fleshy swellings. 7
2a. Body with large, ovate scales, arranged in a double row on each side. Fig. 412. . . . . .Family MICROPTERYGIDAE

The larvae of *Micropteryx* live on wet moss and are characterized by the presence of 8 pairs of segmented abdominal prolegs. The larvae of *Sabatinca* occur among liverworts.

Fig. 412. a, **Micropteryx** sp.; b, a scale.

2b. Body with setae only. 3

3a. Prolegs rudimentary or wanting; crochets absent. 4

3b. Prolegs at least indicated by rudimentary crochets.
Fig. 413. 12

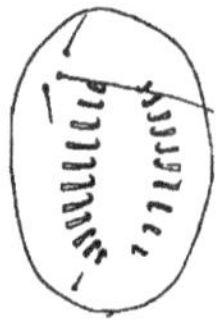

Fig. 413.
Crochets.

4a. Front extending upwards to vertex; small species.
Fig. 414. ....Family COLEOPHORIDAE

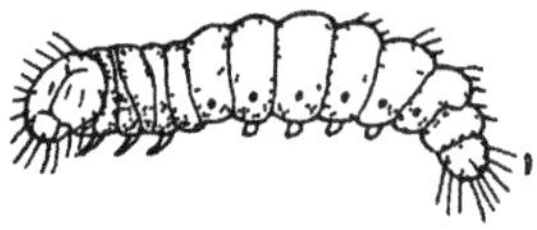

Fig. 414 **Coleophora
malivorella** Riley.

This family contains about 1,000 described species. The caterpillars are known as
leaf miners and case bearers. They feed
on leaves, flowers, fruits and seeds of various plants. Some systematists make this
group a subfamily of the TINEIDAE.

4b. Front not extending to vertex.
Fig. 415. 5

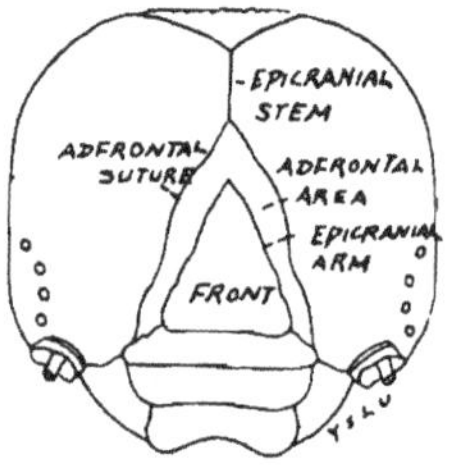

Fig 415 Cephalic as-
pect of head

5a. Head retracted; body often with spines or secondary hairs; primary
setae obsolete; body with obscure incisures and usually with conspicuous pits. Fig. 416. ....Family LIMACODIDAE

Fig 416 Saddle-back-
ed slug caterpillar, **Sabine stimulea** Clemens.

About 850 species are described. The larvae
are slug-like and known as slug-caterpillars. The
body bears tubercles and stinging or poisonous
hairs. They feed on various plants.

5b. Head exposed; body with primary setae and strong incisures....6

6a. Setae iv and v distant on abdominal segments; prolegs present.
Fig. 417. ....(Tegeticula) Family INCURVARIIDAE

Fig. 417. Setal map of an abdominal segment.

About 300 species have been described. The caterpillars of the Adelinae are case-bearers and are known as fairy moths, while that of the Proxodoxinae are borers in seeds and stems of Yucca and other Liliaceae. As used here this includes McDunnough's superfamily IN-CURVAROIDEA.

6b. Setae iv and v adjacent; prolegs absent.
Fig. 418. ....A few GELECHIIDAE

The members of this large family vary rather widely in habits. Some are gall makers, others destructive to stored cereals and still others attack the fruit of living plants.

Fig. 418. a, **Sitetroga cerealella** Oliv.; b, setal map of an abdominal segment.

7a. Body spindle-shaped; head with closed front (separated from the vertex by the epicrania).
Fig. 419. ....Family INCURVARIIDAE

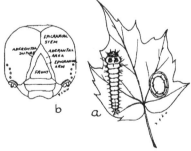

The larvae are known as needle miners and leave a characteristic pattern in leaves. The adults are exceedingly small.

Fig 419 a, Maple case bearer, **Paraclemensia acerifoliella** Fitch; b, cephalic aspect of head, showing the closed front.

151

7b. Body cylindrical or flattened; if somewhat spindle-shaped, the front extends upwards to vertex. 8
8a. Head with 1 ocellus on each side, or none. 9
8b. Head with 6 ocelli on each side. 11
9a. Front triangular; ocellus at front.
Fig. 420. . . . . .Family ERIOCRANIIDAE

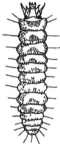

The caterpillars mine in leaves. The pupae possess toothed mandibles. They are closely related to the MICRO-PTERYGIDAE.

Fig. 420. **Mnemonica auricyanea** Wlshm.

9b. Front quadrangular; ocellus lateral. 10
10a. Front widest at posterior end; body usually flattened; prolegs when present, on 3rd to 5th abdominal segments.
Fig. 421. . . . . .Family GRACILARIIDAE

The larvae are of two types: the young have a flat head, ocelli very small and variable in number. They are miners of leaves, bark, or fruits. The full-grown caterpillars are cylindrical, with normal head, prolegs well developed on the 3rd to 5th abdominal segments. They mine, or web, or skeletonize the leaves. The azalea leaf miner, *Gracilaria azaleella* Brants imported from Japan to the United States is a pest in green house.

Fig. 421. **Litho-colletis hamadry-adella** Clemens (round form larva).

10b. Front widest at anterior end; body cylindrical; prolegs on 2nd to 7th abdominal segments. Fig. 422. . . . . .Family NEPTICULIDAE

They are called serpentine miners. The caterpillar is minute, about 2.5 to 10 mm. long. They mine in leaves and sometimes in fruits and bark. The mines are linear or serpentine. Certain species of *Ectoedemia* are gall makers. Pupation occurs in a cocoon in the soil.

Fig. 422 Plum leaf-miner, **Nep-ticula slinger-landella** Kft

11a. Abdomen with rudimentary prolegs, bearing crochets on 3rd to 6th segments. Fig. 423. ....Family TISCHERIIDAE

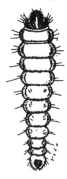

The caterpillars make blotch mines in the leaves of oak. But *Tischeria malifoliella* Clemens makes trumpet leaf mines on apple.

Fig. 423. **Tischeria malifoliella** Clemens.

11b. Abdomen without prolegs on 6th segment.
Family GRACILARIIDAE

12a. Body with tufted or secondary hairs; at least 2 setae on tubercle vi of 6th abdominal segment, or with additional setae on proleg. Fig. 424. 41

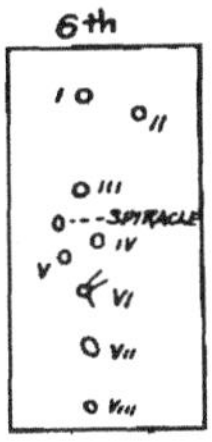

Fig. 424. · Setal map of 6th abdominal segment.

12b. Body without tufted or secondary hairs; tubercle vi with a single seta; tubercle vii with at most 3 setae, unless the proleg has a multiserial circle of crochets. Fig. 425. 13

Fig. 425 Setal map of 6th abdominal segment.

13a. Without prolegs on 6th abdominal segment.
Family GRACILARIIDAE

153

13b. With prolegs on 6th abdominal segment. 14

14a. Crochets of prolegs arranged in a circle or ellipse (sometimes incomplete), or in transverse bands. Fig. 426. 15

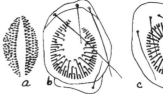

Fig 426 Crochets· a, in transverse bands, b, in incomplete circle, c, in complete circle

14b. Crochets forming a single band (sometimes with a few vestigial ones in addition). Fig. 427. 37

Fig. 427. Crochets in single band.

15a. Prespiracular wart of prothorax with 2 setae. Fig. 428. ....Family **PYRALIDIDAE**

This family is the second largest of the order and about 10,000 species have been described. The larvae are largely phytophagous and some feed upon dried vegetable matter. The meal moth, *Pyralis farinalis* (L.) feeds on cereal and cereal products. The caterpillars of the subfamily Schoenobiinae are borers in water plants, while *Nymphula nymphaeta* (L.) and *N. stagnata* Donovan are semiaquatic species living in silk-lined sacs on water plants in Europe.

Fig 428 a, Garden webworm, **Loxostege similaris** (Guen), b, beet webworm, **Loxostege sticticalis** (L), c, setal map of prothorax

15b. Prespiracular wart of prothorax with 3 setae. Fig. 429. 16

Fig. 429 Setal map of prothorax.

16a. Crochets of prolegs arranged in 2 transverse bands.
Fig. 430. 17

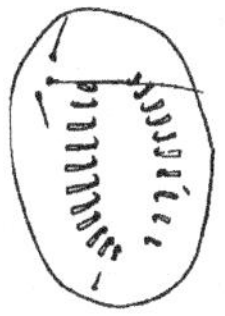

Fig 430 Cro-
chets in two
bands

16b. Crochets of prolegs arranged in
a circle or ellipse, sometimes
broadly interrupted.
Fig. 431. 22

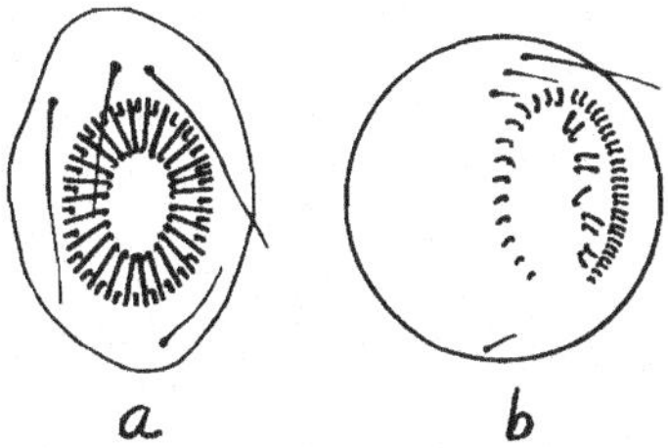

a.   *b.*

Fig 431 Crochets a, in complete circle, b, in incomplete
circle.

Fig. 432. Cro-
chets in a single
series.

17a. Prolegs with a single series of crochets, or with
2 bands formed of several series of alternate
crochets.
Fig. 432. ....Family INCURVARIIDAE

17b. Prolegs with 2 simple series of crochets.
Fig. 433. 18

Fig 433. Crochets
in two series

18a. Abdominal setae iv and v remote. Fig. 434. (Compare with Fig.
435). ....(*Bucculatrix*) Family LYONETIIDAE

Fig. 434, **Lyonetia speculella** Clemens.

The caterpillars frequent forested areas and orchards. They are
mostly leaf miners. Those of *Bucculatrix* are first miners and later
skeletonizers. Pupation takes place
in a cocoon. The cocoon of *Bucculatrix* is ribbed and surrounded
by a palisade of erect silken filaments.

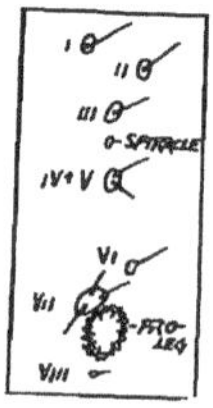

Fig. 435. Setal map of an abdominal segment.

18b. Abdominal setae iv and v adjacent.
Fig. 435. 19

19a. Crochets of anal prolegs arranged in 2 groups.
Fig. 436. ....Family GELECHIIDAE

Fig. 436. Potato tuberworm, **Gnorimoschema operculella** (Zeller).

The larvae pictured here is scattered very widely and does heavy damage to the fruit of tomatoes as well as to potato tubers. It attacks still other members of the nightshade family also.

19b. Crochets of anal prolegs in a single series. 20

20a. Front extending about one third way to vertex.
Fig. 437. ....(Cossula) Family COSSIDAE

Fig. 437 **Cossus liquiperda.**

The common goat moth, Cossus cossus (L.) of Europe, is an example. The caterpillars bore into the trunks and limbs of broad-leaved deciduous trees and large shrubs. They make large tunnels in the trunk. The larvae of the carpenterworm, Prionoxystus robiniae (Peck) of America, make large galleries in trees which usually cause the death of the trees.

20b. Front extending at least two thirds way to vertex. 21

21a. Spiracles elliptical, normal in size; those of 8th abdominal segment located higher than the others.
Fig. 438. ....Family AEGERIIDAE

Fig. 438. Squash-vine borer, **Melittia satyriniformis** Hubner.

The caterpillars live as borers in roots, trunks and limbs of shrubs and trees and herbaceous plants. Aegeria apiformis (Clerck) is a common species which infests poplars and willows chiefly. The too well known squash borer belongs here.

156

21b. Spiracles circular, very small; the last pair about in line with others. ....Family COLEOPHORIDAE

22a. Abdominal setae iv and v remote, or v absent in a few small species. Fig. 439. 23

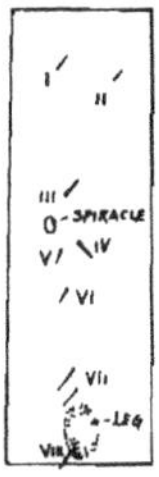

Fig 439 Setal map of an abdominal segment.

22b. Abdominal setae iv and v adjacent, often on a common tubercle. Fig. 440. 27

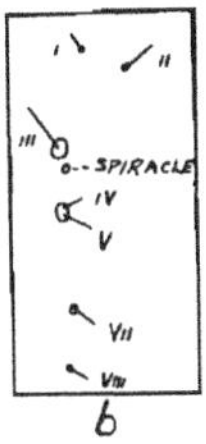

Fig. 440 Setal map of an abdominal segment.

23a. Prolegs with crochets arranged in a single complete ellipse. Fig. 441. 24

Fig 441. Crochets in a single complete ellipse.

23b. Prolegs with crochets arranged in a broken ellipse, or with additional rudimentary series at the base of normal ones. Fig. 442. 26

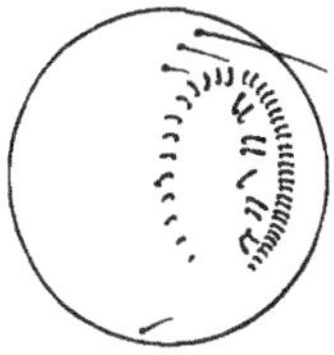

Fig 442 Crochets in broken ellipse.

24a. Prespiracular setae of prothorax about as far from its spiracle as from each other; abdominal seta i higher than ii. Fig. 443. ....Family LYONETIIDAE

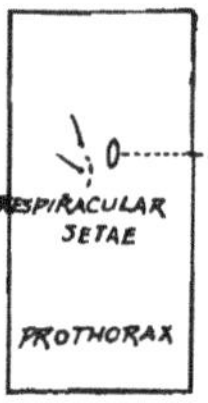

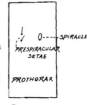

This small family of ribbed case bearers live as tiny leaf miners or skeletonizers. They are often flattened. The adults are usually brightly colored.

Fig. 443. Setal map of prothorax. .

24b. Prespiracular setae of prothorax about twice as far from its spiracle as from each other. Fig. 444. 25

Fig. 444 Setal map of prothorax.

25a. Abdominal setae i much lower than ii. Fig. 445. ....Family TINEIDAE

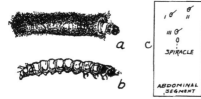

Fig 445 Casemaking clothes moth, **Tinea pelionella** (L) a, larva with case; b, larva; c, setal map of an abdominal segment.

The larvae of the case-making clothes moth, Tinea pellionella (L.), live in portable parchment-like cases. The webbing clothes moth, Tineola biselliella (Hummel), is characterized by its larvae making webs with particles on which they feed. Both feed on wool, hair, skin, feathers and other animal matter.

25b. Abdominal setae i not lower than ii. Fig. 446. ....Family HELIODINIDAE

The caterpillars are tiny either herbivorous or predacious. They feed on fruits and leaves and some mine in fruits. Some species are believed to be predators of mealybugs and scale-insects. They are known as "sun moths."

Fig 446. Setal map of an abdominal segment.

26a. Meso- and metathorax with seta ia in front of ib and well separated; abdominal seta iv above level of spiracle.
Fig. 447. ....Family HEPIALIDAE

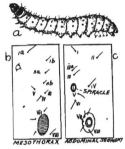

Fig 447 a, **Hepialus - humuli;** b, setal map of mesothorax, c, setal map of an abdominal segment.

The caterpillars are all plant borers including roots, stems, twigs of grasses, shrubs and trees. Some species are quite large and often somewhat wrinkled. Rather numerous hairs arise from tubercules. The larvae are usually dusky, whitish or tinged with yellow. The adults are narrow winged medium to large sized moths and are known as swifts.

26b. Meso- and metathorax with seta ia and ib closely associated; abdominal seta iv below level of spiracle.
Fig. 448. .. . . Family YPONOMENTIDAE

Fig 448 a, Diamondback moth, **Plutella maculipennis** (Curt); b, setal map of mesothorax; c, setal map of an abdominal segment

The caterpillars are often found gregariously living in webs or mining in leaves, twigs and fruits. They are destructive to conifers and other trees. The species here pictured feeds on members of the mustard family. The small green caterpillars start as miners but presently feed on the surface of the plant.

27a. Last pair of abdominal spiracles placed dorsally and closer together on middle line. Fig. 449. ....Family CARPOSINIDAE

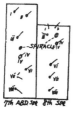

This family consists of about 100 described species. The caterpillars are fruit-borers. One species bores in peaches in Japan.

Fig 449. Lateral aspect of 7th and 8th abdominal segments.

27b. Not as 27a. 28

28a. Mesothorax with 2 setae vii located above base of leg. Fig. 450. 29

Fig 450 Setal map of mesothorax

28b. Mesothorax with 1 seta vii. 30

29a. Prothoracic spiracle with long axis vertical.
....Family THYRIDIDAE
The caterpillars of this family are concealed feeders.

29b. Prothoracic spiracle with long axis horizontal.
Fig. 451. ....Family PSYCHIDAE

The caterpillars are called bagworms because they make portable cases with leaves, twigs and other debris. They feed upon leaves, flowers, and even bark. Pupation occurs in the larval case in which the female may remain until the eggs are laid.

Fig: 451 **Thyridopteryx ephemeraeformis** Haworth

30a. Setae ii of 9th abdominal segment closer together than on any other segments, frequently on the same plate. Fig. 452. 31

Fig. 452. Setal map of 9th abdominal segment.

30b. Setae ii of 9th abdominal segment as far apart as on other segments. Fig. 453. 32

Fig 453. Setal map of 9th abdominal segment

31a. Crochets of prolegs uniordinal; abdominal setae iv and v horizontally placed. Fig. 454. ....Family PHALONIIDAE

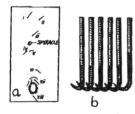

The caterpillars bore in plants or feed in seeds. They and their adult moths are small.

Fig. 454. a, Setal map of an abdominal segment; b, uniordinal crochets

31b. Crochets of prolegs usually multiordinal; abdominal setae iv and v in a diagonal or vertical line.

Fig. 455. .... Family TORTRICIDAE

a

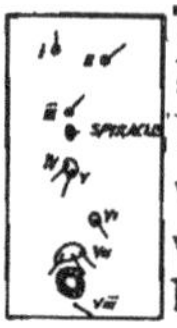

b

Fig. 455. a, Clover-seed caterpillar, **Laspeyresia interstinctana** Clemens; b, setal map of an abdominal segment.

The caterpillars are leaf rollers. They are destructive to many kinds of trees and other plants. The larvae when disturbed wriggle violently and may escape backwards from the nests of rolled leaves. The spruce budworm, *Archips fumiferana* (Clemens) and the fruit tree leaf roller, *Archips argyrospila* (Walker) are important pests.

32a. Abdominal setae i and ii close together.

Fig. 456. .... *(Schreckensteinia)* Family HELIODINIDAE

Fig 456 Setal map of an abdominal segment.

The members of this genus of sun moths are plant feeders. All are of small size. The family is interesting in that a few species are apparently predacious on scale insects.

32b. Abdominal setae i and ii widely separated.

Fig. 457. 33

Fig. 457. Setal map of an abdominal segment.

33a. Front reaching less than half way to vertex: crochets triordinal. Fig. 458. ....Family COSSIDAE

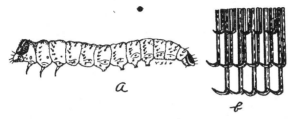

Fig 458 a, Leopard moth, **Zeuzera pyrina** L , b, triordinal crochets

The caterpillars are mostly borers in the heartwood of various kinds of woody plants. The leopard moth, Zeuzera pyrina (L.), the larvae bore in the branches and stems of apple, beech, birch, cherry, currant, elm, maple, oak, pear, plum, walnut, etc. The life cycle needs two years to be completed.

33b. Front reaching more or less two thirds way to the vertex, and ending in an attenuate point: crochets uniordinal or biordinal: small species. Fig. 459. 34

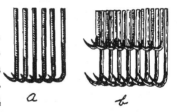

Fig 459 Crochets a, uniordinal, b, biordinal.

34a. Crochets of prolegs biordinal. Fig. 460. 35

Fig 460 Biordinal crochets

34b. Crochets of prolegs uniordinal. Fig. 461. 36

Fig. 461. Uniordinal crochets.

35a. 3 ocelli arranged closely together, more widely separated from the other one. Fig. 462. ....Family OECOPHORIDAE

Fig. 462. **Depressaria heracliana** De Geer.

The caterpillars usually live in webs or rolled leaves. One species is destructive to parsnips.

35b. Ocelli evenly spaced. Fig. 463. ....Family GELECHIIDAE

Fig. 463. Pink bollworm, **Pectinophora gossypiella** (Saunders).

The larvae pictured here is a widely distributed and serious pest of cotton. It made its first appearance in our country in 1917.

36a. Setae iii on 8th abdominal segment usually placed just above and slightly before the spiracle.
Fig. 464. ....Family GLYPHIPTERYGIDAE

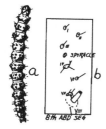

This family includes about 550 known species, largely oriental. The habits of the caterpillars are known as leaf rollers, leaf skeletonizers, leaf miners, stem borers and some live on webs.

Fig 464 a, Apple and thorn skeletonizer, **Anthophila pariana** (Clerck), b, setal map of 8th abdominal segment.

36b. Setae iii on 8th abdominal segment usually placed above and behind the spiracle. Fig. 465. ....Family BLASTOBASIDAE

Fig. 465 **Valentinia glandulella** Riley: a, acorn with a hole, b, caterpillar in acorn; c, head and thorax; d, an abdominal segment.

Some larvae are known as borers in nuts, some scavengers, and some are predacious on scale-insects.

37a. Prespiracular wart on prothorax with 3 setae.
Fig. 466. ....Family YPONOMEUTIDAE

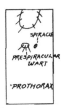

Fig 466 Setal map of prothorax

37b. Prespiracular wart on prothorax with 2 setae. 38
38a. Tubercle vii on meso- and metathorax with 2 setae. 39
38b. Tubercle vii on meso- and metathorax with 1 seta.
Fig. 467. ....Family NOCTUIDAE

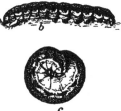

c

Fig. 467. a, Setal map of mesothorax, b, Tomato fruitworm, or corn earworm, **Heliothis armigera** (Hbn), c, variegated cutworm, **Peridroma margaritosa** (Haworth). (U.S.D.A)

About 20,000 species have been described. The caterpillars are commonly known as armyworms, cutworms, etc. Night is their usual feeding time, but when very numerous they often spread out during the day as well. Some feed on seeds and some are stem borers while the great majority are foliage feeders. They are notorious pests of agricultural crops. The corn earworm, *Heliothis armigera* (Hubner) is a cosmopolitan pest.

39a. Setae minute; tubercle reduced to obscure rings; head usually wide; prolegs reduced. Fig. 468. ....Family THYATIRIDAE

Fig. 468. **Thyatira derasa.**

The larvae of this small family are spanworms traveling like the geometrids. There are known as the beautiful mining moths, the "beauty" belonging to the adults. The naked caterpillars sometimes live gregariously in webs. They pupate in a cocoon.

39b. Setae heavy, almost always spinulose; with conspicuous tubercles. 40
40a. Tubercle iii of abdomen with 2 setae.
Fig. 469. ....Subfamily Lithosiinae, ARCTIIDAE

Fig. 469. **Oenistis quadra.**

The caterpillars possess tufted hairs which are much reduced in the last instar. This subfamily includes about 50 North American species. The caterpillars feed upon lichens.

40b. Tubercle iii of abdomen with 1 seta.
Fig. 470. .. ..(*Utethesia*) Family ARCTIIDAE

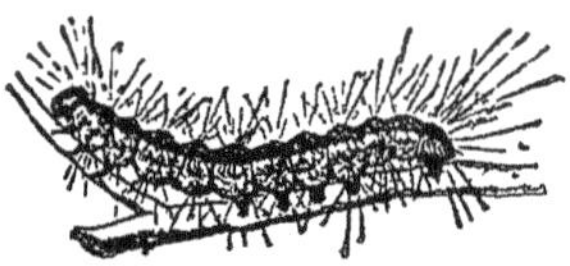

Fig. 470. Fall webworm, Hyphantria cunea (Drury). (U.S.D.A.)

The caterpillars of this family are covered with dense tufted hairs often reddish-brown and black. When disturbed they often curl into a compact mass and are called woolly bears or hedge hog caterpillars. The cocoon are made of silk and the no-longer-needed body hairs. They feed upon a wide variety of plants. The fall webworm, *Hyphantria cunea* (Drury) lives gregariously in webs.

41a. Less than 4 pairs of abdominal prolegs; sometimes anal prolegs reduced. Fig. 471. ....Family GEOMETRIDAE

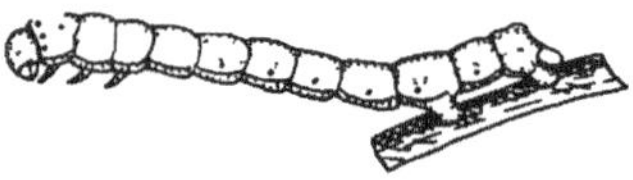

Fig. 471. **Paleacrita vernata** Peck.

About 2,000 species have been described. The caterpillars are called loopers, measuring worms, or spanworms because of their methods of locomotion. They feed chiefly on living plants but a few are able to subsist upon dry vegetable matter.

41b. 4 pairs of abdominal prolegs or more. 42

42a. Crochets on prolegs uniordinal.
Fig. 472. 43

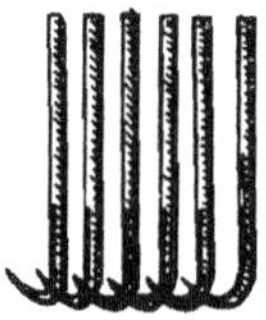

Fig. 472 Uniordinal crochets.

42b. Crochets on prolegs biordinal or triordinal. Fig. 473. 52

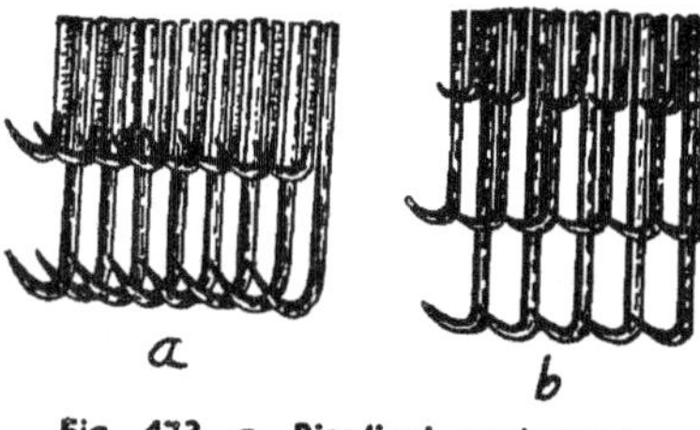

a   *b*

Fig. 473. a, Biordinal crochets; b, triordinal crochets.

43a. Warts rudimentary or absent, or obscured by secondary hairs...44

43b. At least wart vi (subventral) many haired and distinct; secondary hairs sparse or absent above prolegs. 49

44a. Anal plate bifurcated; head roughly papillose; 3rd ocellus very large. Fig. 474. ....Family SATYRIDAE

Fig. 474 Oeneis macounii Edw

About 60 described species are recorded in North America. The caterpillars chiefly live on grasses and cereals. The rice butterfly, *Melanitis leda* (L.), is a pest of rice, barley, bamboo and sugar cane in Asia.

44b. Anal plate simple; head smoother; 3rd ocellus rarely much enlarged. 45

45a. Spiracles elliptical, larger; prolegs short. 46

45b. Spiracles circular, small; prolegs slender, more or less stem-like, with expanded planta. Fig. 475. ......Family PTEROPHORIDAE

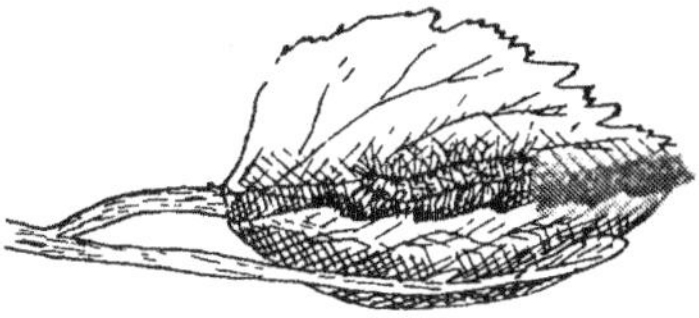

Fig. 475. Grape-vine plume **Oxyptilus periscelidactylus** Fitch.

More than 350 species have been described. Most larvae are stem borers and leaf rollers. Some are of economic importance as pests of ornamental plants and agricultural crops. The adults are the plume moths so named because of their finely split wings.

46a. Body with dense secondary setae. Fig. 476. 47

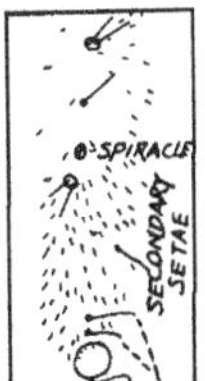

Fig 476 A body segment showing the primary setae and secondary setae

46b. Secondary setae very sparse or absent above prolegs; with simple setae or a few subprimaries. 48

167

47a. Notch of labrum deep, with parallel sides; anal prolegs as large as others; with warts, more or less overshadowed by the secondary hairs. Fig. 477. ....A few NOCTUIDAE

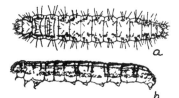

Fig 477. a, Corn earworm **Heliothis armigera** (Hbn); b, cutworm, **Euxoa auxiliaris** Grote. (USDA)

This family of owlet moths is an exceedingly important one, economically. Cutworms hide in the earth of gardens, cultivated fields, etc., by day and come out at night to cut off young plants at ground level. The corn earworm not only causes heavy loss by feeding at the tips of the maturing ears of corn but also tunnels into tomatoes.

47b. Notch of labrum acute, with convergent sides; anal prolegs much reduced and not used; warts rudimentary and dominated by a single hair (*Melalopha*) or absent (*Datana*). Fig. 478. ....Family NOTODONTIDAE

Fig. 478. Yellow-necked caterpillar, **Datana ministra** (Drury).

These caterpillars are gregarious, and pose often with the anterior and posterior ends raised into the air and attached only by median prolegs. They frequently possess dorsal humps or tubercles on the body and are often brightly colored. Their chief feed is the leaves of deciduous trees.

48a. Tubercle iv at about the same level on abdominal segments 6th, 7th and 8th. Fig. 479. ....(Doa) Family LYMANTRIIDAE

Fig. 479. **Hemerocampa vetusta** Bdv.

This family includes many destructive species. The gypsy moth, *Porthetria dispar* (L.) and the brown-tail moth, *Nygmia phaeorrhoea* (Donovan) may occur in such large number as to completely overrun and defoliate large areas of trees.

48b. Tubercle iv of 7th abdominal segment much lower than on other segments; anal prolegs more or less reduced or modified. Fig. 480. ....Most NOTODONTIDAE

Fig. 480. **Cerura vinula** (L.)

The caterpillar here pictured is a "puss moth". They never fail to attract attention. The backward projecting parts are anal tubes. This species feeds on the leaves of the willow family.

49a. With eversible mid-dorsal glands on 2nd abdominal segment. Fig. 481. ....Family LYMANTRIIDAE

Fig. 481. Notolophus antique L. (U.S.D.A)

The caterpillars of this comparatively small family are usually clothed with long hair-like scales which are often sting producing. They feed on the foliage of forest trees.

49b. No eversible mid-dorsal glands. 50

50a. Spiracles circular, small. ....Family PTEROPHORIDAE

50b. Spiracles elliptical, normal in size. 51

51a. Wart or seta iv much lower on 7th abdominal segment, or absent. Fig. 482. ....Family NOCTUIDAE

Fig. 482 Setal map of 6th, 7th and 8th abdominal segments.

51b. Wart or seta iv about the level on 7th abdominal segment as on the 6th and 8th. ....Family ARCTIIDAE

52a. Body without noticeable secondary hairs; with not more than 8 hairs on each proleg. ....(Ethmia) Family ETHMIIDAE

52b. Body with numerous secondary hairs, at least on the prolegs. .53

53a. Setae very irregular in length, some ten times as long as the others; with obscure warts, at least in the earlier stages; sometimes provided with scale-like hairs. Fig. 483. ....Family LASIOCAMPIDAE

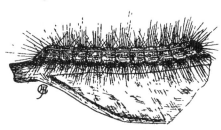

Fig. 483. **Malacosoma americana** Fab.

About 1,355 species have been scribed. The canterpillars possess long hairs and are brightly colored. They live in forested areas and orchards and feed on the foliages of various trees. The tent caterpillars, *Malacosoma* spp. occur in large numbers and lie in webs. The Syrian silkworm, *Pachypasa otus* Drury belonging here was reared for its silk by the Greeks and Romans.

53b. Setae subequal or sometimes with setae and prominent warts and spines. **54**

54a. 8th abdominal segment with a dorsal horn, or plate, or tubercle. **55**

54b. 8th abdominal segment without a dorsal horn, or plate, or tubercle. **58**

55a. Body with numerous branching spines or enlarged tubercles....**56**

55b. Body with at most 2 pairs of small spines on thorax. **57**

56a. Head angulated or spined dorsally, or abdomen with several mid-dorsal spines; crochets of prolegs usually triordinal.
Fig. 484. ....Family NYMPHALIDAE

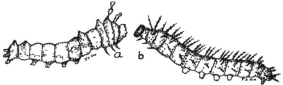

F**i**g. 484. a, **Basilarchia astyanax** Fab ; b, **Vanessa antiopa.**

About 4,000 species have been described. The caterpillars are usually spiny but some are naked. The chrysalises are suspended by the cremaster and the head is held downwards. They are often marked with silver or gold ornamentations. The adults are butterflies.

56b. Head rounded; crochets biordinal.
Fig 485. ....Family SATURNIIDAE

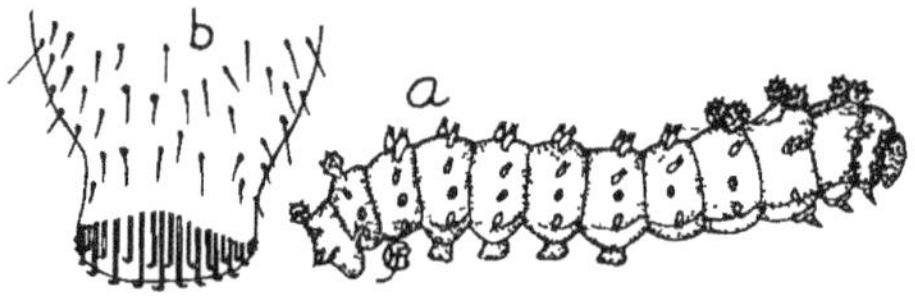

Fig 485 a, **Samia cecropia** L.; b, a proleg with crochets.

The caterpillars chiefly feed on broad-leaved deciduous and evergreen trees. They are called giant or wild silkworms. No less than 30 species in oriental Asia are able to produce usable silk.

57a. Segments with 6 or 8 annulets; prolegs not widely separated.
Fig. 486. ....Family SPHINGIDAE

Fig. 486 Tobacco hornworm, **Protoparce sexta** (Johanssen).

About 900 species have been described. The caterpillars are called hornworms because of the presence of a horn-like process on the 8th abdominal segment. Some larvae assume grotesque attitudes which are thought to be responsible for the name "sphinx moth" or "sphinx caterpillar".

57b. Segments with 2 or 3 obscure annulets; prolegs widely separated. Fig. 487. . . . . .Family BOMBYCIDAE

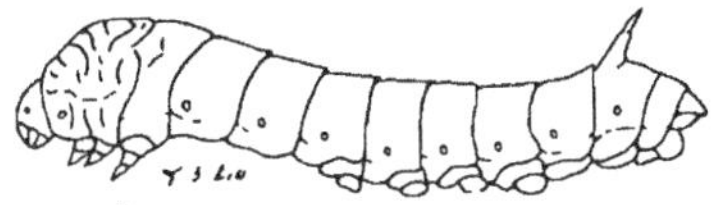

Fig 487 Chinese silkworm, Bombyx mori L.

The Chinese silkworm, *Bombyx mori* L. is an important beneficial insect which has been domesticated for more than 2,000 years. It was estimated about 70 million pounds of raw silk are produced each year.

58a. Head elevated, triangular . . . .*(Lapara)* Family SPHINGIDAE

58b. Head not so. 59

59a. Crochets on prolegs forming an ellipse, at most narrowly interrupted. Fig. 488. . . . . .Family HESPERIIDAE

Fig 488. Epargyreus tityrus Fab.

About 3,000 species have been described. The head of the caterpillars is much larger than its prothorax which forms a narrow "neck" and makes them readily recognized. Its body is widest at middle and tapering toward both ends. They live exposed on plants or within rolled and webbed leaves. They feed chiefly on cereals and grasses. The adults are known as skippers.

59b. Crochets arranged in one band, occasionally interrupted, or rarely forming 2 separated bands. 60

60a. Bands of crochets on prolegs reduced or interrupted at middle and with a narrow spatulate, freshly lobe arising near the interruption. Fig. 489. . . . . .Family LYCAENIDAE

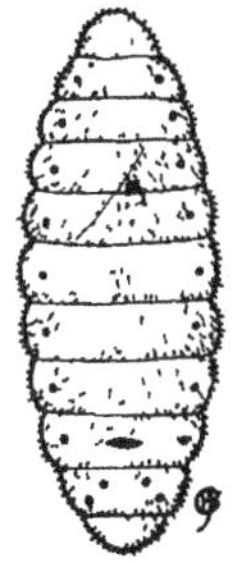

The caterpillars are largely phytophagous and often found on leguminous plants. Some are predacious and feed on scale-insects and other homopterous nymphs. A few are myrmecophilous. The body is short and broad, slug-like and the head is smaller and narrower than the body.

Fig. 489. Lycaenid larva.

60b. Prolegs with band of crochets continuous, without a fleshy lobe near the middle. 61

61a. Dorsum of prothorax bearing an eversible, forked scent gland. When the gland is retracted a transverse groove is revealed: body not hairy or spiny, but sometimes with fleshy filaments. Fig. 490. ....Family PAPILIONIDAE

Fig. 490. Papilio cresphontes Cramer.

About 800 species have been described. The caterpillars feed on a number of plants, but chiefly on *Citrus* and Umbelliferae. The thorax of the larva is usually enlarged, and sometimes possesses two eyespots. A protrusible scent gland on the dorsum which is called *osmeterium*— is often present and is ejected when the caterpillar is disturbed. The adults are the swallowtail butterflies.

61b. Not as 61a. 62

62a. Head and body entirely without spines, high tubercles, or fleshy filaments. 63

62b. Body with spines, high tubercles, or fleshy filaments. 65

63a. Anal plate entire, rounded. 64

63b. Anal plate bifurcate at tip, bearing 2 distinct processes. ....Family SATYRIDAE

64a. Head apparently larger than prothorax. ..Family NYMPHALIDAE

64b. Head smaller than prothorax. Fig. 491. ....Family PIERIDAE

Fig. 491. Cabbageworm, Pieris rapae (L.)

About 1,000 species have been described. The caterpillars feed on many kinds of plants but are especially fond of cabbages and other cruciferous crops. The cabbage butterfly, *Pieris rapae* (L.) is a cosmopolitan species and the rape butterfly, *Pieris napi* (L.) is also common to both Europe and North America.

65a. Mesothorax and sometimes several other segments bearing fleshy
filaments. Fig. 492. ....Family DANAIDAE

Fig. 492. Danaus plexippus L.

The caterpillars chiefly
feed on milkweeds. The
monarch butterly, Dan-
aus plexippus (L.) is nearly a cosmopolitan species.
Its caterpillar is black and
yellow. The chrysalis is
pale green and iridescent.

65b. Body without fleshy filaments. ....Family NYMPHALIDAE

Key to the PUPAE of the more important families of LEPIDOPTERA
(Chiefly from E. Mosher, 1916)

1a. With functional mandibles crossing in front of head.
Fig. 493. ....Families MICROPTERYGIDAE & ERIOCRANIIDAE

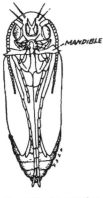

MANDIBLE

The pupation of Micropterygidae takes place
in a dense, parchment-like cocoon. The pupation of Eriocraniidae takes place in a tough
cocoon in the ground. The pupa uses its large
mandibles to cut its way out of the cocoon and
to dig up to the surface.

Fig. 493. Mnemonica
auricyanea Wlshm.

1b. Without functional mandibles, or indicated only as small tubercles
or lobes. 2

2a. 4th abdominal segment movable on the 3rd; or appendages free
from each other. 3

2b. 4th abdominal segment fixed to 3rd; appendages fused to each
other. 19

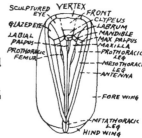

3a. Maxillary palpi present, separated from maxillae by a suture.
Fig. 494. 4

Fig 494 Cephalic aspect of head and thorax.

3b. Maxillary palpi absent. 11

4a. Dorsum of abdomen provided with fine spines, but not arranged in rows. 5

4b. The anterior edge of some abdominal segments covered with a row of spines, sometimes with a second posterior row of spines. 7

5a. Maxillary palpi extending as a band along posterior margin of eyes. (See Fig. 497). 6

5b. Maxillary palpi not extending along posterior margin of eyes.
Fig. 495. ....A few GRACILARIIDAE

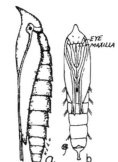

Fig 495 a, Litho-colletis hamadryadel-la Clemens, b, Litho-colletis argentinotel-la Clemens ♀.

Hibernation takes place either in adult stage or in pupal stage. When in pupal stage, the adult is well developed inside.

More than 200 species of the genus pictured are known. Many of them are highly economic.

6a. Spiracles of 1st abdominal segment covered by wings.
Fig. 496. ....Family INCURVARIIDAE

Pupation takes place in a silken cocoon at the mouth of the larval burrow.

Fig 496 **Pro-
doxus quinque-
punctellus** Cham.

6b. Spiracles of 1st abdominal segment exposed.
Fig. 497. ....Family NEPTICULIDAE

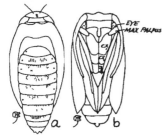

When the larva is full-grown it drops to the ground and spins a dense flattened silken cocoon within the rubbish or on the surface of the soil.

Fig. 497. **Nepticula platanella**
Clemens ♂.. a, dorsal aspect;
b, ventral aspect.

7a. Middle abdominal segments, each with 2 rows of spines. 8

7b. Middle abdominal segments, each with 1 row of spines. 10

8a. Cremaster absent, or indicated only by a tuft of spines; anal rise without spines. Fig. 498. ....Family AEGERIIDAE

Pupation takes place in the tunnel which is made by the larva.

This is a comparatively small family. The species pictured lives on lilac and ash.

Fig. 498. **Podo-
sesia syringae**
(Harr.) ♀ .

8b. Cremaster well developed, forming a definite process; or anal rise with spines. 9

9a. Last abdominal segment with a group of angular nodules.
....Family PHALONIIDAE

9b. Last abdominal segment with setae only.
Fig. 499. .... .Family TORTRICIDAE

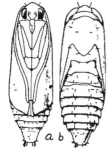

Pupation takes place in rolled leaves or on the bark of the host plant. Some spin cocoons which are attached to other objects or put within debris.

Fig. 499. **Laspeyresia interstinctana** Clemens. a, dorsal aspect; b, ventral aspect. (U S.D.A.)

10a. Notum of mesothorax prolonged into a long lobe.
Fig. 500. ....Family GLYPHIPTERYGIDAE

The information of the pupae of this family is very limited.

Fig. 500 **Anthopila pariana** Clerk.

10b. Notum of mesothorax not prolonged into a long lobe.
Fig. 501. ....Family TINEIDAE

Pupation takes place in a silken cocoon or larval case.

Fig. 501 **Tinea pellionella** (L) ♂

11a. Dorsal head-piece much longer than the prothorax.
(See Fig. 502). 12

11b. Dorsal head-piece not longer than the prothorax. 15

12a. 4th abdominal segment free from 3rd; antennae and hind legs
not in subequal length. 13

12b. 4th abdominal segment rigidly fastened to 3rd; antennae and
hind legs subequal in length. 14

13a. Labial palpi visible. Fig. 502. ....Family TISCHERIIDAE

The early stages are leaf-miners. Pupation takes
place in the Spring in the larval mine.

Fig. 502. **Tisch-
eria malifoliella**
Clemens. ♀

13b. Labial palpi invisible. Fig. 503. ....Family LYONETIIDAE

Pupation takes place in a
cocoon which formed on the
leaf under two bands of
silk, or is sometimes naked
and suspended by a few
silk threads to a bent leaf.

Fig 503. **Lyonetia speculella** Clemens.

14a. 3rd to 7th abdominal segments each with 2 deep punctures at
the anterior margin near the mid-dorsal line; 7th longer than 8th
to 10th together. ....(Phyllocnistis) LYONETIIDAE

14b. Not so. ....Family GRACILARIIDAE

15a. Cremaster with a distinct stem. ..   (Peronea) TORTRICIDAE

15b. Cremaster without a stem, its hooks attached to body. 16

16a. 1st abdominal spiracles invisible; dorsal spines or setae arranged
in transverse rows...17

16b. 1st abdominal spiracles visible; dorsal spines or setae irregular. Fig. 504. ....Family LIMACODIDAE

Pupation takes place in a smooth silken cocoon which is attached to the host plant.

Fig 504 **Euclea chloris.** ♀.

17a. Mesothorax less than twice as long as metathorax; maxillae quadrangular, widely separated. Fig. 505. ...Family HEPIALIDAE

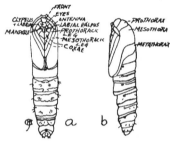

The pupa is slender, fitting the larval burrow. Its mandibles are rudimentary, but sharply defined. Before emergence, the pupa leaves the larval burrow.

Fig 505 **Sthenopis thule** Stkr a, ventral aspect; b, lateral aspect.

17b. Mesothorax more than twice as long as metathorax; maxillae longitudinal. 18

18a. 3rd abdominal segment movable on 2nd; abdominal segments with an anterior row of spines and a posterior row of setae. Fig. 506. ....Family PSYCHIDAE

The pupation takes place in the larval bag attaching to the host plant. The species pictured is the most common one of its family in our country. The family is a fairly large one.

Fig. 506. **Thyridopteryx ephemeraeformis** Haworth.

18b. 3rd abdominal segment fixed on 2nd; abdominal segments with both rows of spines. Fig. 507. . . .. Family COSSIDAE

The pupal stage passes in the burrow which was made by the larva.

This, our most important species, was introduced from Europe and infests many species of trees.

Fig 507. Leopard moth, **Zeuzera pyrina** L. ♂

19a. Labrum with 3 lobes (pilifers distinct). Fig. 508. 20

Fig 508 Anterior part of pupa

19b. Labrum simple or bilobed (pilifers absent). 28

20a. Maxillary palpi present. (See Fig. 509). 21

20b. Maxillary palpi wanting. 22

21a. Epicranial suture wanting; no deep dorsal groove between 9th and 10th abdominal segments; 8th abdominal segment free on 7th in male. ....(Atteva) YPONOMEUTIDAE

21b. Epicranial suture distinct at sides; or with a deep dorsal groove between 9th and 10th abdominal segments; 8th abdominal segment fixed on 7th in both sexes. Fig. 509. ...Family PYRALIDIDAE

Pupation takes place in various ways: some spin cocoons in dead leaves or under rubbish. The aquatic species spend their pupal stage in a cocoon beneath the surface of the water.

Fig 509 European corn borer, **Pyausta nubilalis** (Hubner)

179

22a. With a deep dorsal groove between 9th and 10th abdominal segments. ....Subfamily Epipaschiinae, PYRALIDIDAE

22b. Not so. 23

23a. Prothoracic femur exposed; antennae not swollen.
Fig. 510. ....Family PTEROPHORIDAE

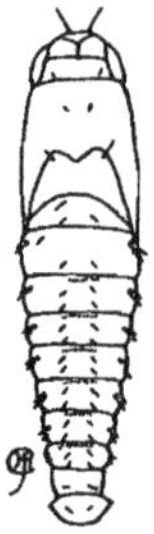

Pupae usually suspend themselves by their tail on the host plant.

They are often spiny. The adults have divided wings.

Fig. 510. **Pterophorus tenuidactylus** Fitch.

23b. Prothoracic femur concealed; antennae swollen. ... .24

24a. Maxillae in contact with eyes; tip of mouth parts beyond tip of wings; pupa usually in a cocoon.
Fig. 511. ....Family HESPERIIDAE

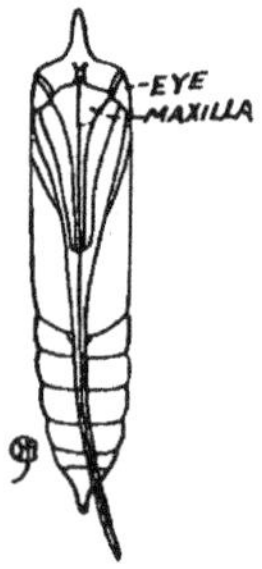

Pupa is rounded, suspended by a Y-shaped girth in a cocoon.

This family has some 3000 known species some of which are economic.

Fig 511. **Calpodes ethlius** Cr.

24b. Maxillae separated from eyes; tip of mouth parts not beyond tip of wings; pupa usually exposed. 25

180

25a. Pupa normally exposed, rarely in cocoon; mesothoracic legs reaching forward to eyes. Fig. 512. .....Family NYMPHALIDAE

Pupa suspended by the tail or in a girded thin cocoon. They are sometimes dull colored but are often marked with silver or gold.

Fig 512 Bren-
thia pavonacel-
la Clemens ♀ .

25b. Pupa normally girded at middle, rarely in cocoon; mesothoracic legs not reaching forward to eyes. 26

26a. Body rounded; mouth parts not reaching the tip of wings. Fig. 513. ....Family LYCAENIDAE

The body of pupa is short, rounded and closely girded. It is usually smooth and small. Our smallest butterflies belong to this family.

Fig 513. Lycae-
nopsis ladon.

26b. Body elongate; mouth parts reaching the tip of wings. 27

27a. Anterior end of pupa with 2 points. Fig. 514. ....+.......Family PAPILIONIDAE

Pupa loosely girded and with two points at the anterior end.

Most of the members of the family pass the winter in.this stage.

Fig. 514. Papilio
cresphontes Cra-
mer.

27b. Anterior end of pupa with 1 point.
Fig. 515. ....Family PIERIDAE

The shape of pupa is angular ending in a single spine and is girded loosely. Many species go through several generations a year, making the pupal stage very short.

Fig 515 **Calli-dryas eubule.**

28a. Tip of fore wings far beyond the posterior edge of the 4th abdominal segment; prothoracic femur exposed. 29

28b. Tip of fore wings not beyond the posterior edge of the 4th abdominal segment; prothoracic femur concealed. 31

29a. Maxillary and labial palpi concealed; pupa without movable segments. ....Family LYONETIIDAE

29b. Maxillary and labial palpi exposed; with several movable abdominal segments. 30

30a. Caudal end of abdomen with lateral projections; maxillary palpi wanting. Fig. 516. ....Family COLEOPHORIDAE

Pupation takes place in the larval case ordinarily fastened on the host plant.

Fig 516. **Coleo-phora malivorel-la** Riley

30b. Caudal end of abdomen without lateral projections; maxillary palpi present. Fig. 517. ....Family YPONOMEUTIDAE

Pupation takes place in a cocoon which is spindle-shaped and suspended in its larval web.

Fig 517 **Scy-thris eboracen-sis** Zeller

31a. Fore wings usually extending beyond 4th abdominal segment; if not, then the body depressed, antennae adjacent on the middle; first 4 abdominal segments usually longer than the remainder; epicranial suture always present. 32

31b. Fore wings not extending beyond 4th abdominal segment; if beyond, then the maxillary palpi never present; first 4 abdominal segments rarely longer than the remainder; epicranial suture rarely visible. 36

32a. Antennae 4/5 as long as fore wings, meeting only at apex; labial palpi distinct. ....(Scythris) YPONOMEUTIDAE

32b. Antennae reaching almost to the tip of wings, meeting at middle and sometimes diverging at apex; labial palpi usually concealed. 33

33a. Antennae not diverging at apex. 34

33b. Antennae diverging at apex. 35

Fig 518 **Depressaria heracliane** De Geer.

34a. Prothoracic legs longer than mouth parts.

Fig. 518. ....(Ethmia) ETHMIIDAE

34b. Prothoracic legs shorter than mouth parts. ..A few GELECHIIDAE

35a. Fronto-clypeal suture complete. Fig. 519. ..Family GELECHIIDAE

Pupation takes place in a silken cocoon.

The family is a large one with several thousand species and numerous genera. The several species of Recurvaria mine within the needles of the conifers. The other species pictured is a widely distributed pest of stored grain, feeding and pupating within the grains.

Fig 519 a, Spruce leaf-miner, **Recurvaria piceailla** Kearf, b, **Sitotroga cerealella** Oliv (U S D A)

35b. Fronto-clypeal suture obsolete in middle.
Fig. 520. ....Family OECOPHORIDAE

Pupation takes place in hollow stem, or larval web, or folded leaves, varying differently with the larval habits.

The larvae are often case makers.

Fig. 520 **Cryptolechia quercicella** Clemens.

36a. Labial palpi exposed, lanceolate. 37

36b. Labial palpi invisible or reduced to a small area............41

37a. Body with secondary setae (often minute), not arranged around larval warts. Fig. 521. ....Family LASIOCAMPIDAE

Pupation takes place in a silken cocoon hidden in debris or other objects. Both the' pupae and the eggs have a smooth exterior. The nearly 30 members of this genus do serious damage to trees.

Fig. 521. **Malacosoma disstria.** Hubner.

37b. Body with primary setae only, or with setae around larval warts. 38

38a. Prothoracic femur exposed. 39

38b. Prothoracic femur concealed. 40

39a. Tip of abdomen with a group of pyramidal points, setae obscure; mesothoracic legs touching maxillary palpi; 5th abdominal segment without special ridge. ....(Diatraea) PYRALIDIDAE

39b. Tip of abdomen with a cremaster or hooked cremastral setae; mesothoracic legs not touching maxillary palpi; 5th abdominal segment with a special ridge. Fig. 522. .....Family NOCTUIDAE

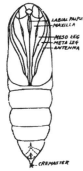

Fig. 522. **Papaipe-ma nebris** Gn. ♀

The pupal stage passes in various ways: some make loose cocoons in leaves, some enter the soil for pupation, many pupate under debris on the surface of the ground.

The more than 20,000 species of this great family vary so widely in size and habits that anything said about the family must be of a general nature. Many of the species are highly economic and some of the most destructive plant pests fall in this group. Any collecting trip is likely to turn up some of their pupae.

40a. The scars of larval warts with setae not arranged in circles. ....Family NOCTUIDAE

40b. The scars of larval with setae arranged in circles. Fig. 523. ....Family LYMANTRIIDAE

Fig. 523. **Hem-erocampa leucos-tigma** S. & A.

Pupation takes place in a silken cocoon which is sometimes mixed with body setae.

The pupae of the white marked tussock moth, here taken as an example of the family, are easily located since they are often wrapped in a dead leaf attached to the tree or other food plant. The wingless female after emergence and fertilization usually deposits her eggs upon the cocoon and covers them with a white coat which is weatherproof but which makes the whole assembly more conspicuous.

41a. Maxillary palpi present; on thorax and base of abdomen with a crest; cremaster present.

Fig. 524. ....Subfamily Galleriinae, PYRALIDIDAE

The caterpillars live ordinarily in the nests of bees and wasps. The bee moths or waxworms sometimes do serious damages in beehives. The pupae have well-marked appendages and are enclosed within a thick, tough cocoon.

Fig. 524. Wax moth, **Galleria melonella** (L.) ♂

41b. Not as 41a. 42

42a. Antennae club-shaped; cremaster wanting.
...................................(Oeneis) NYMPHALIDAE

42b. Antennae not club-shaped; if so, cremaster present. 43

43a. The larval warts with setae arranged in circles. 44

43b. The larval warts with setae arranged not in circles. 46

44a. Antennae reaching beyond the half of fore wings. 45

44b. Antennae reaching less than half of fore wings.
....A few LYMANTRIIDAE

45a. Cremaster as long as 9th and 10th abdominal segments together; with hooked setae. ....Subfamily Pantheinae, NOCTUIDAE

45b. Cremaster if present, then abdomen with flanged plates.
Fig. 525. ....Family ARCTIIDAE

The cocoon is usually formed by coarse silk and larval body hairs. The pupation takes place mostly under leaves or within debris on the ground.

The pupa shown here comes from the very common brick-red and black "banded woolly bear" caterpillar so much in evidence in the Fall.

Fig. 525. Isia isabella S. & A.

186

46a. Body with secondary setae. 47
46b. Body with primary setae or none. 48
47a. Body with rather coarse, short secondary setae; cremaster rudimentary. Fig. 526. ....Family BOMBYCIDAE

Pupation takes place in white or yellow thick silken cocoon. The Chinese silkworm yields 70 million pounds of raw silk annually.

Fig. 526. Bom-
byx mori L

47b. Body with fine, soft secondary setae; cremaster well developed. Fig. 527. ....Family NOTODONTIDAE

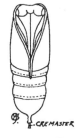

The pupa is often naked and protected by an earthen cell. Other species spin a scanty cocoon which frequently contains some of the debris in which it is placed.

Fig. 527. Phry-
ganidia califor-
nica Pack.

48a. Antennae not pectinate; spiracular furrows often present; fronto-clypeal suture distinct at ends. 49
48b. Antennae pectinate; spiracular furrows rarely present; fronto-clypeal suture wanting. Fig. 528. ....Family SATURNIIDAE

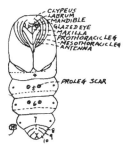

Pupation takes place in dense silken cocoons which have been utilized for silk by man.

Fig. 528. Samia cecropia
L

49a. Antennae usually filiform, the greatest width rarely greater than that of the prothoracic legs, if greater, then cremaster always present; antennae never more than ¾ the length of wings; epicranial suture always wanting; scar of dorsal horn of 8th abdominal segment usually present; labial palpi never visible. Fig. 529. ....Family SPHINGIDAE

Fig 529. Tobacco hornworm, **Protoparce sexta** (Johansen)

Pupation takes place in the ground in an earthen cell which is made by the soil and the body fluid. A few species pupate on the surface of the ground in a simple cocoon composed of leaves fastened with silk.

49b. Antennae usually broader near the proximal end, their greatest width usually greater than that of the prothoracic legs; antennae usually more than ¾ length of wings, if not, then epicranial suture is present, or the cremaster is wanting, or if present then bifurcate at the distal end or bearing hooked setae; dorsum of abdomen usually with a deep groove between 9th and 10th abdominal segments; scar of dorsal horn of 8th abdominal segment never present; labial palpi sometimes visible. 50

50a. Maxillae usually more than 3/5 length of wings; if not, then the caudal end of body with hooked setae, or 3rd abdominal spiracle concealed by wings; prothoracic femur often exposed; a deep furrow usually present on the dorsum of abdomen between the 9th and 10th segments. Fig. 530. ....Family GEOMETRIDAE

Fig 530 Brephos infans Moesch.

Pupation takes place in the soil with or without a silken cocoon.

This rather large family includes some 2,000 species, many of which are well known.

50b. Maxillae seldom more than 3/5 length of wings; if so, then the posterior margin of mesothorax with a row of deep pits or entire body punctate; 3rd abdominal spiracle never concealed by wings; prothoracic femur never exposed; cremaster T-shaped. ·· ....Family NOTODONTIDAE

ORDER DIPTERA

Key to the LARVAE of the more important families

(After John R. Malloch, 1917)

1a. Mandibles moving horizontally; head complete,
if not, the posterior portion with deep longitudinal incisions, or the thorax and abdomen
together consisting of 13 segments. Fig. 531.
................Suborder ORTHORRHAPHA,
series NEMATOCERA....3

Fig. 531. Head of **Culex** sp

1b. Mandibles moving vertically; head incomplete,
without a strongly developed upper arcuate plate.
Fig. 532. 2

Fig. 532. Anter-
ior part of body,
showing the man-
dibles.

2a. Maxillae well developed, palpi distinct; mandibles
normally sickle-like; antennae well developed on
the upper surface of a slightly arcuate sclerotized
dorsal plate. Fig. 533.
Suborder ORTHORRHAPHA,
series BRACHYCERA......16

Fig. 533. Dor-
sal aspect of
head.

2b. Maxillae poorly developed, palpi visible only in a few larvae;
mandibles short and hook-like; antennae poorly developed or
absent, when present situated upon a membranous surface.
Fig. 534. ....Suborder CYCLORRHAPHA*

Fig 534 a, **Drosophila melanogaster** Meigen (Calif. Exp Sta), b, Hessian fly, **Phytophaga destructor** (Say) (U S D A), c, **Eris-
talis bastardi** Macq , d, **Toxomerus politus** Say, e, **Leucopis
griseola** Fall (U S D A), f, Common cattle grub, **Hypoderma
lineatum** De Vill) in host skin (U S D A); g, Mediterranean
fruit fly, **Ceratitis capitata** (Wied) with an anterior respiratory organ (Calif. Exp. Sta).

*Key to families is not available.

3a. Head incomplete; thorax and abdomen combined consisting of 13 segments; larvae peripneustic; usually with a sclerotized plate on ventral surface of mesothorax. Fig. 535. . .Family CECIDOMYIDAE

Fig 535 **Retinodiplosis inops** O S

The larvae are mostly gall-makers, but some are predacious on scale-insects and others live in decaying organic matter. The Hessian fly, *Phytophaga destructor* (Say) is a serious pest of wheat. The larvae live and feed on the stem beneath the leaf sheaths, where pupation also takes place.

3b. Not so. 4

4a. Head and thorax and 1st and 2nd abdominal segments fused; larvae with minute abdominal spiracles; abdomen with a ventral longitudinal series of sucker-like discs.
Fig. 536. . . . . .Family BLEPHAROCERATIDAE

The adults are called net-winged midges. The larvae live in swift-flowing streams and feed on algae and diatoms. They may be found clinging to the rocks. Pupation takes place in the water.

Fig. 536 **Biblo-
cephala** sp.

4b. Head free, or if retracted within or fused with prothorax the other thoracic segments are distinct. 5

5a. Head complete; mandibles opposed. 6

5b. Head incomplete posteriorly, either with 3 deep wedge-shaped slits (2 on dorsum and 1 on venter), or ventral surface very poorly sclerotized and the dorsal one posteriorly in the form of 4 slender heavily sclerotized rods, with a weakly sclerotized divided plate on anterior half of the dorsum. Fig. 537. ....Family TIPULIDAE

Fig 537 **Tipula eluta** Loew

There are about 6,000 species of crane flies described. The larvae are commonly called leather jackets. They are aquatic, semiaquatic, and some are terrestrial. They feed upon decaying wood, decaying vegetations, fungi, moss, and roots of many plants. A few are leaf miners.

6a. Thoracic segments fused and dilated, forming a complex mass. Fig. 538. ....Family CULICIDAE

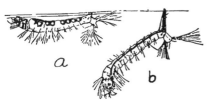

Fig 538 a, **Anopheles** sp ; b, **Culex** sp.

Around 2,000 species of mosquitoes have been described. The larvae are aquatic and live in various types of fresh water and even in brackish and salt water. The culicine larvae rest under water surface with the body obliquely placed while the anophelines are horizontally placed. Many species of female mosquitoes are the vectors of human diseases. Anopheles are responsible for malaria and Aedes carry the causative agent of yellow fever and dengue.

6b. Thoracic segments distinct. 7

7a. Larvae peripneustic, or with at least rudimentary abdominal spiracles. 8

7b. Larvae amphipneustic or metapneustic. 11

8a. Larvae with rudimentary abdominal spiracles; mouth with a large articulated process on each side which bears a number of long hairs and closes, fan-like, when at rest; posterior abdominal segments dilated, the last one armed on venter with a sucker-like disc which bears concentric series of bristles; aquatic species. Fig. 539. ....Family SIMULIIDAE

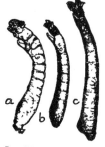

Fig 539 a, Simulium pictipes Hagen, b, S. venustum Say, c, S. sp (Utah Agr Exp. Sta.)

About 300 species of buffalo gnats or black flies are described. The larvae live mostly in swift fresh water and congregate in masses on their webs on rocks in water. The larvae are often so abundant as to completely cover the rocks to which they are attached. The female bites and causes painful swellings. They are disease carriers.

8b. Larvae with distinct though sometimes small abdominal spiracles; mouth without fan-like processes; posterior abdominal segments not noticeably dilated, the last one without sucker-like disc; terrestrial species. 9

9a. Antennae elongate; body armed with conspicuous bristles or hairs. 10

9b. Antennae usually short and inconspicuous, sometimes apparently absent; body without conspicuous bristles. Fig. 540. ....Family MYCETOPHILIDAE

Fig. 540. Exechia netive Johannsen.

Around 2,000 species of the fungus gnats have been described. The larvae inhabit damp places in large numbers. They are active and able to leap. Their food is decaying vegetation and fungi. Some species are recorded as pests of mushrooms.

10a. Anal spiracles at the apices of a pair of long stalk-like processes. Fig. 541. ....Family SCATOPSIDAE

Fig. 541. Rhegmoclema atrata Say.

The larvae live in dung, in decaying organic matter, or under the loose bark of decaying trees. Their adults are known as dung midges, or minute black scavengers.

10b. Anal spiracles not noticeably elevated, situated near base of dorsal surface of caudal segment.
Fig. 542. . . . . .Family BIBIONIDAE

Fig. 542. **Bibio albipennis** Say.

About 500 species of the March flies have been described. The larvae live in and feed on decaying vegetable matter, dung, and the roots of grasses, cereals and vegetables. They are sometimes very abundant.

11a. Dorsal surface of 1st and 2nd abdominal segments each with 2 wart-like elevations. Fig. 543. . . . . .Family DIXIDAE

Fig. 543. **Dixa sp**

Only around 10 species have been described in the United States. The larvae are aquatic and feed on algae. The body is bent and moves by alternate thrusts of the two ends of the body, the bent portion is foremost.

11b. Dorsal surface of 1st and 2nd abdominal segments without elevated processes. 12

12a. All or some of the dorsal segments with narrow, sclerotized strap-like transverse bands; or the apical segment in the form of a short sclerotized tube; rarely the ventral abdominal segments bear a central series of sucker-like discs.
Fig. 544. . . . . .Family PSYCHODIDAE

Fig 544 **Psychoda superba** Banks

The larvae are aquatic or terrestrial and some live in drain pipes. They feed on decaying matter, dung, fungi and sewage. The adults are called sand flies or moth flies. Some sand flies are the carriers of human diseases. *Flebotomus argentipes* Annandale & Brunnetti, *F. major* Annandale, *F. chinensis* Patton & Hindle are the carriers of kala azar.

12b. Dorsum without narrow, sclerotized, strap-like bands; apical segment not in the form of a short sclerotized tube; ventral abdominal segments never with sucker-like discs. .13

13a. Antennae undeveloped, appearing as pale round spots on side of head; ventral surface of head with sclerites contiguous anteriorly, widely separated posteriorly. . . .Family MYCETOPHILIDAE

13b. Antennae pedunculate, usually well developed; ventral surface of head with sclerites contiguous for entire length, not separated widely posteriorly. 14

14a. Abdominal segments not subdivided. 15

14b. Abdominal segments subdivided by means of transverse constrictions. ....Family TIPULIDAE

15a. (a) Aquatic larvae very slender, tapering towards both ends; without thoracic or anal pseudopods or surface hairs (except about 8 at apex of abdomen). (b) Terrestrial larvae stout, with well-defined segments which are armed with strong bristles, some of which are lanceolate; pseudopods present.
Fig. 545. ....Family CERATOPOGONIDAE

The members of this family are called biting midges, punkies, or sand flies. Their larvae are aquatic, semi-aquatic or terrestrial. The latter live in moist humus soil or under bark. The aquatic species inhabit various types of water including seashore and salt lakes. The adults suck blood from other insects and mammals. Some species are the vectors of filaria worms.

Fig 545. **Forcipomyia specularis** Coq

15b. Larvae rarely very slender, generally of an almost uniform thickness, rarely with the thoracic segments appreciable swollen but not fused; abdominal and thoracic segments frequently with rather noticeable soft hairs, the last segment almost invariably with a conspicuous tuft of hairs on dorsum near apex; pseudopods almost always present, sometimes (very rare) only the thoracic one distinguishable in terrestrial forms.
Fig. 546. ....Family CHIRONOMIDAE

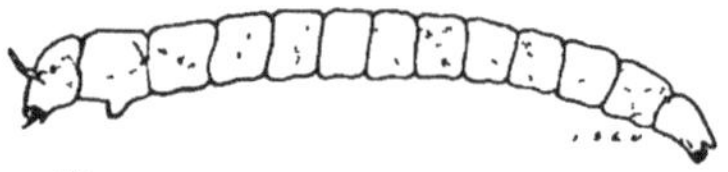

Around 2,000 species of the midges have been described. The larvae are aquatic or terrestrial. The aquatic species live in various types of water including salt lakes and open sea. Some feed on the water surface, others make silken cases and attach to rocks or other objects on the bottom or in mud. The blood worms are red colored larvae. The terrestrial species live in dung, fungi, mosses and decaying vegetation.

Fig. 546 **Camptocladius byssinus.**

194

16a. Posterior spiracles approximated, situated within a terminal or subterminal cleft or chamber, usually concealed; body entirely shagreened or wholly or in part longitudinally striated. 17

16b. Posterior spiracles rather widely separated, visible, situated on apical segment, which may be truncated, sclerotized, or armed with apical processes; or upon penultimate or antepenultimate segment; body not shagreened or visibly striated. 18

17a. Head not retractile; body flattened, surface finely shagreened, sometimes with lateral abdominal spiracles, without vestigial pseudopods; spiracular fissure transverse, sometimes rather small; pupae enclosed in larval skin.
Fig. 547. . . . . .Family STRATIOMYIDAE

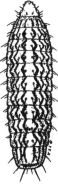

About 1,200 species of the soldier flies have been described. Some larvae live in water and feed on decaying matter and algae or prey on small aquatic animals. Some possess a long breathing tube on the caudal end. Some live in mud, in fruit, in dung or rotting wood.

Fig. 547 **Geosargus viridas** Say.

17b. Head retractile; body cylindrical, surface not shagreened, usually longitudinally striated; abdomen with a girdle of pseudopods on each segment; spiracular fissure vertical; pupae free.
Fig. 548. . . . . .Family TABANIDAE

Around 2,500 species of the horse flies have been described. The larvae are spindle-shaped, living in water or damp places. The flies are blood-sucking insects and biting on warm-blooded animals including man. Some of them are disease carriers.

Fig. 548. **Tabanus atratus** Fab.

19a. Projecting portion of head and flattened apical plate of terminal abdominal segment heavily sclerotized, the former cone-shaped, entirely closed except at extreme apex, not retractile; the latter obliquely truncate and with projecting processes.
Fig. 549. ....Family XYLOPHAGIDAE

The larvae are found in the soil or under the bark of rotten trees. They feed upon the larvae of other insects.

The members of this small family are related to the better known soldier flies and to the horseflies.

Fig. 549 Xylo-
phagus lugens
Loew.

19b. Projecting portion of head more or less retractile, not cone-shaped, the movable portion not enclosed; apical abdominal segment without a heavily sclerotized flattened terminal plate. 20

20a. Apical abdominal segment ending in 2 long processes which are fringed with long soft hairs; abdomen with paired pseudopods and fleshy dorsal and lateral appendages.
Fig. 550. ....Family RHAGIONIDAE

Fig 550 Atherix sp.

Some larvae live in fresh water with flattened body while others live in dung, wood or fungi with cylindrical body. They are predacious and feed on small animals. Some *Vermileo* can make ant-trapping pits in dust or sand similar to those of the ant-lions. The adults are known as snipe flies.

20b. Apical abdominal segment not as above; paired abdominal pseudopods usually absent; other appendages always absent...21

21a. Apical abdominal segment ending in 4 short pointed processes or 2 fleshy lips; internal portion of head with a large, arched, sclerotized upper plate, the longitudinal rods and other cephalic parts on a horizontal plane. ....Family RHAGIONIDAE

21b. Apical abdominal segment not as above, or the internal portion of head without arched upper plate, and the longitudinal cephalic rods and other cephalic parts meet at right angles. 22

22a. Apical abdominal segment without projecting processes, spiracles very small; parasites of spiders.
Fig. 551. ....Family CYRTIDAE

Around 200 species of the humpbacked flies are known. The first instar larvae are caraboid in form with distinct segments and two long anal bristles. They feed on spider eggs and spiders. They change to eruciform larva which is not so active as the first instar.

Fig. 551 **Ptero-dontia flavipes** Grag 1st instar.

22b. Apical abdominal segment frequently with projecting processes, spiracles large; species live in water, mud, earth, or decaying vegetable matter.
Fig. 552. ....Family EMPIDAE and family DOLICHOPIDAE

Empidae: About 1,600 species of the dance flies are known. The larvae live in water or in decaying vegetation, dead wood, soil and mosses where they feed upon small animals.

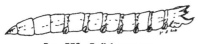

Fig. 552. **Dolichopus sp.**

Dolichopidae: About 2,000 species of the long-legged flies have been described. The larvae are mostly aquatic and feed on other insects. Some are found in plant stems or under tree bark.

23a. Posterior spiracles situated upon the antepenultimate segment; abdominal segments 1-6 subdivided, the body apparently consisting of 20 segments exclusive of the head. 24

23b. Posterior spiracles situated upon penultimate segment; abdominal segments simple, the body apparently consisting of 11 or 12 segments exclusive of the head. 25

24a. Posterior dorsal internal extension of head spatulate at apex; ventral posterior projections in the form of 2 short sclerotized rods. Fig. 553. ....Family THEREVIDAE

About 300 species have been described. The larvae frequent sandy soil, fungi and decaying wood. They feed upon earthworms and other soft-bodied insects or decaying organic matter. The adults are known as stilleto flies.

Fig. 553. **Psilocephala haemorrhoidalis** Macquart.

24b. Posterior dorsal extension of head not spatulate at apex; ventral posterior projections absent. Fig. 554. ....Family SCENOPINIDAE

Fig 554 Ventral aspect of head of **Scenopinus fenestralis** L.

About 50 species have been described. The larvae are sometimes found in houses under carpets or in furniture and also in decaying wood. Their food habits are thought to be predacious. One species is thought to destroy the larvae of carpet beetles.

25a. Penultimate abdominal segment longer than ultimate, with a deep transverse depression near its apex giving it the appearance of 2 distinct segments; ultimate segment terminating in a sharp ridge with a median sharp point, on either side of which dorsally and ventrally are situated 4 very closely approximated hairs. Fig. 555. ....Family MYDAIDAE

Around 100 species have been described. Both adults and larvae are predacious. The larvae are found in decaying wood. The adults are known as mydas flies and are often conspicuously marked.

Fig. 555. **Mydas clavatus** Drury.

25b. Penultimate abdominal segment shorter than ultimate, or if longer, then without a deep transverse depression; apical segment
not as above, the hairs not closely approximated. 26

26a. Thoracic segments each with 2 long hairs, one on each side on
ventro-lateral margin; apical segment with 6 or 8 long hairs;
head well developed, forwardly protruded, and more or less cone-
shaped when viewed from above, appearing flattened when viewed from side; penultimate segment usually shorter than ultimate
or not much longer; body straight in life.
Fig. 556. ....Family ASILIDAE

Around 4,000 species of the
robber flies have been described. The larvae inhabit soil
with decaying organic matter
where they prey upon other
insect larvae.

Fig. 556 **Promachus vertebratus** Say.

26b. Thoracic segments without hairs, if present, they are very weak;
apical segment without distinguishable hairs; head not much
protruded, directed downward, not cone-shaped, with a dorsal protuberance when viewed from side; penultimate segment distinctly
longer than ultimate; body usually curved in a half circle in life.
Fig. 557. ....Family BOMBYLIIDAE

About 1,800 species of bee
flies are known. The first instar larvae are slender and
legless with hairs on thorax
and anal region which disap-
pear in the latter instars. They
are predacious or parasitic on
the larvae of bees and wasps,
pupae of tsetse flies, caterpillars and also on the eggs of
beetles and grasshoppers. Some
Hemipenthes have been reared
f r o m ichneumonid cocoons.
That would suggest that they
are hyperparasitic.

Fig. 557. **Sparnopolius fulvus** Wied.

Key to the PUPAE of the more important families of DIPTERA

(After John R. Malloch, 1917)

1a. Pupa not enclosed within the larval skin, if so, the head is distinct
as in the larva, or the puparium is slightly flattened dorso-ventral-
ly, its texture leathery, not sclerotized, and the anterior respiratory
organs not distinguishable; adult or pupa emerges through a rectangular split on dorsum of larval skin.
Suborder ORTHORRHAPHA 2

1b. Pupa enclosed with the larval skin; head always retracted, the sclerotized portion occupying a position on the inner side of the ventral surface of the puparium; anterior respiratory organs distinct, either protruded from the antero-lateral angles of the cephalic extremity or from dorsum of base of abdomen; adult usually emerges by forcing off the rounded anterior extremity of the puparium in cap-like form, or the dorsal half of the thoracic portion — the lines of cleavage being along the lateral margins to a point at base of abdomen; rarely emergence is through a rectangular splitting of the dorsum of the puparium.
Fig. 558. ....Suborder CYCLORRHAPHA°

Fig 558 a, **Toxomerus politus** Say, b, **Phytophaga destructor** (Say) (USDA), c, Sheep bot fly, **Oestrus ovis** L (Ohio Exp Sta); d, **Rhagoletis pomonella** (Walsh), e, **Leucopis griseola** Fall (USDA)

2a. Antennae much elongated, distinctly visible beneath the pupal skin, normally curving well over upper margin of eyes and extending to or beyond base of wing, in some cases almost to apex of wing; head without strong thorns (except in some Cecidomyiidae and a few Tipulidae); thoracic respiratory organs much elongated or sessile; abdomen sometimes unarmed in the species with short antennae. ....Series NEMATOCERA......3

2b. Antennae shorter, projecting downward and outward, not curving over the eyes or reaching nearly to base of wing; head usually with strong thorns or horns; thoracic respiratory organs sessile, rarely stalk-like; abdomen usually armed with strong spines or bristles, or if unarmed there are only 4 or 5 distinct pairs of abdominal spiracles. ....Series BRACHYCERA......21

3a. Head with several strong thorns in a vertical series on the median line; pupae living in galls, sometimes in the hardened larval skin and resembling a flaxseed. Fig. 559. .....Family CECIDOMYIDAE

Fig. 559. **Monardia** sp.

Pupation takes place in different ways: some pupae are naked, some are borne in puparia and a few in silken cocoons.

*Key to families is not available.

3b. Head without strong thorns, or if at base of each antenna with a protuberance, thus not sharp; pupae not living in galls, but usually free and not enclosed in larval skin, if enclosed the larval moult does not resemble a muscoid puparium. 4

4a. Thoracic respiratory organs sessil; abdomen without strong thorns or leaf like elevations; legs straight. 5

4b. Thoracic respiratory organs stalked, or if sessile the abdomen with strong thorns or leaf-like elevations, or the legs are recurved against base of abdomen and apex of thorax, or the coxae do not conceal the sternopleura and the scape of the antennae is almost globose; legs straight or recurved. 8

5a. Legs short, apices of hind tarsi projecting slightly beyond apices of wings; antennae short, curved across middle of eye. Fig. 560. ....Family BIBIONIDAE

Pupation takes place in an earthen cell in the ground.

This family, numbering some 500 species, contains a few members which are sometimes exceedingly numerous. The species pictured is our most common one. All of the members of the family seem to be vegetable feeders.

Fig. 560 **Bibio albipennis** Say.

5b. Legs elongate, usually all tarsi projecting for a considerable distance beyond apices of wings; antennae elongate, extending to or beyond base of wings. 6

6a. Thorax conspicuously swollen, almost globose, its anterior profile declivous; sternopleura concealed.
Fig. 561. ....Family MYCETOPHILIDAE

Pupation takes place mostly in delicate cocoons and a few are suspended by some loose silk from the surface of fungi or other objects.

Fig. 561. Leia oblectabilis Loew.

6b. Thorax not conspicuously swollen, the anterior profile not sloping downward. 7

7a. Scape of antennae much swollen, globose; abdominal spiracles small or absent; sternopleura enlarged, not concealed by fore coxae and femora. Fig. 562. ....Family CHIRONOMIDAE

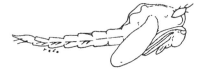

Some pupae are active and float at water surface, but some remain in the larval tube. The respiratory organs either consist of a pair of branched filaments or of a simple tube.

Fig. 562 Tanypus illinoensis Mall.

7b. Scape of antennae not much swollen; abdominal spiracles distinct; sternopleura not visible, concealed by large coxae and femora of the fore legs. ....Family CECIDOMYIDAE

8a. Thoracic respiratory organs slender, long and tube-like; legs straight, extending well beyond apices of wings; body without armature except a pair of hairs on anterior margin of head; sternopleura concealed. ....Family CECIDOMYIDAE

8b. Species not in such combination of characters; abdomen usually with hairs or spines, or sternopleura exposed. 9

9a. Pupa in a pocket-shaped or slipper-shaped cocoon consisting of coarse threads, thoracic respiratory organ projecting from the wide open end. Fig. 563. ....Family SIMULIIDAE

Fig 563 **Simulium venustum** Say, pupa and cocoon.

Pupation takes place in the pocket-like cocoon which is made by the larva. The respiratory organs are tube-like filaments which protrude from the cocoon.

9b. Pupa free, or if enclosed or partly so the cocoon is not pocket-like and respiratory organs do not consist of tube-like filaments..10

10a. Pupa when seen from above oval in outline; the abdominal base not conspicuously narrower than thorax, so that the lateral outline is continuous; dorsal surface with strong integument. 11

10b. Pupa with abdomen well differenciated from thorax; the dorsum membranous, or if strong and almost sclerotized, then surface with well developed spines. 12

11a. Thoracic respiratory organs lamelliform, consisting of 4 flat plates, the broad sides of which are contiguous.
Fig. 564. ....Family BLEPHAROCERATIDAE

Fig. 564. **Bibiocephala sp.**

Pupation takes place in the place occupied by the larvae often results in large numbers of individuals being produced.

11b. Thoracic respiratory organs simple, tube-like.
Fig. 565. ....Family PSYCHODIDAE

Pupation takes place in the same habitat as that of the larvae. The pupa usually carries the larval exuviae at its caudal end.

Fig 565. **Psychoda superba** Banks

12a. Apical abdominal segment terminating in 2 or 4 paddle-like or fin-shaped organs which are fringed on all or part of outer surface by strap-like hairs; or if the apical segment terminates in 2 long subconical processes, the tarsi are recurved against the ventral surface of the base of the abdomen and apex of thorax so that they do not extend beyond apices of wings. 13

12b. Apical abdominal segment obtuse, armed with short or elongate spines or thorns; or if ending in a pair of long, slender processes they are more or less oval in cross section and without strap-like hairs; tarsi generally entirely straight, rarely the apices of the hind pair incurved slightly, but never recurved as above. 18

13a. Thoracic respiratory organs terminating in numerous thread-like filaments. .... Family CHIRONOMIDAE

13b. Thoracic respiratory organs consisting of a single stem, in some cases with a few long, or many short, scale-like, surface hairs, but never terminating in numerous thread-like filaments; occasionally the thoracic respiratory organs not elevated. 14

14a. Thoracic respiratory organs not elevated; sternopleura exposed. .... Family CHIRONOMIDAE

14b. Thoracic respiratory organs conspicuously elevated. 15

15a. Thoracic respiratory organs situated close to anterior margin of thorax; no stellate hairs on thorax and abdomen. .... Family CHIRONOMIDAE

15b. Thoracic respiratory organs situated close to middle of thoracic dorsum. 16

16a. Apical abdominal segment ending in 2 or 4 broad, flat, paddle-like plates. Fig. 566. .... Family CULICIDAE

The pupae are very active and float at water surface to breath air by a pair of trumpet-like respiratory organs on the thorax. This permits their destruction by oil or poisons placed on the surface of the water.

Fig. 566. **Culex** sp.

16b. Apical abdominal segment ending in 2 long subconical processes. 17

17a. Apical processes armed with short hairs at apices and on middle of outer margin. ....Family CULICIDAE

17b. Apical processes unarmed. Fig. 567. ....Family DIXIDAE

The pupae closely resemble the pupae of Culicidae both in habit and in appearance.

Fig. 567. **Dixa sp.**

18a. Apices of legs not extending beyond apices of wings. 19

18b. Apices of legs extending beyond apices of wings. 20

19a. Apical segment of abdomen ending in 2 conical processes. Fig. 568. ....Family CERATOPOGONIDAE

The information of pupae of this family is **very** limited.

Fıg 568 **Pal-pomyia sp**

19b. Apical segment of abdomen ending in 2 upper and 2 lower short thorns. ....Family PSYCHODIDAE

205

20a. Thoracic respiratory organs long, bifid; apical abdominal segment rounded, without processes; abdominal spiracles pedunculate. Fig. 569. ....Family SCATOPSIDAE

The biology of the pupae of this family is not known.

Fig 569 **Rhegmoclema atrata** Say.

20b. Thoracic respiratory organs simple; apical abdominal segment not rounded, generally armed with protuberances. Fig. 570. ....Family TIPULIDAE

Pupation takes place at the similar situation as the larval.

Fig 570 **Pachyrrhina ferruginea** Fab.

21a. Pupa enclosed within larval skin. Fig. 571. ....Family STRATIOMYIIDAE

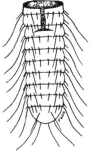

Pupation takes place in soil or under debris near the place where the larvae live.

The family numbers more than 1,000 species. The eggs are variously placed in mud, water or waste materials.

Fig 571 **Neopachygaster maculicornis** Hine

21b. Pupa free. 22

22a. Prothorax with a long aperture mesad of and connected with the spiracle. Fig. 572. ....Family TABANIDAE

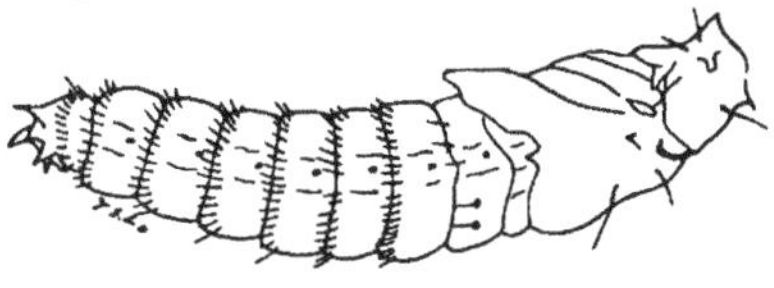

The pupae are cylindrical and elongate with thoracic spiracles connected subcutaneously with a large cavity on the prothorax.

Fig. 572. **Tabanus lasiophthalmus** Macq.

22b. Not as 22a. **23**

23a. Head without strong forwardly directed thorns, at most with 1 thorn on base of antenna which is directed to the side; abdominal armature weak, becoming gradually stronger towards apex of basal abdominal segment; apices of hind tarsi at most extending slightly beyond apices of wings; abdomen with 7 pairs of spiracles. **24**

23b. Head usually with strong thorns, or if absent, the abdominal armature is stronger on basal of 2nd segment than it is on apical, or there are less than 7 pairs of abdominal spiracles; apices of hind tarsi usually distinctly beyond apices of wings. **26**

24a. Antennal sheaths much thickened at base, apical portion slender, styliform, the whole directed almost straight downward. Fig. 573. ....Family RHAGIONIDAE

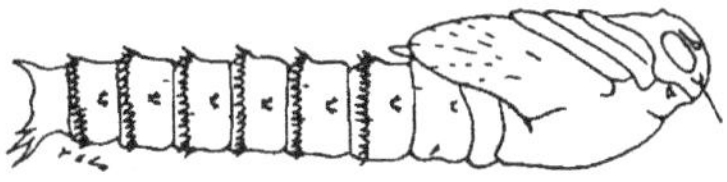

The information concerning the biology of the pupae of this family is quite limited.

Fig 573 **Chrysopilus ornatus** Say.

24b. Antennal sheaths thickened throughout their length, the apical portion generally more or less distinctly annulated, the whole directed either straight sideways or in a slightly downward direction. **25**

25a. Antennal sheaths showing much more than 10 annulations. ....Subfamily Rhachicerinae, RHAGIONIDAE

25b. Antennal sheaths showing not more than 10 annulations. Fig. 574. ....Family XYLOPHAGIDAE

Information about the pupae is very limited.

Fig 574 **Xylophagus lugens** Loew

26a. Head without strong thorns; abdomen with 3 to 4 distinct pairs
of spiracles and without spinose armature.
Fig. 575. ....Family CYRTIDAE

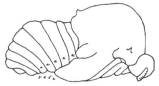

Pupation takes place in web, or burrow, or under some other objects near
the place where the host died.

Fig 575. **Ogcodes costatus**
Loew

26b. Head usually with strong thorns, at least with elevated ridge-
like antennal sheath and several small carinated elevations; abdomen with 7 pairs of spiracles and spinose armature. 27

27a. Head with 2 thorns. 28

27b. Head with more than 2 thorns or with several short tubercles...29

28a. Abdomen with a single transverse series of spines on each dorsal
segment; wing with a long thorn at base.
Fig. 576. ....Family THEREVIDAE

The pupae are free and the pupation takes place
in the soil.

The adults of this small family are known as stilleto flies. The larvae are apparently predacious.

Fig. 576 **Psilo-
cephala haem-
orrhoidalis** Mac-
quart

28b. Abdomen with 2 transverse series of spines on each dorsal segment; wings without thorns at base. .....Family SCENOPINIDAE
Little is known about the biology of the pupae.

29a. Upper pair of cephalic thorns directed sideways and slightly upward; apices of wings extending to or very slight beyond apex of 1st abdominal segment; apices of middle tarsi not extending to apices of wings. Fig. 577. ....Family MYDAIDAE

The available information about the biology of the pupae is very limited.

Fig. 577. **Mydas clavatus** Drury

29b. Upper pairs of cephalic thorns directed forward, at most slightly divergent apically, generally slightly curved downward, or head without strong upper thorn. 30

30a. Head with strong thorns, if absent the abdomen with dorsal transverse armature consisting of very strong thorns and intervening long slender hairs; apices of antennae obtuse. 31

30b. Head very rarely with thorns, 2 carinate elevations present on upper anterior margin; antennae with attenuated apices; body without thorns, sometimes with bristles. 32

31a. Lower median portion of face with a closely approximated pair of stout thorns which are occasionally fused almost to apices; abdomen with transverse armature on dorsal segments consisting of short flattened thorns and long slender hairs, the thorns usually appearing as if attached to, rather than forming part of the abdomen and sometimes turned up at bases and apices. Fig. 578. ....Family BOMBYLIIDAE

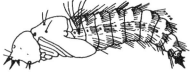

When the parasite is fully grown then it leaves the host and enters the soil for pupation.

Fig. 578. **Spogostylum albofasciatum** Macquart.

31b. Lower median portion of face without thorns; abdomen with transverse armature consisting of alternating long and short thorns. Fig. 579. ....Family ASILIDAE

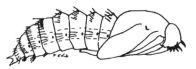

Pupation takes place in soil. However, the pupae have the habit of coming to the surface of soil shortly before the emergence of the adult.

Fig. 579. **Ceraturgus cruciatus** Say.

32a. Cephalic armature consisting of 2 carinated elevations on upper anterior margin, on each of which is a very long hair; antennal sheath raised above level of face, tapering apically, directed downward and slightly outward; proboscis often much elongated. Fig. 580. ....Family EMPIDAE

Pupation takes place in a cocoon which is densely coated with wood particles.

Fig. 580 *Drapetis nigra* Meigen.

32b. Similar to Empidae, but proboscis never elongated. Fig. 581. ....Family DOLICHOPIDAE

Pupation takes place in an earthen cell or in a cocoon made by wooden fragments and silk. The pupa possesses a pair of elongate thoracic respiratory horns which protruded outside of the pupal cell or cocoon.

Fig 581 *Aphrosylus praedator*

ORDER HYMENOPTERA

(From H. Yuasa, 1923)

1a. Body caterpillar-like, thoracic legs usually present; head much more strongly sclerotized than the rest of the body; prolegs usually developed, if absent the body is caterpillar-like; antennae almost always present and more than 1-segmented; mandibles heavily sclerotized almost always with more than 1 tooth; ocelli often present; larvae generally free living, or plant borers, a few are gall-makers (But the members of the family Orussidae is parasitic). ....Suborder CHALASTOGASTRA......2

1b. Body maggot-like, legless; head not strongly sclerotized; antennae soft, unsegmented; mandibles weak almost never more than an apical tooth; ocelli wanting; larvae parasitic, or parasitoidal, or living upon the food supplied by the adult, a few are gall-makers. Fig. 582. ....Suborder CLISTOGASTRA*

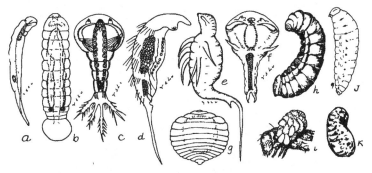

Fig 582. a-f, Some parasitic larvae with hypermetamorphosis, g, **Aphelinus mali** Hald (Aphelinidae, h, **Chelonus** sp (Braconidae); i, **Euplectrus plathypenae** How (Eulophidae), j, **Vespa maculata** Kirby (Vespidae), k ,**Monomorium minimum** Buckley (Formicidae).

2a. Thoracic legs present, either normal in form and distinctly segmented or modified; if modified, fleshy or conical, if conical, head and body depressed. 3

2b. Thoracic legs not distinctly segmented, mamma-like or wanting; if mamma-like, head and body never distinctly depressed. 17

3a. Thoracic legs normal in form, not seta-like, rarely nipple-shaped; prolegs usually present; subanal appendages wanting; antennae usually with less than 7 segments. 4

3b. Thoracic legs seta-like; prolegs wanting; subanal appendages present, setaceous; antennae very long, 7-segmented. Fig. 583. ....Family PAMPHILIIDAE

Fig 583. **Pamphilium** sp.

Around 100 species have been described. The larvae roll leaves or spin webs usually live gregariously together. A few are serious orchard pests.

*Key to families is not available.

4a. 10 pairs of prolegs present on each abdominal segment; antennae 6- or 7-segmented. Fig. 584. ....Family XYELIDAE

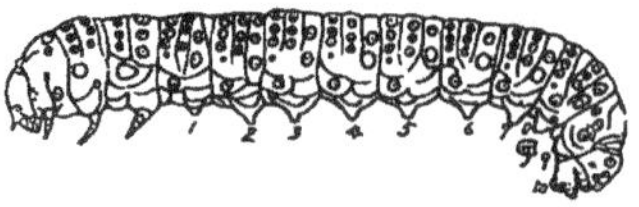

Fig. 584. Megaxyela major Cresson.

About 80 species of the xyelid sawflies have been described. The larvae are free feeders on elms, pines, hickory, butternut, etc. Pupation takes place in an earthen cell in the ground.

4b. 6 to 8 pairs of prolegs, sometimes reduced or absent; antennae never more than 5-segmented. 5

5a. Thoracic legs normal in form, 5-segmented; if modified, tarsal claws always present; prolegs usually developed. 6

5b. Thoracic legs fleshy, indistinctly 4-segmented; tarsal claws wanting. Fig. 585. ...Subfamily Phyllotominae, TENTHREDINIDAE

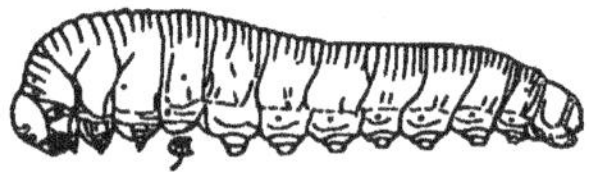

Fig. 585. Caliroa cerasi L.

6a. Prolegs present on abdominal segments 2-8 and 10; antennae elongate, conical, usually 5-segmented. 7

6b. Prolegs present on abdominal segments 2-7 and 10, rarely on segments 2-7 only or 2-6 and 10. 11

7a. Thoracic legs 5-segmented, normal in form. 8

7b. Thoracic legs 4-segmented, modified. Fig. 586. ....Family TENTREDINIDAE

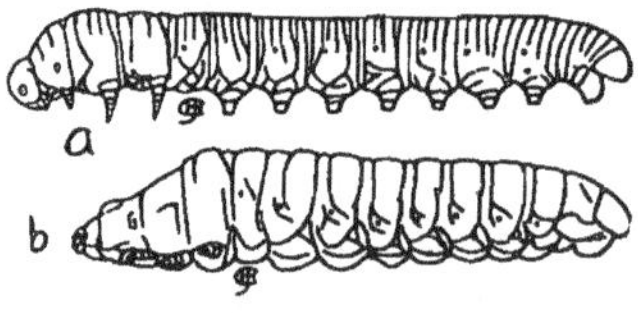

Fig 586. a, Emphytus sp. (Emphytinae); b, Phlebatrophia mathesoni MacGillivray.

About 5,000 species of sawflies have been described. The habits of the larvae are various: leaf feeders, leaf miners, gall makers and some spin webs. Pupation usually takes place in a parchment-like cocoon on or in the ground. Many species are seriously destructive.

8a. 3rd abdominal segment with 6 annulets on dorsum. (See Fig. 587). 9

8b. 3rd abdominal segment with more or less than 6 annulets on dorsum. 10

212

9a. Antennae conical, 5-segmented.
Fig. 587. . . . . .Family TENTREDINIDAE

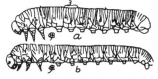

Fig. 587. a, **Tomosthethus bardus** Say (Blennocampinae); b, **Dolerus similis** Norton (Dolerinae).

This includes three subfamilies: Dolerinae, Emphytinae and Blennocampidae. The oaks, members of the rose family and grasses and sedges are frequent food plants.

9b. Antennae not conical, 3-segmented, erect and peg-like.
Fig. 588. . . . . .Family DIPRIONIDAE

Fig 588. **Neodiprion lecontei** Fitch.

About 70 species have been described. The larvae feed on the leaves of pine, spruce, cedar, etc. The body is usually yellowish or greenish with grayish or brownish stripes of with rows of black spots.

10a. Antennae conical, 5-segmented; labrum without secondary longitudinal sutures. Fig. 589. . . . . .Family TENTHREDINIDAE

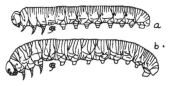

Fig 589 a, **Strongylogaster annulosus** Norton (Selandriinae); b, **Tenthredo** sp. (Tenthredininae).

Here is included 3 subfamilies: Selandriinae, Emphytinae and Tenthredininae. Many broad-leafed trees and shrubs and ferns are attacked by members of these groups.

10b. Antennae not conical, 1-segmented; labrum with secondary longitudinal sutures. Fig. 590. . . . . .Family CIMBICIDAE

Fig. 590. **Abia inflata Norton.**

About 50 species have been described. The larvae are caterpillar-like, body usually curled spirally and covered with a waxy bloom. They feed on the leaves of different kinds of deciduous trees and shrubs. Pupation takes place in a parchment-like cocoon in an earthen cell under ground.

11a. Thoracic legs 5-segmented, normal in form; prolegs on abdominal segment 2-7, either with or without anal prolegs. 12

213

11b. Thoracic legs 6-segmented, or phothoracic legs 4-segmented and others 3-segmented; prolegs on abdominal segments 2-7 and 10, or 2-6 and 10, very small. Fig. 591. ....Family ARGIDAE

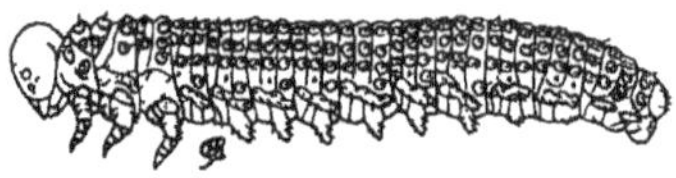

Fig. 591. Hylotoma sp.

About 200 species have been known. Larvae feed on broad-leaved deciduous trees and shrubs. The members of this family are widely scattered.

12a. Prolegs present on the last abdominal segment, either normal or fused on the meson, forming a single prominence. 13

12b. Prolegs absent on the last abdominal segment. Fig. 592. ....Family TENTHREDINIDAE

Fig. 592. Kaliofenusa ulmi Sun devall (Fenusinae).

The subfamilies Fenusinae and Hoplocampinae are included here. A number of leaf miners are included in the species which fall here.

13a. Anal prolegs normal and separated. 14

13b. Anal prolegs united on the meson forming a single protuberance. Fig. 593. ....Family TENTHREDINIDAE

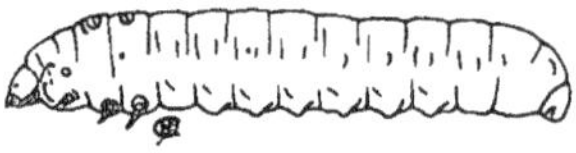

Fig 593. Metallus rubi Forbes.

The subfamily Solioneurinae belongs here. They are leaf miners on members of the rose family.

14a. Antennae 5-segmented; 3rd abdominal segment with 6 annulets; 10th abdominal tergum with several caudal protuberances. Fig. 594. ....Subfamily Hoplocampidae, TENTHREDINIDAE

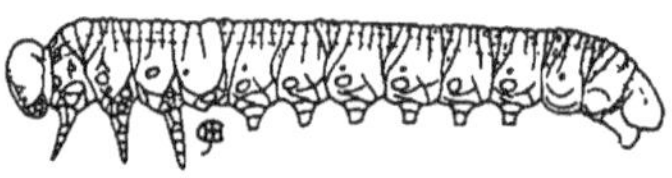

Fig. 594. Henichroa dyari Rohwer.

The larvae feed on the leaves of pear and other Rosaceae.

14b. Antennae 4-, rarely 3-segmented; 3rd abdominal segment usually with less than 6 annulets; 10th abdominal tergum with or without caudal tuberances. 15

214

15a. An eversible gland on ventro-meson of each abdominal segment 1-7; body often with numerous conspicuous setae, setae arising from distinct tubercles; antennae 4-segmented. Fig. 595. .... Subfamily Nematinae, TENTHREDINIDAE

Fig. 595. **Pteronidae ribesi** Scopoli

Some members of this rather large subfamily are gall makers, while others are known to feed on the foliage of broad-leaved trees and shrubs and on grasses and sedges.

15b. Without eversible glands; body never conspicuously setiferous; antennae 3- or 4-segmented. 16

16a. Antennae 4-segmented; 3rd abdominal segment with 5 annulets; abdominal segments 2-4 and 8, or 2-5 and 8 without a postsubspiracular sucker-like protuberance. Fig. 596. .... Family TENTHREDINIDAE

Fig 596 **Cladius pectinicornis** Fourcray (Cladinae).

The subfamilies Hoplocampinae and Cladinae are both included here. Members of the rose family furnish food for some of these species.

16b. Antennae 1-segmented; 3rd abdominal segment with 3 annulets; abdominal segments 2-4 and 8, or 2-5 and 8 with a postsubspiracular sucker-like protuberance. Fig. 597. .... Family ACORDULECERIDAE

Fig. 597. **Acordulecera** sp.

Around 100 species have been described. The larvae are free feeders and gregarious on plant leaves.

17a. Thoracic legs present; last abdominal segment with suranal process. (See Fig. 599). 18

17b. Thoracic legs wanting; last abdominal segment without suranal process. Fig. 598. .... Family ORUSSIDAE

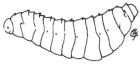

Fig. 598. **Oryssus occidentalis** Cresson.

About 50 species of the parasitic wasps are known. The larvae are parasitic on the larvae of cerambycid and buprestid beetles. The pupae have a long ovipositor which is held over the back.

18a. Subanal appendages present, vestigial and palpiform; ocelli present; antennae 4- or 5-segmented. Fig. 599. ...Family CEPHIDAE

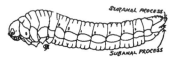

Fig. 599. **Janus integer** Norton.

Around 100 species of the stem sawflies are known. The body of the larvae is C-shaped with a small terminal abdominal appendage. They bore into the stems of grasses, trees and shrubs. Pupation takes place in the larval burrow within a thin cocoon.

18b Subanal appendages wanting; ocelli wanting. 19

19a. Antennae 3-segmented; meta-spiracles functionless, very much smaller than abdominal spiracles. Fig. 600. ....Family XIPHYDRIIDAE

Fig 600. **Xiphydria** sp.

Less than 50 species are known. The larvae are borers in trees. Birches and maples are known to be attacked in our country.

19b. Antennae 1-segmented; meta-spiracles functional, as large as abdominal spiracles. Fig. 601. ....Family SIRICIDAE

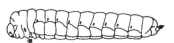

Fig. 601. **Tremex columba** L

Around 50 species of the horntails are known. The larvae are S-shaped and deeply segmented with a horny abdominal process. They bore in the stems of pines and other broad-leaved deciduous trees that are usually not perfectly healthy. Pupation occurs in thin parchment-like cocoon within the burrows of the larvae.

SOME IMPORTANT REFERENCES

GENERAL

Balduf, W. V. 1935. The bionomics of entomophagous insects. 220 pp. John S. Swift Co., St. Louis.

Clausen, Curtis P. 1940. Entomophagous insects. pp. x+668. McGraw-Hill, N. Y.

Felt, E. P. 1917. Key to American insect galls. Bull. N. Y. St. Mus. 200:1-310.

Frost, S. W. 1942. General entomology. pp. x+524. McGraw-Hill, N. Y.

Hayes, Wm. P. 1932. The present status of the classification of immature insects. Tran. Ill. Acad. Sci. 24: 181-202.

Imms, A. D. 1930. A general textbook of entomology. ed. 2. viii+703 pp. Dutton, N. Y.

Karny, H. H. 1934. Biologie der Wasserinsekten. pp. 1-311. Wagner, Wien.

Muesebeck, C. F. W. 1946. Common names of insects approved by the American Association of Economic Entomologists. Jour. Econ. Ent. 39(4):427-448.

Needham, J. G., S. W. Frost, and B. H. Tothill. 1928. Leaf-mining insects. pp. viii+351. Williams & Wilkins, Baltimore.

Needham, J. G. and P. R. Needham. 1941. Guide to the study of fresh-water biology. 88 pp. Comstock Pub. Co., Ithaca, N. Y.

Peterson, Alvah. 1939. Keys to the orders of immature stages of North American insects. Ann. Ent. Soc. Amer. 32(2):267-278.
1949 Larvae of Insects, Part I. 84 plates, 315 pp. Pub. by the author; distributed by Ward's Natl. Sc. Est., Rochester, N. Y.

Torre-Bueno, De La J. R. 1937. A glossary of entomology. pp. ix+336. Brooklyn Ent. Soc., Brooklyn, N. Y.

Order PROTURA

Ewing, H. E. 1940. The Protura of North America. Ann. Ent. Soc. Amer. 33:495-551.

Womersley, H. 1927. A study of the larval forms of certain species of Protura. Ent. Mthly. Mag. 13:140-154.

Order THYSANURA

MacGillivray, A. D. 1893. North American Thysanura. Cand. Ent. 25:173-174, 218-220.

Order COLLEMBOLA

Bacon, G. A. 1912-14. California Collembola. Jour. Ent. Zool. 4:841-845; 5:43-46, 202-204; 6:45-47, 84, 85, 137-179.

Mills, H. B. 1934. A monograph of the Collembola of Iowa. Ia. St. College, Mon. 3:1-143.

Order PLECOPTERA

Claassen, P. W. 1931. Plecoptera nymphs of America (North of Mexico). pp. 1-195. Thomas Say Foundation, Thomas, Springfield, Ill.

Frison, T. H. 1929. Fall and winter stone-flies or Plecoptera of Illinois. Bull. Ill. Nat. Hist. Surv. 18:345-409.

1942. Studies of North American Plecoptera, with special reference to the fauna of Illinois. Bull. Ill. Nat. Hist. Surv. 22(2):235-355.

Order EPHEMEROPTERA

Morgan, Anna H. 1913. A contribution to the biology of Mayflies. Ann. Ent. Soc. Amer. 6:371-426.

Needham, J. G., J. R. Traver, and Yin-Chi Hsu. 1935. The biology of Mayflies. pp. xiv+759. Comstock Pub. Co., Ithaca, N. Y.

Smith, Osgood R. 1935. The eggs and egg-laying habits of North American Mayflies (With a key to the eggs of N. American Mayfles). In Needham, J. G. et al. Ibid. pp. 67-89.

Order ODONATA

Howe, Jr. R. H. 1918. Pictorial key to Zygoptera nymphs. Psche 25:106-110.

1922 and 1925. Pictorial key to Anisopteran nymphs. Psyche 29, Supplement Oct.-Dec.; 32, Supplement Dec.

Hayes, Wm. P. 1941. A bibliography of keys for the identification of immature insects. Pt. II. Odonata. Ent. News 52(3-4): 52-55, 66-69, 93-98.

Kennedy, C. H. 1915. Notes on the life history and ecology of the dragonflies of Washington and Oregon. Proc. U. S. Nat. Mus. 49: 259-345.

1917. Notes on the life history and ecology of the dragonflies of Central California and Nevada. Proc. U. S. Nat. Mus. 52:483-635.

Needham, J. G. 1903. The life histories of Odonata, suborder Zygoptera. In Aquatic insects of New York State. pt. 3 N. Y. St. Mus. 68(18): 199-517.

Needham, J. G. and C. A. Hart. 1901. The dragonflies of Illinois with descriptions of the immature stages. pt. I. Petaluridae, Aeschnidae and Gomphidae. Bull. Ill. St. Nat. Hist. Lab. 6(1):1-94.

Needham, J. G. and E. Fisher. 1936. The nymphs of N. American libelluline dragonflies. Trans. Amer. Ent. Soc. 62:107-116.

Wright, Mike and Alvah Peterson. 1944. A key to the genera of anisopterous dragonfly nymphs of the United States and Canada. Ohio Jour. Sci. 44(4):151-166.

Order ORTHOPTERA

Blatchley, W. S. 1920. Orthoptera of Northeastern America. 784 pp. Nature Pub. Co., Indianapolis.

Tuck, J. B. and R. C. Smith. 1939. Identification of the eggs of Mid-western grasshoppers by the chorionic sculpturing. Kans. Exp. Sta. Tech. Bull. 48:1-39.

Order COLEOPTERA

Anderson, William H. 1939. A key to the larval Bostrichidae in the United States National Museum. Jour. Wash. Acad. Sci. 29(9):382-391.

Boving, A. G. and A. B. Champlain. 1920. Larvae of North American beetles of the family Cleridae. Proc. U. S. Nat. Mus. 57:575-649.

Boving, A. G. 1925. Beetle larvae of the subfamily Galerucinae. Proc. U. S. Nat. Mus. 75(2):1-48.

Boving, A. G. and F. C. Craighead. 1932. Illustrated synopsis of the principal larval forms of the order Coleoptera. Ent. Amer. 11:1-352.

Boving, A. G. 1942. Descriptions of the larvae of some West Indian melolonthine beetles and a key to the known larvae of the tribe. Proc. U. S. Nat. Mus. 92:167-175.

Chu, H. F. 1945. The larvae of Harpalinae, Unisetosae (Carabidae). Ent. Amer. 25(1):1-70.

Cotton, R. T. 1924. A contribution toward a classification of the weevil larvae of the subfamily Calendrinae in North America. Proc. U. S. Nat. Mus. 66:1-11.

Craighead, F. C. 1915. Contribution toward a classification and biology of the North American Cerambycidae. Larvae of the Prioninae. U. S. Dept. Agr. Rept. 107:1-24.
1923. North American Cerambycid larvae. Dom. Cand. Dept. Agr. Tech. Bull. 27. new ser. Ent. Bull. 23:1-151.

Gage, J. H. 1920. The larvae of the Coccinellidae. Ill. Biol. Mon. 6:1-62.

Hamilton, C. C. 1925. Studies on the morphology, taxonomy, and ecology of the larvae of holarctic tiger beetles (Cicindellidae). Proc. U. S. Nat. Mus. 65:1-87.

Hayes, Wm. P. 1929. Morphology, taxonomy, and biology of larval Scarabaeoidea. Ill. Biol. Mon. 12(2):1-119.

Hayes, Wm. P. and H. F. Chu. 1946. The larvae of the genus Nosodendron Latr. (Nosodendridae). Ann. Ent. Soc. Amer. 39(1):69-79.

Glen, Robert, Kenneth M. King, and A. P. Arnason. 1943. The identification of wireworms of economic importance in Canada. Cand. Jour. Res. 21:358-387.

Glen, Robert. 1944. Contribution to the knowledge of the larval Elateridae. no. 3. Agriotes Esch. and Dalopius Esch. Cand. Ent. 76:73-87.

McGillivray, A. D. 1903. Aquatic Chrysomelidae and table of families of coleopterous larvae. Bull. N. Y. St. Mus. 68:288-327.

Murayama, Jozo. 1931. A contribution to the morphological and taxonomic study of larvae of certain May-beetles which occur in the nurseries of the Peninsula of Korea. Bull. Forest-Expt. Sta. Chosen No. XI, pp. 1 - 108.

Fracker, S. B. 1915. The classification of lepidopterous larvae. Ill. Biol. Mon. 2 (1) : 1 - 169.

Rees, Bryant E. 1943. Classification of the Dermestidae based on larval characters, with a key to the North American genera. U. S. Dept. Agr. Misc. Pub. 511:1-18.

Richter, P. O. 1940. Kentucky white grubs. Bull. Kentucky Agr. Exp. Sta. 401:71-157.

1944. Dynastinae of North America with descriptions of the larvae and keys to genera and species. ibid. 467:1-56.

1945. Rutelinae of Eastern North America with descriptions of the larvae of Strigodermella pygmaea (Fab.) and three species of the tribe Rutelini. ibid. 471:1-19.

Sailsbury, Murl Beauford. 1943. The comparative morphology and taxonomy of some larval Criocerinae (Chrysomelidae). Bull. Brooklyn Ent. Soc. 38(3):59-74.

Satterthwait, A. F. 1931. Key to known pupae of the genus Calendra, with host-plant and distribution notes. Ann. Ent. Soc. Amer. 24(1): 143-172.

St. George, R. A. 1924. Studies on the larvae of North American beetles of the subfamily Tenebrioninae with a description of the larvae and pupae of Merinus laevis (Oliv.). Proc. U. S. Nat. Mus. 65:1-22.

Van Emden, F. I. 1938. On the taxonomy of Rhynchophora larvae. Trans. Roy. Ent. Soc. Lond. 87:1-37.

1939. Larvae of British beetles I. A key to the genera and most of the species of British Cerambycid larvae. Ent. Mthly. Mag. 75: 257-273; 76:7-13.

1941. Larvae of British beetles II. A key to the British Lamellicornia larvae. Ibid. 77:117-127; 181-192.

1942. Larvae of British beetles III. Keys to the families. Ibid. 78:206-272.

1943. Larvae of British beetles IV. Various small families. Ibid. 79:209-223; 259-270.

1942. A key to the genera of larval Carabidae. Trans. Roy. Ent. Soc. Lond. 92:1-99.

Order HEMIPTERA

Butler, E. A. 1923. A biology of the British Hemiptera-Heteroptera. 682 pp. H. F. & G. Witherby, London.

Esselbaugh, Charles O. 1946. A study of the eggs of the Pentatomidae. Ann. Ent. Soc. Amer. 39(4):667-691.

Funkhouser, W. D. 1917. Biology of the Membracidae of the Cayuga Lake Basin. Cornell Agr. Exp. Sta. Mem. 11:181-445.

Hart, C. A. 1919. The Pentatomidae of Illinois with keys to nearctic genera. Bull. Ill. Nat. Hist. Surv. 13(7):157-218.

Hungerford, H. B. 1919. The biology and ecology of aquatic and semi-aquatic Hemiptera. Kans. Univ. Sci. Bull. 11:3-328.

Karny, H. H. 1934. Biologie der Wasserinsekten. pp. xv+311. Wagner, Berlin.

Radio, P. A. 1926. Studies of the eggs of some Reduviidae. Kans. Univ. Sci. Bull. 16:157-179.

1927. Studies on the biology of the Reduviidae of America North of Mexico. Ibid. 28:1-291.

Order NEUROPTERA

Ross, H. H. and T. H. Frison. 1937. Studies of nearctic aquatic insects. I. Nearctic alderflies of the genus Sialis (Megaloptera, Sialidae). Bull. Ill. Nat. Hist. Surv. 21(3):57-100.

Smith, R. C. 1922. The biology of the Chrysopidae. Cornell Exp. Sta. Mem. 58:1287-1372.

1923. Life histories and stages of some hemerobiids and allied species. Ann. Ent. Soc. Amer. 16(2):129-148.

Order TRICHOPTERA

Elkins, Winston A. 1936. The immature stages of some Minnesota Trichoptera. Ann Ent. Soc. Amer. 29:65-81.

Lloyd, J. T. 1921. The biology of North American caddisfly larvae. Bull. Lloyd Lib. Bot. Pharm. & Materia Medica. Bull. 21, Ent. Bull. no. 1, pp. 1-24.

Milne, Margey J. 1939. Immature North American Trichoptera. Psyche 46:9-19.

Ross, H. H. 1944. The caddisflies, or Trichoptera, of Illinois. Bull. Ill. Nat. Hist. Surv. 23(1):1-326.

Order LEPIDOPTERA

Buckler, W. 1886-1901. The larvae of the British butterflies and moths. Vols. I-IX. Ray Society, London.

Cook, W. C. — Cutworms and armyworms. Minn. St. Ent. Cir. 52:1-8.

Dyar, H. G. 1893. On the larval cases of North American Psychidae. Ent. News. 4:320-321. .

1894. A classification of lepidopterous larvae. Ann. N. Y. Acad. Sci. 8:194-232.

1895. Additional notes on the classification of lepidopterous larvae. Trans. N. Y. Acad. Sci. 14:49-62.

1895. A classification of Lepidoptera on larval characters. Am. Nat. 29:1066-1072.

1905. A descriptive list of a collection of early stages of Japanese Lepidoptera. Proc. U. S. Nat. Mus. 28:937-956.

Forbes, W. T. M. 1911. Field key to sphingid caterpillars of the Eastern United States. Ann. Ent. Soc. Amer. 4:261-262.

1923. The Lepidoptera of New York and neighboring states. Cornell Agr. Exp. Sta. Mem. 68:1-729.

Jones, F. M. and H. B. Parks. 1928. The bagworms of Texas. Bull. Texas Agr. Exp. Sta. 382:1-36.

Mosher, Edna. 1914. The classification of the pupae of the Ceratocampidae and Hemileucidae. Ann. Ent. Soc. Amer. 7:277-300.

1916. The classification of the pupae of the Saturnidae. Ibid. 9(2):136-156.

1916. A classification of Lepidoptera based on characters of the pupa. Bull. Ill. St. Lab. Nat. Hist. 12:12-159.

1917. Pupae of some Maine species of Notodontoidea. Bull. Maine Agr. Exp. Sta. 259:29-84.

Order DIPTERA

Banks, N. 1912. The structure of certain dipterous larvae with particular reference to those in human foods. U. S. Dept. Agr. Bur. Ent. Tech. Ser. 22:1-44.

Felt, E. P. 1925. Key to gall midges. Bull. N. Y. St. Mus. 257:1-239.

Frost, S. W. 1923. A study of the leaf-mining Diptera of North America. Cornell Agr. Exp. Sta. Mem. 78:1-228.

Greene, C. T. 1922. Illustrated synopsis of the puparia of one hundred muscoid flies. Proc. U. S. Nat. Mus. 60(10):1-39.

1925. The puparia and larvae of sarcophagid flies. Proc. U. S. Nat. Mus. 66(29):1-26.

1926. Descriptions of larvae and pupae of two-winged flies belonging to the family Leptidae. Ibid. 70(2):1-20.

1929. Characters of the larvae and pupae of certain fruit flies. Jour. Agr. Res. 38:489-498.

Hayes, Wm. P. 1938-39. A bibliography of keys for the identification of immature insects. Pt. I. Diptera. Ent. News 49(9):246-251; 50(1): 5-10, 76-82.

1944. A bibliography of keys to immature mosquitoes. Ibid. 55(6): 141-145, 184-189.

Heiss, E. M. 1938. A classification of the larvae and puparia of the Syrphidae of Illinois. Univ. Bull. 16:1-142.

Johannsen, O. A. 1934. Aquatic Diptera. Pt. I. Nemocera, exclusive of Chironomidae and Ceratopogonidae. Cornell Agr. Exp. Sta. Mem. 164:1-71.

1935. Aquatic Diptera. Pt. II. Orthorrhapha-Brachycera and Cyclorrhapha. Ibid. 177:1-62.

1937. Aquatic Diptera. Pt. III. Chironomidae; subfamilies Tanypodinae, Diamesinae and Orthocladiinae. Ibid. 205:1-84.

1937. Aquatic Diptera. Pt. IV. Chironomidae; subfamily Chironominae. Ibid. 210:1-56.

Malloch, J. R. 1917. A preliminary classification of Diptera, exclusive of Pupipara, based upon larval and pupal characters, with keys to imagines in certain families. Pt. I. Bull. Ill. St. Lab. Nat. Hist. 12:161-409.

Phillips, Venia Tarris. 1946. The biology and identification of trypetid larvae (Trypetidae). Mem. Amer. Ent. Soc. 12:1-161.

Thomsen, L. C. 1937. Aquatic Diptera. Pt. V. Ceratopoginidae. Cornell Agr. Exp. Sta. Mem. 210:57-80.

Order HYMENOPTERA

Bischoff, H. 1927. Biologie der Hymenoptera. 597 pp. Springer, Berlin.

Duncan, C. D. 1939. A contribution to the biology of the North American vespine wasps. Stanford Univ. Pub. Univ. Ser. Biol. Sci. 8(11):1-272.

Yuasa, H. 1923. A classification of the larvae of the Tenthredinoidea. Ill. Biol. Mon. 7:1-172.

INDEX AND PICTURED GLOSSARY

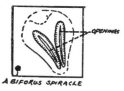

INDEX

INDEX

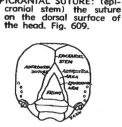

F

FALCATE: sickle-shaped.
FALCIFORM: having the
    form of a sickle.
Fall armyworm 5
Fall webworm 166
False chinch bug 134
False wireworm 13
Feather-winged beetles 80
FEMUR (pl., femora): a seg-
    ment of the leg, between
    trochanter and leg. See
    leg.
Fenusina 214
FILIFORM: slender and more
    or less of equal diameter.
Firebrat 28, 56
Fire-colored beetles 114
Fireflies 97
FISSURE: a slit.
FLAGELLATE: whip-like.
Flat-headed apple tree
    borer 44
Flat-headed borers 94
Flebatomus argentipes 193
Flebatomous chinensis 193
Flebatomus major 193
Florida wax scale 138
FORCEPS: hook or pincer-
    like processes on the
    caudal end of the abdo-
    men.
Forcipomyia specularis 194
Forficula 37
Formicidae 211
FOSSA (pl., fossae): a pit.
FOSSORIAL: fitted for dig-
    ging or burrowing.
Fringe-winged fungus
    beetles 106
Frit fly 40
Froghoppers 137
FRONTAL SUTURE: the arms
    of the epicranial suture.
Fruit tree leaf roller 162
Fulgoridae 136
FUNGIVOROUS: feeding on
    fungi.
Fungus gnats 192

FURCULA: in Collembola;
    the more or less forked
    leaping appendage on the
    4th abdominal segment.
Furniture beetle 119
FUSIFORM: spindle-shaped.

G

GALEA: the outer lobe of
    the maxilla. Fig. 610

Figure 610

Galerucinae 124
GALL: abnormal growth of
    plant tissue, caused by
    stimuli not of the plant
    itself, generally by insects.
Galleria melonella 185
Gallihaetis fluctuans 66
Garden webworm 154
Gelastocoridae 130
Gelastocoris oculatus 130
Gelechiidae 151, 156, 164,
    183
GENITALIA: all of the geni-
    tal structures; the repro-
    ductive organs.
Geocoris 134
Geometridae 166, 188
Geosargus viridas 195
German cockroach 8, 35, 72
Gerridae 131
Gerris remigis 131
Giant water bugs 130
Gibbium psylloides 119
GILL: a special, variously
    formed respiratory organ
    in aquatic insects.
Glischrochilus obtusus 107
Glossosomatinae 147
Glowworms 97
Glyphipterygidae 164, 176
Gnorimoschema operculelle
    156
Goat moth 156
Golden-eye lacewing 50, 144
Goldenrod ball gall 21
Goniocotes gigas 34
Gracilaria azaleella 152
Gracilariidae 152, 153, 174,
    177
GRADUAL METAMORPHOS-
    IS: the growth of insects
    from tre egg through the
    nymph to the adult.
Granary weevil 127
Grape phylloxera 139
Grape-vine plume 167
Grasshopper 7, 10, 70
Greenhouse thrips 38
Greenhouse whitefly 139
Green lacewings 144
Green peach aphid 139
Green stink bug 39
Ground beetle 12

Grouse locust 70
GRUB: the larva of Coleop-
    tera.
Gryllidae 69, 71
Gryllotalpinae 69
GULA: the central part of
    the head beneath, later-
    ally bounded by the genae.
GULAR SUTURE: the line
    between the gula and the
    genae. Fig. 611

Figure 611

Gypsy moth 7, 168
Gyrinidae 74

H

HABITATION (or habitat):
    the region where the ani-
    mal lives naturally.
Haematopinus adventicius 37
Haliplidae 75
Harpalus vagans 29, 49
Harpalus viridiaeneus 76
Helgramites 141
Helieopsyche 49
Heliodinidae 158, 162
Heliothis armigera 13, 47,
    165, 168
Heliothrips haemorrhoidalis
    38
Helmis aeneus 93
Helochares 117
Helodidae 90, 92
Helophorinae 117
Helophorus aquaticus 117
Hemerobiidae 145
Hemerobius pacificus 145
Hemerocampa leucostigma
    13
Hemerocampa vetusta 13,
    168
Hemipenthes 199
Hemiptera 129
Henichroa dyari 214
Hen louse 34
Hepialidae 159, 178
Hepialus humuli 159
Heptagenia 33, 64
HERBIVOROUS: feeding on
    plants,
Hercothrips fasciatus 10
Hesperiidae 171, 180
Hesperobaenus 103
Hesperophylax 17, 40, 52
Hessian fly 189, 190
Heteroceridae 89
Heterocerus ventralis 89
HETEROMETABOLA: a col-
    lective name for the in-
    sects with gradual or in-
    complete metamorphosis
Hexagenia bilineata 33, 63
HIBERNATION: a period of
    lethargy or suspended ani-
    mation in animals occur-
    ing during seasonal low
    temperatures.

INDEX

228

INDEX

M

Machilidae 56
Machilis martima 56
Magaxyela major 212
MAGGOT: larvae of certain Diptera
Magicicada septendecim 4, 39, 136
MALA· a lobe; sometimes applied to the galea and lacinia when fused. Fig. 615

Figure 615

Malacosoma americana 169
Malacosoma disstria 184
Mallophaga 34
MALPIGHIAN TUBES· the excretory organs of the insect, emptying into the hind intestine
MANDIBLE: the first pair of jaws. 73 Fig. 616

Figure 616

MANDIBULO-SUCTORIAL: a type of mouth parts 50 Fig 617

Figure 617

Mantid 8, 69
Mantidae 70
Mantispa styriaca 143
Mantispidae 143
Maple case-bearer 41, 151
March flies 193
Marsh springtail 58

MAXILLAE (sing, maxilla) the second pair of jaws. Fig. 618

Figure 618

MAXILLARY PALPI (sing, palpus or palp). a pair of appendages carried by the maxilla See maxilla
Mayfly 6, 33
Meal moth 154
Mealworm 116
Mealy-bugs 138
Measuring worms 166
Mecoptera 46, 47, 52
Mediterranean fruit fly 189
Megacephala carolina 76
Melalopha 168
Melandryidae 113
Melandrya striata 110
Melandryidae 110
Melanitis leda 167
Melanoplus differentalis 31
Melanoplus femur-rubrum 71
Melasis rufipennis 95
Melittia satyriniformis 156
Melittomma sericeum 128
Meloidae 85
Melyridae 99
Membracidae 137
METAPNEUSTIC having only the last pair of abdominal spiracles open
MENTUM: the distal sclerite of the labium. See labium
MESOPLEURON· the lateral sclerite of the mesothorax
MESOTHORAX the second or middle segment of the thorax
Metaecus paradoxus 86
Metallus rubi 214
METAMORPHOSIS changes of form of insects as they pass from one stage to another
METAPLEURON the lateral sclerite of the metathorax.
METATHORAX the last or third thoracic segment.
Metcalf, Z. P 3
Mesovelia mulsanti 132
Mexican bean beetle 6
Microentomon perposillom 29, 55
Micromalthidae 74
Micromalthus debilis 45, 74
Micropterygidae 149, 173
Micropteryx 149
Midges 194
Migratory locust 71
MINES: galleries made by larvae between the upper and lower covering of a plant leaf 21
Minute brown scavenger beetles 102

Miridae 135
Mnemonica auricyanea 152, 173
MOLA (or molar): the grinding surface of the mandibles. Fig. 619.

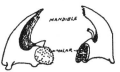

Figure 619

Molamba lonata 14
Molanna uniophila 148
Molar structure 73
Mole cricket 69
Mollanidae 148
Monarch butterfly 173
Monardia 200
Monocesta coryli 124
Monomorium minimum 44, 211
Monotomidae 103, 107
Mordellidae 118
Mormon cricket 71
Mosquitoes 191
Moth flies 193
MOULT (or molt): the periodical shedding of the skin or outer covering of insects as they grow This process is also called ecdysis
MOUTH PARTS. a collective name for the structures of an insect's mouth, including labrum, mandible, maxillae, labium and other related appendages. (See Figs 46 and 47)
MULTIARTICULATE: with many segments
MULTIORDINAL CROCHETS: the hooks on the prolegs when they are of many different lengths but all arranged in a single row.
Murmidiidae 108
Murmidius ovalis 108
Musca domestica 6
Mycetophagidae 112
Mycetophagus punctatus 112
Mycetophilidae 192, 193, 202
Mydaidae 198, 209
Mydas clavatus 198, 209
Mydas flies 198
Myiatropa florea 44
Myochrous denticolli 124
MYRMECOPHILOUS· insects that live in ant nests
Myrmeleon 145
Myremeleontidae 145
Mytilaspis citricola 138
Myzus persicae 139

N

NAIAD· any nymph with aquatic habits

229

Phytophaga destructor 189, 190, 200
PHYTOPHAGOUS· feeding upon plants.
PIERCING AND SUCKING MOUTH PARTS: Fig 621

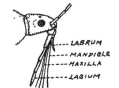

Figure 621

Pieridae 172, 182
Pieris napi 172
Pieris rapae 172
Pigmy crickets 69
PILIFERS: the caudo-lateral projections of the labrum. Fig 622

Figure 622

Pine gall weevil 127
Pink bollworm 164
PLANIDIUM: the newly hatched larva of some chalcids.
PLANTA: the anal clasping legs of caterpillars.
Plant bug 10, 135
PLATYFORM: a type of larvae with short, broad and flat body, with or without short legs. 14
Platyphylax 16
Platypodidae 128
Platypsyllidae 81
Platypsyllus castoris 81
Platypus compositus 128
Platystomidae 128
Plecoptera 59
PLEURON (pl., pleura): the lateral region of any segment of the insect body.
PLICATE: with folds.
Plum curculio 40
Plum leaf-miner 152
Plume moths 167
PLUMOSE. feathered like a plume.
Plutella maculipennis 159
Podapion gallicola 127
Podisus maculiventris 6
Podosesia syringae 175
Poduridae 58
Polymitarcidae 63
Popillia japonica 4
PORRECT: projecting.
Porthetria dispar 7, 168
POSTEMBRYONIC DEVELOPMENT: the development of an insect after hatching.
Pothamanthidae 62
Potato leafhopper 137
Potato tuberworm 156

Potomanthus 62
Praying mantid 70
Predacious diving beetles 77
PREDATOR: an animal that preys on others.
PREPUPA: a quiescent instar between the end of the larval stage and the pupal stage, active but not feeding
Preservatives 25, 26
PRESTERNUM a narrow anterior part of the sternum
PRIMARY LARVA: the newly hatched larva of the insects with hypermetamorphosis. See triungulin. 85
PRIMARY SETAE. the setae borne on setiferous tubercules, definite in number and position.
Prionochaeta opaca 80
Prionocyphon discoideus 90
Prionoxystus robiniae 156
PROBOSCIS· an extended mouth structure.
Prodoxus quinquepunctellus 175
Projapygidae 57
PROLEG· a fleshy unsegmented abdominal leg.
Promachus vertebratus 199
PROMINENCE elevated part.
PRONOTUM. the dorsal face of the prothorax
Prosopistoma foliaceum 62
Prosopistomatidae 62
PROSTERNUM: the ventral face of the prothorax.
PROSTHECA: a mandibular sclerite set with hairs, articulated to the basalis. 80 Fig. 623

Figure 623

Prostomis mandibularis 105
Protentomidae 55
Proterhinidae 125
Proterhinus anthracias 125
PROTHORAX: the first or anterior segment of the thorax.
Protoparce quinquemaculata 17
Protoparce sexta 13, 170, 188
PROTRACTED: extended.
PROTUBERANCE: any elevation above the surface.
Protura 54
Proxodoxinae 151
Psoini 120
Pselaphidae 84
Psephenidae 92
Psephenus 93
Psephenus lecontei 92
Pseudo click beetles 95

PSEUDOCULI: a pair of organs in the head; their nature undetermined.
PSEUDOPOD a soft footlike appendage, as on the abdomen of caterpillars
PSEUDOPUPA (in Coleoptera) the larva in a quiescent coarctate condition which is followed by the true pupa.
Psilocephala haemorrhoidalis 198, 208
Psocids 35
Psychidae 160, 178
Psychoda superba 193, 203
Psychodidae 193, 203, 205
Psylla pyricola 10, 138
Pteraphorus tenuidactylus 180
Pterocrace storeyi 143
Pterodontia flavipes 197
Pteronarcidae 59
Pteronidea ribesii 31, 47, 215
Pterophoridae 167, 169, 180
Pterostichus 12, 40
Ptiliidae 80
Ptilodactyla serricollis 92
Ptilodactylinae 92
Ptilostomis ocellifera 149
Ptinidae 119
PULVILLUS (pl., pulvilli): pad-like structures between the claws.
Punkies 194
PUPA· the resting, inactive stage of holometabolous insects, between the larva and the adult.
Pupae of Diptera 199
Pupae of Lepidoptera 173
PUPARIUM: the next-to-the-last larval skin within which many maggots pupate for greater protection.
PUPATION: the act of becoming a pupa; entering the resting stage.
Puss moth 168
Pygmy locust 70
PYGOPODS: the appendages of the tenth abdominal segment taken collectively
Pyralididae 154, 179, 180, 184. 186
Pyralis farinalis 154
Pyrausta nubilalis 54, 179
Pyrochroidae 114
Pytha niger 115
Pythidae 114, 115

R

Ranatra fusca 130
Range caterpillar 7
Rape butterfly 172
Raphidia hermandi 140
Raphidia oblita 140
Raphidiidae 140
RAPTORIAL· fitted for grasping and holding prey.
RASPING MOUTH PARTS: with a file-like structure.
Rearing insects 26
Rectal tracea 11
Recurvaria piceailla 183
Reduviidae 133

231

INDEX

Stilleto flies 198, 208
Stink bug 39, 133
STIPES (pl., stipetes): **the** basal stalk of the **max-** illa.
Storehouse beetle 119
Stoneflies 34
Stratiomyidae 195, 206
STRIDULATING ORGAN: an organ producing sound by rubbing two parts. Fig. 625

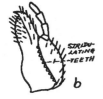

Figure 625

Strongylogaster annulosus 213
STYLET: a small style or stiff process.
STYLI (sing., stylus): the small appendages on the under side of the abdomen in Thysanura. Fig. 626

Figure 626

STYLIFORM: ending in a long slender point.
SUBANAL APPENDAGE: the appendage beneath the anal segment.
SUBIMAGO: a winged stage in Mayflies just after emergence from the pupa and before the last moult.
SUBMENTUM: a sclerite of the labium next to the mentum. See labium. Fig. 627

Figure 627

SUBPRIMARY SETAE: the rimary setae found in later instars but not in the first.

SUBTERRANEAN: existing beneath the surface of the soil.
SUBULATE: awl-s h a p e d; linear at base, attenuate at tip.
Sucking lice 37
Sugarcane leafhopper 6
SULCATE: with deep grooves.
Sun-moths 158, 162
SURANAL PROCESS: the process above the anal segment.
Swallow bug 132
Swallowtail butterflies 172
Sweeping net 22
Sychroini 113
Symphypleona 58
Synchroa punctata 113
Syrian silkworm 169

T

Tabanidae 195, 207
Tabanus atratus 195
Tabanus lasiophthalmus 207
Tagoperla media 60
Tarnished plant bug 135
TARSI (sing., tarsus): see leg.
Tegeticula 151
Tenebrio molitor 116
Tenebrionidae 113, 115, 116
Tenebroides mauritanicus 100
Tenodera aridifolia sinensis 70
Tent caterpillars 169
Tenthredinidae 212-215
Tenthredo 213
TERGITE: dorsal sclerite of a semgent.
TERGUM: the dorsal part of a segment.
Tetraonyx 85
Tettigidae 70
Tettigonidae 71
Therevidae 198, 208
Thermobia domestica 28, 56
Thorn skeletonizer 164
Thrips 38
Throscidae 95
Throscus 95
Thyatira derasa 165
Thyatiridae 165
Thyrididae 160
Thyridopteryx ephemeraeformis 16, 19, 160, 178
Thysanoptera 38
Thysanura 55
TIBIA (pl., tibae) · the apical segments of the leg.
TIBIOTARSUS: the segments of the tibia and the tarsus when fused together. Fig. 628

Figure 628

Tiger beetle 76
Tinea pellionella 158, 176
Tineidae 158, 176
Tingitidae 134

Tipula eluta 191
Tipulidae 191, 194, 206, 153
Tischeria malifoliella 43, 153
Tischeriidae 153, 177
Toad bugs 130
Tobacco hornworm 170, 188
Tomato fruitworm 13, 165
Tomato hornworm 13, 17
Tomostethus bardus 213
Tomoxia bidentata 118
TONGUE (the hypopharynx): a sensory structure attached to the upper surface of the labium.
Tooth necked fungus beetles 102
Topoperla 34
Tortoise beetles 125
Torticidae 162, 176, 177
Toxomeris politus 189, 200
TRACHEA (pl., tracheae): ringed tubes belonging to the respiratory system.
TRACHEAL GILLS: the flattened or hair-like processes in aquatic larvae through which oxygen is absorbed from the water. Fig. 629

Figure 629

Trachykele blondeli 94
Tree-cricket 71
Treehoppers 137
Tremex columba 216
Trialeurodes vaporariorum 139
Triaenodes flavescense 49, 148
Tribolium confusum 116
Trichoptera 52, 146
Tricorythodes allectus 6
Tricorythus 65
Tridactylinae 69
Triodopteryx ephemeraeformis 160
TRIORDINAL CROCHETS: hooks of the prolegs when in three different lenghts but arranged in a single row.
Triphleps tricticolor 39
TRIUNGULIN· the first instar of Meloidae, Mantispidae and Strepsiptera. 85
TROCHANTER: a segment of the leg, between the coxa and femur. Fig. 630

Figure 630

INDEX

Figure 631